Glennyce S. Eckersley is an international angel expert and the author of many successful books, including *An Angel At My Shoulder* and *Saved By The Angels*. She lives in Manchester, UK, and has made many media appearances.

Angels to Watch Over Us

How Angels Help Us from Our Earliest Years

BY GLENNYCE S. ECKERSLEY

RIDER

LONDON • SYDNEY • AUCKLAND • JOHANNESBURG

1 3 5 7 9 10 8 6 4 2

Copyright © Glennyce S. Eckersley 1999, 2006

First published as *Children and Angels* in 1999 by Rider

This revised and updated edition first published in 2006 by Rider
an imprint of Ebury Publishing, Random House
20 Vauxhall Bridge Road, London SW1V 2SA
www.randomhouse.co.uk

Random House Australia (Pty) Limited
20 Alfred Street, Milsons Point, Sydney,
New South Wales 2061, Australia

Random House New Zealand Limited
18 Poland Road, Glenfield,
Auckland 10, New Zealand

Random House South Africa (Pty) Limited
Isle of Houghton, Corner of Boundary Road & Carse O'Gowrie,
Houghton 2198, South Africa

Random House UK Limited Reg. No. 954009

Papers used by Rider are natural, recyclable products made from wood
grown in sustainable forests.

Typeset by SX Composing DTP, Rayleigh, Essex
Printed and bound in Great Britain by Cox and Wyman Ltd, Reading, Berks.

A CIP catalogue record for this book is available from the British Library

ISBN 1846040302 (until Jan 07)
ISBN 9781846040306

In memory of Daniel Greenberg

When angels speak spiritually with me from heaven,
they speak just as intelligently as the man
by my side . . .

EMANUEL SWEDENBORG, philosopher
and theologian

Contents

Preface

The meaning of the word 'angel' is messenger. Every spiritual path and culture has references to these magnificent beings. According to these sources, the primary work of the angels is to mediate between ourselves and God. They bring us messages of reassurance and love, as well as the powerful, abiding knowledge that we are never alone. Indeed, angels have been recorded and illustrated for thousands of years, and they have always been perceived as beings who offer guidance, help or comfort.

Many religions teach that we each have our own personal guardian angel, and that children are particularly close to their specially assigned angel. In the stories collected in this book, angels appear to have many roles: they may rescue us, soothe us, accompany us to the next world, or send us messages of love when we are most in need of them. There is a theory that angels were formerly human beings who have now proceeded to the next stage of life to develop as angels. This is supported by the many tales of angel encounters as visits from loved ones in angelic form.

The eighteenth-century philosopher and theologian Emanuel Swedenborg taught that angels can also be found within ourselves. We need not search outside, we only need to discover what is already within, albeit well hidden. In searching for our inner angel, we may perhaps uncover many positive childlike qualities, such as the ability to play, trust, and express feelings spontaneously and openly. As we grow older, scepticism, ridicule and peer pressure can often gradually force us to leave such innocent spirituality behind.

Could it be that civilisations follow a similar pattern – the more sophisticated they become, the less spiritual? Happily, nowadays many advanced societies look back towards the past and are willing to explore ancient religions and the spirituality of indigenous peoples, wishing to absorb some of the wisdom and insight that these traditions retain.

Perhaps we are born with a spiritual blueprint – DNA of the divine, passed on intact through the ages, only to be suppressed from our consciousness as we grow? It has been revealed that symbols, signs and myths are more powerful if they have been meaningful in one form or another through the preceding ages. Of all symbols, angels must surely be among the most potent.

Angels have communicated with mankind throughout history and they can appear in many forms, as gentle guides, joyful envoys or wise guardians. As the inspiring stories in this book reveal, the angels watch over us from our earliest years. It is wonderful to know that they are always with each and every one of us, offering comfort and hope throughout our lives.

GLENNYCE S. ECKERSLEY

Acknowledgements

I am indebted to my friend and colleague David Lomax for his considerable help and support with research, and for giving his advice and precious time. To my editor Judith Kendra, a huge thank you for her understanding and encouragement. To Emma Heathcote, thanks for her considerable practical help and generosity; also to the staff at New Church College for their tolerance. Finally a big thank you to my family, Ross and Gillian, who have to live with me during the process of writing books. In particular a special thank you to my daughter Rachel for her practical help and patience.

Without my contributors there would not be a book of course and I cannot thank enough these special people. Firstly the children and staff of Walverden County Primary School, Nelson; also the children and staff of Stand Unitarian Sunday School, Manchester. Last, but by no means least, the people who gave me their very personal stories. Thank you to: Diane Balshaw, Nancy Bennet, Janice Brace, Victoria Bradley, Maggy Brook, Enid Case, Margaret Cook, Helen Coyle, Judith

Cosgrove, Carol Cox, Laura Deakin, Bella Forman, James Giles, Gillian Gordon, Lesley Gorton, Josh Green, Ray Grindall, Jean Hess, Liam Humphreys, Diane Infanti, Natasha Law, Wendy Lawday, Ian Lennox Martin, Thomas Lloyd, Sue Lucas, Mary McKee, Molly Mallory, Daniel Martin, Lisa Masters, Pam Moffat, Susan Moss, Fozia Mohammad, Nizamuddin, Karen Parsons, Jean Peart, Melody Poole, Valerie Porter, Suzanne Price, Catherine Scott, Lucy Sheldrake, Rebecca Shepherd, Judith Shrimpton JP, Paul Spence, Jean Stilwell, Jenny Tozier, Glenys Veal, Yvonne and Louise Waddington, Irene Wheeldon, Maeve Whitfield, Joyce and Paul Wiggins, Jane Wilde. I must also thank Anna, Rita, Amanda, Nick, Pamela and Holly.

Babies and Angels

It is a common belief that babies have a profound connection with angels, and an innate ability to 'see' at a spiritual level. This ability gradually decreases as the child grows, until by adulthood few of us retain the spiritual connection. Gaining knowledge in other spheres apparently bolts the door on the spiritual world.

In researching this book, I have lost count of the number of people who told me they were convinced that babies had the ability to see angels. They had seen an infant stare at a spot in the room, often the ceiling, and break into the most wonderful smile or chuckle, delighted by some form of unseen communication. Often a baby would lift its arms towards this source as if wanting to be lifted. Adults could find no explanation for this and certainly could see nothing themselves.

Since the beginning of time, across all cultures and all religions, from the frozen wastes to the desert heat, there have been accounts of angels and their contact with children. The stories in this book span the globe, cover every family and social background. I feel they

are quite remarkable, but read on and judge for yourself.

One very old lady wrote to me telling me of the
heartbreak her whole family suffered when her great-
granddaughter died at only a few months old. Seconds
before she died this very sick baby suddenly opened
her eyes, beamed at a spot on the ceiling and stretched
out her arms. The grieving family concluded that an
angel must have appeared to the baby to take her to
heaven. It was the only consolation they had on that
distressing day.

In many rescue stories that involve babies and very
tiny children, angelic intervention seems to be the
only explanation. Two dramatic stories were
reported in the press during the summer of 1998
which left everyone involved quite astonished.

Firstly you may recall the sad occasion in the UK
when a grandfather, taking his small grandson on a ride
in the English countryside, plunged down the side of a
mountain after apparently losing control of the car.
Tragically the grandfather was thrown from the car and
killed, leaving his thirteen-month-old grandson alone
for three days and nights. The newspapers reported
that the little boy was protected from the hot sun by

day and the rain and cold at night by being hidden in thick bracken. Eventually a young boy found him in amazingly good health considering his ordeal. Everyone talked of miracles, including the coroner involved in the case. I was most impressed, however, by the words of the senior police officer conducting the investigation. He said, 'Something or somebody not of this world was looking after that little boy.' Many people commented that it must have been his guardian angel.

The second incident occurred in France when a young English couple on holiday watched in horror as their car plunged down a ravine with their baby still strapped into his car seat. Believing they must certainly have lost their baby, they scrambled down the steep slope to where the vehicle had finally come to rest. Astonishingly, the baby was unhurt. He was still sitting safely in his car seat. Again the headlines talked of miracles and guardian angels.

Rescue stories, almost identical in nature, have reached me from all corners of the world. They include accounts of babies in runaway prams and toddlers wandering into danger only to emerge unscathed, rescued by unseen hands. Gill's is very typical of these stories. Pushing her new-born baby to the shops one spring morning along an extremely busy road, Gill reached the window of the local estate agents. Desperate to find another house away from the non-stop heavy traffic, she paused to look into the window. The pram was as new as the baby, and perhaps the brake needed firmer pressure than Gill had applied, for suddenly it rolled swiftly towards the busy road. Gill turned in time to see the pram with its precious occupant roll into the centre of the road. Dashing forward, she caught the pram and, heart beating, returned with it to safety. It was only moments later when she had calmed down that she realised that, for the first time anyone could remember, the road had been totally clear of traffic for those few moments. Normally, huge lorries were thundering past; heavy traffic was non-stop from early morning until late at night. Gill could scarcely comprehend the complete lack of traffic at the precise moment her baby was in such danger, but believed the baby's guardian angel must have intervened.

Another young mother faced with an identical accident saw with relief a man rush into the road to rescue her child in its pram. When the pram was returned to her, she exclaimed, 'Thank God!' The man replied, 'Yes, indeed,' and then he disappeared.

Mavis has few doubts about babies' ability to commune with angels, after the story of her granddaughter's christening. The day was bound to be filled with joy and sadness, since Robert, Mavis's husband, had died only days after Faith had been born. It was a perfect spring day. Daffodils and blossom filled the church grounds; new life in all its forms met the happy family. Mavis entered the elegant old church filled with the thought that Robert would have loved to be there with them.

Quietness fell on the family group as the service started. A spiritual atmosphere encompassed the congregation, including Faith, who gazed intently into the minister's eyes. At six months old Faith was usually extremely lively and wriggled constantly, so it was a surprise to everyone, especially her mother, to see her so calm and intent on the proceedings. The water was poured over Faith's head, and still she did not murmur.

As the service was drawing to a close, the minister held Faith whilst speaking some closing words. The family stood in a semicircle surrounding the font – parents, godparents, grandparents, and finally on the very edge of the semicircle, Mavis. Slowly and quite systematically, Faith gazed around the gathering. She stared intently at each face in turn. Her gaze met

Mavis's. Mavis found herself thinking, 'Robert, I know she would have loved you so much.' Faith's gaze moved on to the empty space at the side of Mavis, her face broke into a huge smile, and at the same moment Mavis felt the sensation of an arm around her waist. Robert is here after all on a visit from the angelic realms, she thought.

Miraculous Rescues

At certain times in our lives we all feel in need of rescue. Childhood can be a particularly hazardous time. Oblivious to the probable consequences, a child will climb the highest rock on the seashore, dive into rivers on hot days, and ride a bike like a demon through the heaviest of traffic. Parents cannot always be two steps behind, waiting in case an accident looks likely. Some children are, it seems, fortunate enough to receive extra help and protection.

For a very short period in my early teens I was the owner of a bicycle. The co-ordination required to ride the machine successfully largely eluded me. I had little skill and even less road sense, and after a few months my cycling days were over. Freewheeling down a very steep hill, I came into contact with a raised iron cover. The resulting somersault convinced me forever that bicycles and I were never intended to mix.

Jean recalls a truly remarkable rescue, one which amazed me when I heard it. At fifteen years of age she was an excellent cyclist, travelling almost everywhere by bike. She was confident, skilful and felt very safe. One busy stretch of road near her home was particularly familiar. Jean regularly used this route and knew every metre thoroughly. There was a large factory along this road where heavy lorries rumbled in and out of the gates at all times. She was always extra vigilant when approaching these gates.

One day Jean cycled along this familiar route to visit a friend for lunch. A fellow cyclist overtook her, and reached the entrance of the gates just ahead of her. Turning his head, he shouted over his shoulder to Jean that all was clear for her to proceed, and signalled to her to keep pedalling.

Suddenly, a single-decker bus hit Jean's bicycle side on with a huge impact. The chances of Jean surviving such an impact were very slim. To her astonishment, however, she felt herself lifted from the bike a fraction of a second before the impact. Unseen hands carried her some six metres from the scene ahead of the bus, and deposited her gently on the grass verge by the roadside next to a hawthorn bush.

Reality was suspended as she tried to come to terms with what had happened. Gazing up at the hawthorn bush and then at her bike, which was now a crushed lump of metal, she could only stare in utter bewilderment. She explained that the feeling she had experienced was like being lifted into the air by an invisible giant. Today, Jean is convinced that those invisible arms belonged to her guardian angel, who carried her swiftly out of danger. She is forever grateful and certain that whatsoever befalls her, she is never alone.

Miracles take place every day of the week in hospitals. A patient receives a new kidney or heart, a hip joint is replaced, or a baby is born. These are all miracles, especially for the people involved. For one small girl of just four years of age a miracle occurred which totally bewildered staff and family alike.

Lucy was carried into St Mary's Hospital at Paddington in London on a stretcher and in a very dangerous condition. Following the stretcher was a small procession of people, including her distraught parents accompanied by a grey-faced policeman and a third man, anxious and agitated. It was clear some dramatic event had occurred.

Two medical students in the casualty department braced themselves of the worst. As third-year students they were not new to emergencies, but the sight of this small girl tugged at their heart strings. The policeman told them what had happened. Lucy had run on impulse into the middle of the extremely busy Edgware Road, before anyone's reactions were quick enough to prevent her. With a sickening thud a large lorry had run over the small girl, the wheels going completely over the small body not once but twice, as the rear wheels also could not avoid Lucy.

Judith and Jenny were practical and professional medical students, and at the end of a thorough examination they were surprised to find that apart from one small bruise on her shoulder Lucy appeared to be unmarked. All exchanged confused glances. How could this be possible? The next stage would have to be X-rays and the doctor was just about to organise this procedure when to everyone's astonishment Lucy opened her eyes. She smiled broadly at everyone and asked, 'Where is the man in white?' The doctor stepped forward. 'I am here,' he said. 'No, no,' she replied, 'I mean the man in the long white shiny dress.' Judith held her hand and stroked her face. 'The man did that,' Lucy said to the startled crowd. 'He stroked my face as he picked me up, and the lorry wheels did not touch me.'

At this point Lucy fell into a completely normal sleep. Over the next twenty-four hours full medical examinations took place, but revealed nothing untoward. Only the small bruise on the shoulder gave evidence of anything at all having happened.

To say everyone involved was baffled would be an understatement. The lorry driver was still insisting he felt two distinct bumps. The policeman and the witness still insist they saw it all clearly. Lucy herself never wavered in her account of the man in white who held the lorry off her small frame. Medical staff could offer no logical explanation. Judith explained that as a medical student, angels were normally out of her field of expertise. She still tells the story, however, and adds that miracles certainly do happen in hospitals.

Extensive research has taught me that angels appear in all shapes and sizes. People seem to see what they can cope with, particularly children. Whilst a gentle light or sweet smell are enough to comfort some, others cope extremely well with a more dramatic sight. It is often when someone is in great danger that a more dramatic figure of an angel will appear. Children often encounter tiny angels or see children who have gone on before them to heaven.

Occasionally I have been told about a series of events which are far from the normal pattern, and which one would assume would frighten a child. Not so in the case of Victoria, who calmly coped with the most dramatic sighting I have ever heard of. Victoria was five years old when these remarkable events took place in Sussex, England. Like most children she fiercely resisted bedtime. It was rapidly becoming a nightly battle to get her in bed and asleep. Her mother became increasingly weary of this constant battle, trying every tactic she knew to try and settle the little girl.

On this particular occasion Victoria's mother was desperate. Weary and at her wits' end, she resigned herself to the situation and limply asked, 'Please go to sleep.' She walked downstairs quite at a loss as to what to do next to resolve the situation. Victoria flew into a tantrum, which eventually blew itself out when she realised that her mother was not responding. She was beginning to realise that her mother could not take much more that day.

Still full of mischief however, Victoria slipped out of bed and crept to the bedroom doorway, shouting defiantly 'I am coming downstairs.' There was no reply. Her mother hoped if she simply ignored her she would go back to bed. At this moment Victoria was literally struck dumb by an awesome sight. There in the doorway blocking her way was a huge African warrior! He was immensely tall, even by a little girl's standards, and carried a spear. He was dressed in the traditional grass skirt. Yet Victoria felt no fear at all, just a sense of peace and love, which washed over her until she was filled with a great desire to snuggle up in bed and sleep. Climbing into bed she smiled at the figure, closed her eyes and fell into a deep sleep.

For years Victoria kept this a secret, thinking no-one would ever believe her. When she told her mother, she suggested that it was perhaps her mother's guardian angel sent to give her a little peace and respite from her daughter. Her mother answered, however, that she was fairly certain that it was Victoria's own guardian angel protecting her from a nasty fall. Had Victoria continued on her determined route along a small corridor and down the stairs, there was a good chance that she might have fallen – and immediately at the bottom of the stairs was a large glass door, lethal to anyone falling against it.

Angels may appear in all shapes and sizes and indeed in different forms, as we have seen, but for some children a voice is all they need to keep them from harm.

Fairgrounds had never been Amanda's idea of fun, but she realised that for her sons they were the nearest thing to heaven. After a great deal of pleading, she eventually promised a trip to the fair. The evening was far from ideal. A persistent drizzle filled the air, making everywhere misty and unpleasantly damp. As she backed the car down the drive, Amanda thought with relief that at least they had not far to go. A few minutes' drive would be sufficient to reach the field, where the fair was in full swing. Adam, aged four, and Ben, only six, chatted excitedly as they set out.

Initially the road was narrow, but soon it opened out to reveal fields on either side and a clear view of the main road ahead. Switching on the windscreen wipers and polishing the inside of the window to afford a better view, she was startled when Ben suddenly shouted, 'Stop, Mummy, now!' There was such urgency in his voice that Amanda did an automatic emergency stop. It flashed through her mind that perhaps Ben was feeling ill or in pain.

Seconds later, however, they were hit by another car, which had inexplicably crossed the road to their side and hit the driver's door full on. The impact pushed Amanda's car into the field where it came to a juddering halt. Fortunately, little damage had occurred and all were uninjured. It was revealed that the oncoming driver had skidded on a patch of oil. He was also unhurt and relieved to see that the occupants of their car were in good shape. He remarked that had they been moving at the time of impact, the collision would have been so much worse.

They returned home and told their father of the event. Sipping a hot drink and glad to be in one piece, Amanda asked Ben why he had shouted. Had he seen the oncoming car skid? Was that why he had shouted as loudly as he did? 'No,' said Ben, 'the voice told me.' Everyone fell silent until Ben's father said, 'I do believe you have a guardian angel.'

It was hot, even for Arizona. The pool was the only place to feel comfortable, and Gloria was grateful for her air-conditioned home. It was therefore a fairly easy decision when her daughter Jody's birthday was approaching for her parents to plump for a pool party — outdoor fun, and lots of space for the children to let off steam. Jody and her two brothers were very excited at the prospect, and eagerly became involved in the preparations.

The birthday arrived, and soon the garden was full of excited children, splashing and laughing in the hot sun. Most children living in that environment can swim as naturally as they walk, but Carolyn was a notable exception. No-one understood why, but she was afraid of the water. To her mother's knowledge there had never been a frightening incident that could have provoked such fear, but the fact remained that she was very reluctant to go anywhere near water, and certainly would not join the other children in the pool. However, she enjoyed herself, and joined in everything except the swimming competition.

Feeling that the heat and all the cheering was giving her a sore throat, Carolyn walked to the far side of the pool to help herself to a soft drink. Eagerly running back around the poolside in order not to miss any of the fun, she suddenly caught her foot on a chair, and before she knew it she was in the water and sinking. It was her worst nightmare come true. Incredibly, no-one witnessed this, nor even heard her through the laughter, especially as they all had their backs to the pool, engrossed in a game. Feeling the bottom of the pool beneath her, Carolyn thrashed in blind panic.

Only seconds later, she became aware of arms

15

holding her, strongly gripping her from behind and lifting her to the surface. A clear memory of rising from the water and being placed gently on the poolside remains with her. At last she cried out and sobbed loudly, attracting attention. A surge of people dashed to her aid.

Carolyn's mother was quite distraught, and when the commotion had subsided thought it best that they should go home. Recapping what had happened slowly and step-by-step, she talked Carolyn through the incident. Finally Carolyn said she had not even seen who had lifted her from the pool, she was so upset. Her mother stared at her daughter in disbelief, having turned and witnessed her crying on the side of the pool. She concluded that she had merely slipped in from the steps and had climbed out herself. There was no-one on the far side of the pool, and no-one could have reached the other side quickly enough without other people seeing them.

Carolyn still insisted that she had been lifted by very strong hands from the water. 'Did you see no-one at all?' her mother asked. 'No-one,' she replied. 'In that case,' said her mother, 'we can only thank God for sending one of his angels.'

Sue and her husband were so exhausted from sleepless nights that they decided to take their child Rebecca into their own bed. The bliss was instantaneous, and all three fell into a deep sleep.

Morning came all too soon. Sue's husband climbed out of bed with a huge effort, and prepared to go to work. They lived in an old, but very pleasant flat, over-looking the sea in Brighton on the south coast of England, a bracing and scenic place to bring up a baby. From deep within the covers Sue heard her husband dashing off to work, but still extremely tired she dozed on, drifting in and out of sleep for some time. A voice penetrated her dreamy state. On waking, Sue thought that she had been dreaming or that her imagination had run away with her. Not so! The voice was there again, clear, loud, and the most beautiful voice she could ever recall hearing. The message, however, was stark: 'Your baby is going down the garden path.' Fully awake by now, Sue realised with a jolt that the bed was empty – no sign of Rebecca. Rushing to the bedroom window, she saw to her horror Rebecca shuffling at great speed towards the road.

With the speed of light, Sue dashed down the path and caught her daughter. Hugging her tightly, she then pondered on what had happened. On close inspection she deduced that the old front door had not closed properly. In his hurry to get to work on time her hus-band had not been aware of this. Yet what was she to make of the voice, and where had it come from? There was no-one in the bedroom or anywhere else in the flat, so it was improbable that the voice had come from outside. The most remarkable thing of all was the nature and tone of the voice. It was the most beautiful Sue had ever heard, and the quality was decidedly unearthly. Sue is in little doubt that her daughter was saved by an angel that morning.

Angels sit on stars wearing their sandals, because the stars are spiky and would hurt their feet.

GILLIAN, 4

Ever since she could remember, stars had fascinated Sarah. She would implore her mother to leave her bedroom curtains open, so that she could fall asleep with the stars twinkling down at her. Living in the country, with no major cities for miles, made the night sky spectacular.

One night, just before Christmas, Sarah stared at the night sky through her large bedroom window. The night was cold and clear, and the velvet sky was full of stars. With her imagination fired, she decided to get out of bed in order to get a closer look and to decide which route Santa's sleigh would take. Shivering a little, she climbed onto the rather high window sill. Full of mounting excitement at the thought of Christmas Eve, she gave a little jump for joy, and found herself catapulting backwards from the window sill, yelling as she fell towards the hard floor. She did not, however, come into contact with the floor, but instead was conscious of a floating sensation and gentle arms placing her into bed. She recalls that the bed was several feet from the window, too far for her to have simply fallen back into it. No-one was in the room and it was several seconds later that the bedroom door opened and her mother appeared to find out what the matter was.

Switching on the light, she came and sat on her daughter's bed. 'Did you have a bad dream?' she asked. Sarah told her what had happened, but her mother would not believe it was real. 'Simply a dream, darling' was all she said. Sarah knew even at that young age that it was definitely not a dream. She went to sleep, but on waking the next morning noticed that the toys that normally sat on the window sill were scattered on the floor – proof at least that she had stood on the window sill, and dislodged them in her fall.

Twenty years later the events of that night are as clear as if they had happened recently, and no-one will ever convince Sarah that she was not rescued by angel arms that night long ago.

Nick was a toddler of three when his parents took him to a fantastic fair. Eyes like saucers, he tried to take in all the wonderful sights and sounds, longing to dash in all directions at once with the sheer excitement of it all. Despite his insistent tugging for freedom, Nick's mother held firmly onto his hand. The crowds were dense, and a toddler would be lost in seconds.

A magnificent traction engine rolled past, its sheer size commanding awe. Following the monstrous engine, there was to be a display of talent in handling a coach and horses. It was a magnificent sight, the coach polished to perfection, as the hooves of the horses thundered down the display field. Nick was entranced at the sight and sounds of the horses. Without warning and with one great tug, he broke free from his mother's grip and dashed onto the field, and directly into the path of the oncoming coach and horses.

The crowd yelled, and Nick's mother screamed. It was obvious that no-one could reach him before the coach bore down. It knocked the little boy off his feet, and although the horses' hooves missed his body, the heavy coach wheels rolled right over his tiny frame.

Silence fell on the crowd. Nobody moved or seemed to know what to do next. Only Nick's parents dashed forward. To this day no-one can fully explain why, or indeed how, Nick was able to survive unharmed. In fact he was still as full of beans as ever only minutes before the event. How could this possibly be? How on earth could a huge carriage wheel roll right over the little boy and there be no evidence of it having happened? Nick, his parents, and all those who witnessed this extraordinary scene are completely at a loss as to what possible explanation there might be.

They do ask themselves from time to time: 'Did the angels rescue Nick?' You will have to decide for yourselves.

Some people are clearly close to the spiritual world from birth – or in Helen's case even before it. Helen's mother was waiting anxiously for her birth, with just three weeks to go. Sleep at this point in time was not an easy state to achieve, and on this particular night it seemed impossible. A previous baby had been born with a mental handicap, and although much loved, she hoped this baby would be perfectly normal in every way.

At last she managed to doze, only to awake suddenly with a jolt for no apparent reason. There then appeared to her, sitting at the foot of the bed, a tall figure of a man dressed in a long white robe. He had shoulder-length brown hair, and his piercing blue eyes radiated pure love and compassion. An index finger was raised to his lips as if to warn her not to shout in surprise. In a voice no louder than a whisper, he told her that the baby would be perfect. He then faded away slowly, leaving Helen's mother full of wonder, but perfectly at ease. Subsequently Helen was indeed born perfect.

Helen loved to hear her mother tell the story of that

night. She felt as if there would always be a guardian angel there for her, and a strong sense of protection stayed with her throughout childhood. Many small incidents seemed to bear this out as she grew.

In her teens Helen began to enjoy greatly outdoor sports. Growing up in Australia was a great bonus for someone who loved being outside. It was therefore a real hardship to stay indoors at the age of sixteen and study for her school exams. Helen was keen to perform well even so, and wished the whole family to be proud of her. It became a great source of worry to her, and as the exams drew close she found herself in a state of high anxiety.

One night a short time before the exams were due to start, Helen lay in bed feeling quite drained. A faint glow began to appear in the room, spreading until it was above her bed. In the centre of this glow a sensitive and beautiful face appeared. At once Helen felt calm and comforted and fell into a deep refreshing sleep. To her amazement and delight, this angel face appeared every night until the exams were completed. Helen passed the exams with flying colours, without the slightest worry, but the angel face never appeared again.

Life continued as normal, but there often seemed to be an unseen presence warning Helen; sometimes it was only a feeling or a slight sensation of a hand stopping her in her tracks. One dramatic incident took place when Helen was about to climb on board a chair lift. The lift was of the type which swung around in a continuous loop without stopping and one had to jump on as it swung behind you, so you had to be nimble.

Helen waited for her turn to climb on the chair, but it arrived so swiftly she scarcely had time to sit in it securely before she was whisked away. Climbing sharply and with speed, Helen struggled to gain a secure seat-hold, but slid off the edge. Plunging to the ground in terror, she felt sure some terrible injuries would ensue, as did the horrified crowd of bystanders who screamed involuntarily. Immediately before coming into contact with the ground, from several metres high, she had the sensation of hands catching her. Gaining consciousness was her next memory. She had fainted with shock, but did not have a single scratch as a result of the fall.

The final story of Helen's continuing protection took place one hot sunny day when a crowd of friends headed for the beach. Heading for Oberon Bay in Wilson's Promontory National Park, they walked down the path to the shore amongst beautiful scenery. A feeling of being held back suddenly overcame Helen, and she stopped dead in her tracks in time to see a poisonous snake slide across their path. Silently saying thank you, she continued to the beach. This was Helen's favourite place and swimming was her favourite outdoor sport. She was usually the first into the water and the last to come out.

The crowd of young people raced to the water, and

several of Helen's friends swiftly swam past her going further out into the bay. They yelled at Helen to follow them, and were slightly puzzled when she hesitated, as it was completely out of character. Normally there would not have been a moment's hesitation. Again Helen was feeling that some force, unseen and unheard, was preventing her from going any further. Turning she swam back to the beach and joined some of her less adventurous colleagues.

No more than ten minutes had elapsed, when to everyone's horror a huge freak wave sent Helen's friends in the water crashing onto the outlying rocks. Scrambling to try and secure a hold, they were unaware that a second large wave was descending on them. People on the shore watched helplessly as one of the friends was swept away by the force of the wave. It was more than twenty-four hours before his body was found. A happy end-of-term picnic had turned into a tragedy. However, for Helen, it seemed once more that she had been warned and protected.

One glorious autumn day Lucy decided to go for a long ride on her pony Clover. The pony had been a thirteenth birthday present for Lucy, and she loved him dearly. Since she lived in a fairly quiet open part of the country, she started her ride trotting down the leafy lanes behind her home, enjoying the crunchy sounds of the fallen leaves under Clover's hooves. Presently they came to a fork in the road where Lucy would usually turn right, which would take her on a long circular route back to the starting point. Today, however, she was feeling a great deal more adventurous, and decided Clover was ready for a much longer ride. They would have to cross a rather busy road at this point, but Clover was used to traffic, and it would only be a very short stretch of road before they could turn into the quiet lanes once more.

Turning to the left, they heard the buzz of traffic, and slowed to a walk as they approached the road. Clover behaved impeccably, halting on command at the busy road. Calmly crossing the road when a break in the traffic allowed, they walked along the far side of the road until they could reach the turning point to leave the busy traffic behind. Passing under a railway bridge should be no problem and they would be there. But trotting under the bridge both Lucy and Clover were startled by being overtaken by a very fast and noisy car. The fact that they were in a short tunnel must have amplified the noise, and Clover was very scared. Panicking, the pony reared, and threw Lucy into the road where she landed heavily.

Traffic screeched to a standstill, a mobile phone was used to call an ambulance immediately, and in record time help arrived. The ambulance personnel were examining Lucy before taking her to hospital. Lucy, however, was astonished to find that she was watching this scene from the underside of the bridge. She was looking down on her own body lying in the road, and could see and hear the ambulance men making their checks. A woman had taken hold of Clover and was calming him, but Lucy was apparently floating above it all. She was aware of a warm light surrounding her and the sensation that it was supporting her. A voice then spoke to her gently and told her not to be afraid.

Her next memory is one of cold and pain washing over her as she was lifted onto a stretcher. She realised that she was back in her body and on the way to hospital. There were no serious injuries, and recovery was fairly swift. Soon she was home, and then had time to reflect on the incident. Her parents pondered on what it could mean and what the voice could have been. Lucy, however, has no reservations. She states categorically that she was cared for by an angel.

It has often been said that we are all psychically gifted, but untutored and underdeveloped in the art. It does seem to be a phenomenon which comes more easily to some people than others, though from time to time we all have premonitions. For certain people the warning or premonition is so powerful there is no mistaking the message. Valerie is one of those people. She will often get not only a feeling that something may be wrong, but also a clear voice in her head telling her what action to take. Valerie firmly believes this is her guardian angel, and can recall six or seven times since childhood when the voice has spoken to her. On several occasions she has been led to situations where as a trained nurse she feels she was needed at that particular time.

The last time Valerie heard this voice it was especially welcome, as it involved the safety of her twelve-year-old son David. She had left him playing with a group of boys happily if noisily in their neighbour's garden to visit the local supermarket. The neighbour had built his own sons an excellent treehouse.

Ten minutes later Valerie was parking her car at the supermarket. Sighing, she switched off the engine, and collected her thoughts along with the shopping list. Turning to open the car door she was shaken by the insistence and clarity of the voice speaking to her. 'Go home at once,' it said, twice. Quickly fastening her seatbelt, Valerie set off for home as fast as the traffic and the speedlimit would allow. Dashing down the path to her neighbour's garden, she saw her son on the ground, surrounded by white-faced children and very concerned adults. David had fallen from the treehouse, landing heavily, and it was apparent to Valerie that he had broken his leg. An ambulance was on its way but

Valerie took over in a professional mode that curtailed the rising panic of her parent role.

Days later, when the confusion had died down and David was in plaster, her friend next door asked 'By the way, what made you come dashing home so quickly from the supermarket that day?' 'A message from on high,' was Valerie's enigmatic answer.

G lenys and her parents were planning a trip to the seaside, and the excitement was intense for the little girl. A picnic was planned, and so sandwiches and a flask were placed in the car and they set off in high spirits.

Approximately half way to their intended destination, Glenys was watching the sky for any sign of rain that might spoil the day. She then saw the most fascinating formation. Against the blue sky a huge cloud had formed into a giant figure. Glenys decided that this must be Jesus. Leaning forward she tapped her mother on the shoulder and said, 'We must not worry, everything will be all right. Jesus is watching over us.' Her mother was startled, to put it mildly, but she smiled at the little girl and said 'Yes dear, of course, thank you.'

Only a few moments after this conversation, the car hit an object close to the curb and Glenys's father lost control. Over and over the car rolled, before landing on its side several hundred metres away. No-one could believe that all three members of the family were completely unhurt, escaping without a scratch. Glenys, however, was not in the least bit surprised.

I am sure we all recall getting into scrapes as children because we disobeyed parental instruction. Kind people rescue some of us, whilst others flounder alone as best they can. For some children, however, it seems very special help is at hand. Margaret can recall several occasions throughout her life when she feels extra special help was at hand, and so she feels truly blessed.

At the age of eight, Margaret was allocated to take her little sister for a walk in the pushchair. She was joined by her good friend Peter. Margaret was more than old enough to understand the rules when going out unaccompanied by an adult, but she was especially warned on their departure not to go anywhere near the canal. This was completely out-of-bounds and to be avoid in all circumstances.

Curiosity is never far away in childhood, and inevitably they found themselves at the canal. There were numerous nooks and crannies to be explored, and Margaret and Peter decided to climb up the steep sides of the bank. They left her sister in her pushchair, and told her to stay put and sit still while they scrambled up the bank. She sat still for less than a minute, and pulling the pushchair after her, tried to follow the other two children up the steep bank. The inevitable happened, and she let go of the chair which immediately ran down the steep slope and straight into the canal. Margaret heard the loud splash and was gripped with fear. Not only was the expensive pushchair in the canal, but it was festooned with coats and hats. Panic and guilt rose in Margaret in equal measures at the thought of her mother's reaction. She had disobeyed a strict instruction, and it was a miracle that her little sister had not fallen into the canal also.

Margaret burst into tears, and found herself praying. What she expected to happen she did not quite know, but it was the only thing she could think of under the circumstances. It seemed that an answer to her prayers appeared in the form of a tall boy carrying a long carved pole. In a trice he had retrieved the pushchair from the water, complete with belongings.

The boy disappeared as quickly as he had come, and Margaret could only stand and stare with amazement. She reflected later that it was far too much of a coincidence that a boy with exactly the right implement to help had arrived at the precise time he was needed. He had a rather special air about him, and was certainly a little mysterious. She concluded that he must have been an angel in disguise.

The protection continued for Margaret as she grew. She was once saved by millimetres from a speeding car completely out of control. Walking down her garden path one day, a huge ridge tile fell and missed her head by a fraction. These and similar incidents have followed Margaret all her life, but the most dramatic incident happened on holiday fairly recently in Keflonica, Greece. Travelling with friends in a car along a very twisty and winding road through the hills, she was only too aware of the sheer drop on each side of the road and the fact that there was not a single barrier to help prevent accidents. The day was wet and misty and the drive distinctly hazardous.

Everyone's worst nightmare was realised when the car skidded on the wet road, and spinning out of control went backwards at speed over the edge and down the steep slope, which was almost a sheer drop. The car thundered through dense foliage until eventually it hit an olive tree. Lurching violently it came to rest on its side in the tree. Rescuers were quickly on the scene, and were surprised and relieved to find all the occupants of the car shaken but completely unhurt.

On reaching the top of the gorge again, Margaret and her friends reflected on just how fortunate they had been. Miraculously they had missed by only a metre or so a giant rock protruding from the hillside. The olive tree was the only tree on that slope, yet it had caught them and effectively prevented them from hurtling down the sheer drop to certain death at the bottom of the valley.

Little wonder that Margaret believes her guardian angel is watching over her still.

'Please, Mum, can I have rollerblades for Christmas?' Mary groaned. Three times in one week she had heard Liam's plaintive cry, and it was only October. She was very worried at the prospect of rollerblades. The local park had provided an area where the youngsters could rollerblade, but to reach it a very busy main road had to be crossed, and Mary had often seen boys dicing with death crossing this road with their rollerblades on their feet.

Inevitably the parents succumbed, and on Christmas morning Liam found his much desired rollerblades under the Christmas tree. He was beside himself with excitement and could scarcely wait to be off to test them. However, he had to promise faithfully not to cross the busy road wearing the blades, but to put them on when he arrived at the park. He promised, of course, and for the next few days the blades scarcely left his feet. Mary watched him go, uttering a silent prayer for his safe keeping.

Soon Liam had become extremely proficient on his

rollerblades, and was capable of performing all kinds of skilful manoeuvres. He began to believe he was almost invincible and was as safe wearing blades as he was on two feet. One evening as dusk was falling, Liam set off for home, leaving the park with his friends. He reasoned that surely by now he did not need to keep removing his blades before crossing the road; he was after all something of an expert at this point, confident and in control. Waving to his friends and glancing only perfunctorily in both directions, he launched himself into the momentarily clear road.

To this day Liam has no idea where the car came from, he only recalls a large red vehicle bearing down on him at great speed. The car struck him virtually head on, but instead of the full impact one would have expected, it felt like a glancing blow, and Liam found himself being lifted high enough for the car to pass underneath his body. He soared through the air in an arc-like movement, and found himself being lowered gently onto his feet. He was safe and sound on the opposite pavement, shocked but in one piece.

A family friend who witnessed the accident told Liam's mother it had been like watching a film with special effects. The boy appeared to float across the road high in the air with no visible means of support. Liam insists that he had a definite sensation of hands holding him until he was out of harm's way. Mary concludes that her prayer had been heard and indeed answered by his guardian angel.

Heaven Scent

I always think that certain smells and fragrances are as powerfully evocative as music or photographs. They whisk us back to childhood, or provoke memories of a certain person in our lives. I am sure each one of us has experienced such sensory triggers. In recent years when people have been a good deal more forthcoming about angelic encounters and experiences, I hear more and more stories involving a fragrance with an angelic source. It appears that the beautiful aroma people experience at time of trouble or when comfort was needed had never previously been connected to a heavenly intervention. When stories began to emerge, it was obvious that at last people had an explanation for their own personal, inexplicable fragrance. For example, one woman who could frequently smell her husband's tobacco smoke, years after his death, was delighted to read another similar story. At last she realised it was not her imagination but as she had always hoped – her husband assuring her whenever she felt particularly low that he was never far away.

J ane will never forget the fragrance that changed
her life, but she struggles to identify it. If you have
ever been marooned in a caravan with rain relent-
lessly beating on the roof, you will know how depressing it can be. Add to this mixture two frustrated small
children, and you will begin to understand how Jane
was feeling. The idea of a caravan holiday had sounded
most attractive, however, when her friend said she
thought a break would be beneficial. It was a beautiful
area and the caravan was comfortable and tastefully
furnished, but no sooner had they arrived and settled
in, than it began to rain. The heavy downpour turned
to torrential rain, and two whole days passed with very
little respite.

Miraculously the third day dawned dry with fairly
clear skies. Like greased lightning, they dashed from
the caravan and down the mountain in the car to the
nearest seaside town. By mid-afternoon the light was
beginning to fade, so Jane thought it best that they
should return to the caravan, and then head for home
while it was still dry. Packing their things into the car,
they felt that at least they had enjoyed one fine day, and
set off in good spirits. The road was quite muddy from
all the recent rain and Jane drove with extra care.

It could not have been more than half an hour from

leaving the caravan site that the rain started again. High winds added to her problems, and the rain became so heavy that the windscreen wipers could scarcely cope. They were in the midst of a storm, and the light had gone completely. Scarcely able to see, Jane stopped the car for a moment, although what she could do about the situation she had no idea. Tears ran down her face as she looked at the two little girls on the back seat. The three-year-old was fast asleep, oblivious to their predicament, but her five-year-old daughter smiled perkily at her. This made Jane cry all the more. It was then that this wise little girl leant forwards, placed her hand on her mother's shoulders and said, 'Don't cry mummy, the angels will help us.' Smiling at the little one, she replied 'Of course, dear.' Drying her eyes on a tissue, she started the car again and was prepared to struggle on. The rain did seem less heavy now, and within minutes it had stopped completely.

Astonishment gripped Jane when suddenly the car was filled with the most powerful aroma. It was almost impossible to identify, like no other smell she had ever encountered. Perfume, flowers and spices all mixed together was the nearest she could come to a description, and it filled her with hope and confidence. The fragrance engulfed them completely for about a minute before gradually fading. Jane drove on with renewed confidence and composure.

Safe in bed at home Jane relived the events of the night. She found herself thinking, 'Where on earth did that fragrance come from?' but she knew in her heart that it was not of this earth at all.

Every raindrop that falls is accompanied by an angel,
for even a raindrop is a manifestation of a being.
MOHAMMED

Death is never easy to cope with, and the loss of someone close and much loved is the hardest thing we ever have to face emotionally. Adults find the experience daunting and emotionally draining, but what about children? How does one begin to explain, comfort and reassure a grieving child?

Rebecca was nine years old when her mother died, and people told her that her mother was now an angel in heaven. All Rebecca knew was that her mother was no longer there, and the only tangible evidence left was a wardrobe full of her clothes and personal effects. Opening the wardrobe, Rebecca could smell her mother's perfume, which made her feel close for a moment. Along with her elder sister, she resolved to be brave and pull together with their much loved father.

Months and years passed, and eventually the pain eased, though Rebecca never forgot her mother. There were moments when she felt low and missed her dreadfully. It was on one of these days that Rebecca felt slightly unwell as well as missing her mother. Late in the afternoon she lay on the sofa in the lounge, home alone for a while. Sinking back into the comfortable cushions, she relaxed and started to think about the days in the past when if she was feeling unwell her mother would pamper her for a while.

Suddenly, through the door from the hall came the most wonderful fragrance. It completely enveloped Rebecca before wafting on through the lounge. It was instantly recognisable to her; she had no doubt at all it was her mother's. Not only did it contain her perfume but also all the other fragrances and smells which composed her mother's life – the medicine she had taken when she had been ill, her shampoo and lots of other smells. She was in no doubt that this was an indication of her mother's presence, an unmistakable way of letting her daughter know that she was not alone and still loved very much.

Since that time, on several occasions and in different places, Rebecca has experienced the all-enveloping aroma, usually at times when she needs comfort or when she feels a little weary. She knows for certain that throughout her life her mother will never be far away.

Maggy suffered the loss of her mother when she was only twelve years old. Her father was a devout Christian, and had decided that he wanted the funeral service in the family home. The coffin was brought into the lounge for several days before the service.

After the funeral, Maggy was amazed to find the room where her mother's coffin had lain full of the perfume of spring flowers. She would frequently go into the room to experience the most wonderful scent she could ever recall.

It was only later when she was an adult that she fully realised that this was a most unusual phenomenon. True, there had been flowers at the time of her mother's funeral service and when the coffin was laid in the lounge. When flowers are removed, however, the fragrance does not last for more than a few hours. The fragrance of spring flowers in Maggy's home lasted for more than twelve months.

I have been informed over and over again recently that the perfume of yellow roses accompanies prayers answered by St Theresa. Yellow roses are apparently a calling card of the saint and feature prominently in stories of help attributed to her.

Enid Case wrote a fascinating book some twenty years ago entitled *The Odour of Sanctity*; she kindly gave me permission to retell one of her stories here.

At the age of five, Cynthia was diagnosed as having a heart murmur. The aortic valve leading from the heart was giving great cause for concern and a close watch would have to be kept on the little girl. For years she was carefully monitored, and at the age of twelve was taken into Blackpool's Victoria Hospital for surgery. This was the only course to be taken if she was to live, yet it carried a huge risk. Friends and family gathered around to pray for the little girl. Many people prayed specifically to St Theresa as the child underwent the ten hours of intensive surgery.

Arriving home, Cynthia's parents walked up the path to the front door. They were a little bewildered at a fine mist which appeared from nowhere and completely surrounded them. It was decidedly aromatic, and as they stepped into the house they were overcome by the scent of roses. There were no flowers of any description in the house. The garden had no roses in bloom, though in her confusion Cynthia's mother went outdoors to check. It was then that Cynthia's sister arrived home and asked, 'What is that wonderful smell? It followed me all down the path and into the house.'

Needless to say the operation was a huge success. In fact after only seventeen days, and to everyone's astonishment, Cynthia came home from the hospital. The entire family to this day are amazed at the events of that evening. Time after time they hear people talk about the smell of roses being an answer to prayers directed to St Theresa, and they would certainly not disagree.

Communication with angels starts if you recognise
they are there.
MURRAY STEINMAN

Irene liked the smell of her little baby boy, especially after his evening bath. She felt a very special bond with her son, so was overcome with shock and grief when he died. However in time, much to her joy, another baby arrived, another son whom she named Zac. A healthy child, he grew swiftly into a toddler. Irene could not help but wonder what her first child would have looked like at this stage; she knew they would still have been close. Pondering on this thought and remembering just how close they had been, she tucked her son Zac into his bed for the night.

A strong feeling of a presence in the room took Irene by surprise. This was accompanied by a fragrance so powerful and beautiful that words fail to describe it, she says. It had appeared quickly and it vanished with equal speed leaving her bewildered. The thought came into her mind subsequently that this was her first-born son contacting her and telling her he was near.

Zac grew up and to Irene's delight over the years on many significant occasions, the fragrance would engulf her as completely as on that first night. The day arrived when Zac was independent enough to leave home, and he decided to acquire a house of his own. It came as no surprise to Irene when Zac's girlfriend told her that on entering the house for the first time, she was amazed to find it full of the most beautiful fragrance, one she had never encountered before.

Angels are beautiful and they have a lovely smell.
FAYE HILTON, 11

Debbie's young son lay seriously ill in hospital, and she felt completely numb. On the way to the hospital she would have to stop at her grandmother's house to give her the news. Her grandmother, Martha, was quite frail and very old, so Debbie wondered how she would react. As she slowly told Martha the awful news, for a time the old lady simply sank back into her chair white-faced. Sitting up straight suddenly she said, 'Well Debbie, I will do the only thing I can and that is pray for Simon. The hospital I know will do their very best for him, but even they can use some help from above.' Debbie smiled and thanked her grandmother, then, declining the usual cup of tea, she quickly left for the hospital.

Hurrying down the hospital corridors she began to worry about what condition he would be in that morning. She too started to pray that her child would recover and return to them. The day wore on, and Simon's father joined Debbie at the hospital. He suggested she went home for a while, but Debbie could not bring herself to leave Simon's bedside.

Eventually a doctor arrived to check up on Simon and after examining him said he could actually detect a slight improvement. It was a ray of hope for them to cling to. Over the course of the night, Simon seemed to be slowly gaining in strength until in the early hours of the morning he opened his eyes. Parents and staff were thrilled, and in the case of the doctors more than a little surprised. 'He is a fighter,' one remarked.

By mid-morning there was a huge improvement, and the consensus was that Simon was out of danger. They still advised that he had a long way to go before a full recovery, but all the signs were now much more positive. At last Debbie broke down in tears, and the tension and grief she had blocked out of her mind flooded over her. She told her husband that she would briefly call in on Martha on the way home to give her the much more cheerful news. Martha, standing erect, answered the door. 'It's good news, Grandma,' Debbie said. 'There has been a considerable improvement in Simon's condition. We feel sure he will now make a full recovery.'

Martha smiled knowingly, 'I know,' she said, 'come in and I will explain.' It had been a long day, filled with worry and Martha had known there would be no point in her going to bed, since sleep would have been impossible. She had sat in her armchair listening to the radio for a long time, and then in the early hours she had decided to pray again. She had asked God to send his angels to help Simon, because he was so precious to

43

them all. 'In that instant the room filled with a heady perfume, completely enveloping me and the whole room,' she said. It had faded very quickly but Martha had known her prayers had been heard. 'Could you say exactly when this was?' Debbie asked. 'I think it must have been around 2 a.m.,' she replied, 'for that was when I had switched off the radio.' Debbie thought with a great degree of certainty that it would have been around that time Simon had opened his eyes. A shiver ran through her. 'Thank you, Grandma,' she said. 'You really did help.' 'We were all touched by angels,' her grandmother replied.

It was a wet and windy Wednesday afternoon, and the sky was positively leaden, not a silver lining in sight. Celia was feeling low and wobbly after a fierce bout of influenza. Not very robust at the best of times, she knew regaining her health and strength would be a slow process. The need for fresh air at this point was, however, uppermost in her mind and she was determined to go outdoors for a little while, no matter how wet.

Pulling on her wellingtons and waterproof anorak, she set out for a short stroll to the village. Barely a soul was in sight, but somehow that suited Celia's mood, she felt even a chat would be a huge effort. It was nearly ten years since she had settled in this lovely part of the country. As an artist and illustrator of books the peace and quiet suited her well, and the beautiful scenery inspired her to work. Celia's parents had died when she was only a teenager, and she and her brother had become very close, living together for many years until the day he married and went to live abroad. Celia missed him very much but was nevertheless very happy with her life.

Finding herself at the door of the tiny bookshop in the village, she wandered inside for a browse. Aroused from her browsing by the loud, old-fashioned bell of the shop, she saw a young mother and two small boys enter. They were not local or she would have known them, and she gazed curiously as they looked around.

A large book about angels in art had taken Celia's eye, and she had it open at a particularly attractive picture. She was taken by surprise when one of the small boys sidled up to her and asked 'Is that a fairy?' Smiling she answered 'No, it's an angel,' and proceeded to tell the little boy all about angels and their functions. She realised with a jolt that he reminded her very much of how her brother had looked at that age. The youngster was clearly fascinated, and Celia told him angels were never far away.

At that instant, the old dusty bookshop was filled with the most wonderful fragrance of spring flowers, spices and dew on grass. Celia could not identify it, as it was unlike anything she had ever experienced before. The young mother looked up in surprise, and remarked that there were no flowers in sight. So where was the beautiful fragrance coming from? The door was firmly closed, and it was still drizzling. Quite a mystery it seemed.

Saying goodbye, the mother and her sons left the shop still remarking on the wonderful smell. Celia bought the book and slowly began to walk home. The little boy had indeed been introduced to angels on that wet and windy Wednesday, she thought with an inner glow. No doubt about it, she felt very much better.

Early in the hot summer of 1966, Emma was sitting under her grandmother's lilac tree, inhaling the fragrance and gazing at the beautiful blossom. Lilac had always been her favourite colour, and gazing up at the deep blue sky through the lilacs was a heady experience.

Chatting to her grandmother under the lilac tree brought them back once again to the by now more than familiar story of Emma's stay in hospital when a small child. Emma's mother, Rosemary, had told her the story many times over the years, and Florence, her grandmother, too was always ready to discuss it.

Apparently one minute Emma had been a happy, laughing child, the next dangerously ill with only a small chance of pulling through. The word 'meningitis' had hit Rosemary as hard as a brick, and she had scarcely been able to comprehend what was happening. Emma had been about four at the time, and does not recall the details, only being taken to hospital feeling very ill.

With her parents and grandmother at her bedside, and the doctors and nursing staff doing all they could to help, the night had worn on. Rosemary's husband had returned to take care of the younger child, and she and Emma's grandmother had sat by the bed during the night. The night had seemed endless, but eventually the sky had begun to lighten. Gazing through the window, tears pricking her eyes, Rosemary had found herself praying, something she had not done in a very long time: 'God send your angels to help my child.'

Turning, she had noticed that Florence was awake and looking confused. 'Where is that lovely smell coming from?' she had asked. The room had filled with the strong scent of lilac. Behind the little girl's bed a light had begun to grow, until a large ray of light fanned out over the whole room. It had lasted for about a minute or so, and then gradually had faded along with the perfume. Rosemary and Florence had stared in silence at each other. They had no idea what on earth had happened.

Shortly after this a nurse had come to check on

Emma. She had said that she was stable, and that in itself was a good sign. Telling the nurse about the incident, Rosemary had noticed a slow, knowing smile spread across her face. 'It is not the first time I have heard such a story,' the nurse had replied. 'The lilac or violet smell has been described to me on several occasions and is known as the scent of angels in the hospital.'

4

Hospital Angels

It seems to me that the most difficult pain to endure is that of one's children. Watching a child in pain and feeling helpless is infinitely worse than anything one might endure oneself, and it is particularly frightening when a child is taken to hospital. Friends and family will say the child is in the most appropriate place for a speedy recovery, and they are probably correct. The problem for the parent, however, is the knowledge that the child must be seriously ill to be taken to hospital in the first place.

This was certainly how Yvonne felt when she heard the awful news that her daughter had been taken to hospital. Struggling to take in the news, she was told that Louise had been taken ill, and no-one was sure what the problem was. The school had sent for an ambulance and then called her.

A brain haemorrhage was diagnosed as the problem, and Louise was very ill indeed. She lay in her hospital bed, her mother holding her hand and feeling completely helpless. Looking up, Yvonne was delighted to see two of her closest friends arriving to give support. The friends looked at the girl not sure of what to say. Not more than a minute or two elapsed when one of the friends jumped up swiftly and fled from the room. Initially taken aback, Yvonne concluded that the sight of Louise ill had upset her friend, who could not cope. It was quite understandable, and she sat with her remaining friend for some time.

To everyone's joy and relief, Louise slowly recovered until eventually she was able to return home, her usual happy self. It was only now that Yvonne discovered what had really happened that night. Whilst chatting, both of her friends had seen angels at the head of Louise's hospital bed, who had appeared in balls of light to the two girls. One friend had interpreted their presence as messengers coming to take Louise to heaven, because at any moment she would die. She had not been able to cope with this, and not realising that the other girl had also seen the angels, she had run from the room in distress. Yvonne's second friend, however, had interpreted the angels' presence completely differently, assuming that they were there to heal and comfort and that Louise would be sure to recover.

Five years have passed, and Louise is a bright, healthy girl. She believes that the angels were certainly messengers that night, and is eternally grateful that the message was in fact so positive.

Bella Forman is a very special lady from Philadelphia, USA, where she not only lectures on the subject of angels but also runs workshops and meditation groups. She very successfully helps many people and she helped one particular lady at times of great need.

Bella became a friend to this lady when she joined her meditation group. She was pregnant and had more than her share of worries about the pregnancy and delivery of the baby. She definitely found meditating a great help. Bella told her the angels would be only too willing to help and that she must never forget they were close. She asked Bella if her baby would have a guardian angel, and Bella replied she felt certain it would. The pregnancy continued a good deal more smoothly after this.

At last the day arrived, labour started and Bella's friend left for the hospital praying for a healthy baby. Placing her trust in the hospital staff, she went through her preparations calmly enough. This calm was not to last, for soon lots of things started to go wrong, the labour dragged on and was proving very painful and difficult. All her old fears flooded back.

Remembering Bella's words, she started to try and meditate, hoping that if she could become a little

51

calmer it might help the situation. She also recalled Bella assuring her that the angels were ever near, and she found herself asking the angels for help. Breathing deeply, she suddenly glanced up, and to her amazement in the mirror on the wall opposite her bed she saw not one but two angels – the guardians of her and her baby. From that moment on the delivery went swiftly and smoothly, much to the surprise of the hospital staff, and to the sheer delight of the proud and grateful new mother.

Janice was just three years old when her story begins, but she is absolutely certain of the events that took place, and the memory is crystal clear to this day.

Christmas was rapidly approaching and the house was filled with all the sights and smells a child associates with this time of year. Janice stood in the kitchen watching her mother bake, and distinctly remembers starting to feel unwell. Temperature soaring, she was placed in her bed and the doctor summoned. After prescribing medicine to bring her temperature down, he left saying he would call again later because he was quite worried about her condition. Janice did not respond to the medicine and grew worse. The doctor on his return said she was seriously ill, and that if morning brought no relief or improvement they would have to admit her to hospital.

It looked like Janice might be spending Christmas in hospital, and this thought distressed her mother terribly. Morning dawned but brought little comfort, for Janice was no better, in fact she was decidedly worse. Her mother prepared herself for the certainty of having to take her daughter to hospital, and waited nervously for the doctor to arrive. Janice distinctly remembers the doctor arriving and talking to her mother downstairs. The curtains were still closed in the little bedroom and the light switched on.

Looking around the room, she saw a sight which would remain with her forever, for there looking directly at her and floating gently in the air were several small angels. She thinks that there must have been at least seven of these lovely creatures, hovering on either side of her bed. They wore long gowns of shining blue, and they definitely had wings, for she can remember the fluttering movements they produced. Most unusually, these angels were very tiny in stature – only the size of a child's doll – and appeared to be female. She even recalls their eyes, kind, intelligent and twinkly as they focused on Janice. It occurred to the little girl that they had come to take her to heaven, and when her mother returned she told her that Jesus wanted her for a sunbeam, repeating a hymn she had learned in Sunday school.

To her mother's surprise, and indeed the doctor's and all the family's, Janice looked considerably better, and in the following days made a swift and complete recovery. She told her mother about the angels' visit and her mother understood completely, never once telling the little girl she had imagined it or that she had been dreaming. Fearing that she would be laughed at, Janice kept the story a secret as she grew, but decided as an adult to tell her story in order to encourage others. She reasons that she saw such tiny beings because, as a very sick small child, an encounter with a much larger vision would have frightened her.

> *Angels have a map of the stars so that they can find you when you're poorly and make you better.*
> NICKY, 10

How often have you heard the expression 'appearances can be deceptive'? We frequently find just how off-beam our assumptions are. It happened to me with Joyce. On first meeting her, I concluded that she was a happy industrious person, socially aware, content with life, and probably had not a care in the world. Nothing could have been further from the truth. She was a contented wife and mother all right, but had come through more trauma than most of us ever have to face. At the age of thirteen her son Paul became seriously ill. The diagnosis was every parent's nightmare: malignant cancer. They were warned that the prognosis was not favourable and to be prepared for the worst possible outcome.

In a state of emotional turmoil, Joyce was sent home to try and get some rest. She and her husband went to bed that night with heavy hearts, exhausted with worry. Sleep was impossible for Joyce, and she found herself sitting up in bed as her husband dozed fitfully. She had tossed and turned for hours, but sleep was not to come.

Suddenly she felt wide awake and alert – something was happening in that bedroom. There was a strong sensation of a presence filling the room, and there was a misty cloud forming at the foot of the bed, growing brighter by the minute. From the centre of this bright mist came a voice: 'Paul will be all right. Do not worry. Have faith.' Gradually the light and the mist cleared, and Joyce felt uplifted and supremely confident.

Shaking awake her bewildered husband, she told him excitedly that Paul was going to be fine and make a full recovery. Being a level-headed, practical man, he tried to calm Joyce, and warned her that the hospital had said no such thing, so her optimism might be totally unfounded. Joyce would not be swayed from her conviction. 'I was visited by an angel,' she told him, 'and I know for certain the message was clear, and I did not imagine or invent it. Paul will be well.'

At the hospital the following day Joyce learnt that

the doctors had reversed their decision not to treat Paul, and now wished to go ahead with chemotherapy to see if it might make a difference, although they still offered little hope. To everyone's amazement, not least the medical staff, Paul responded to treatment better than anyone's wildest dreams. All the treatment went extremely well, and his health improved in leaps and bounds. He was eventually declared clear, and came home to lead a normal life.

Today Paul is a strong young man, enjoying life to the full, and extremely grateful to the hospital staff and all who played a part in his recovery. His mother never once doubted the outcome from that special night, for she had received the message that all would be well from the highest authority of all.

Rain lashed the windows, and the damp seemed to seep under the door. Winter that year was proving to be cold and miserable for Mary. She was unwell, and getting worse by the minute. Not quite four years old, she was suffering from 'double pneumonia'. So severe did Mary's condition become that her mother was informed it was unlikely that her daughter would survive another night.

Although extremely ill and very young, Mary

nonetheless vividly recalls the events of the following night. From being weak and frail and very miserable she suddenly felt great happiness. The room was filled with the most wonderful music, unlike any she had ever heard before or since. It remains in her memory so clearly that she often finds it playing in her head.

To her delight, she then saw what she thought was a fairy in the corner of her room. She recalls a long white robe and a deep red cord around its waist. She called out to her mother to come and see, but when she arrived the figure had disappeared and nothing could be heard of the celestial music. What was clear for all to see, however, was the dramatic change in Mary's condition. Mary told her the whole story, and her mother could see how happy and excited the little girl was, and how it had brought about a miraculous change in her. For the first time in days Mary fell into a deep natural sleep, and astounded the doctor on his return with her marked improvement. He later confessed to her mother that he had held out no hope at all for her.

Mary realises how fortunate she is, and the feeling of happiness she experienced that night has for the most part remained with her. She believes that it is her mission and duty to try and spread this happiness, and has a strong sense of trying to do good and help as many people as possible. She sees this as sharing her gift from the angels, and as a way of saying thank you.

Angels to Watch Over Us

> *The angel is actually the message himself. His*
> *appearance is the message that heaven is intensely*
> *concerned with us, and that God cares for us like a*
> *father for his children.*
>
> H. C. MOOLENBURG

Artists receive inspiration from many sources. For some the countryside and nature are the primary source, whilst others need busy cities, people or even their own inner visions to help them create. Lesley feels strongly that her main source of inspiration comes from angelic sources. For many years angels have been part of her life, assisting her first of all in a quite dramatic way many years ago in Africa.

As a young woman of twenty-two she met and married a Nigerian and went to live in Nigeria, full of happiness and excitement for the future. Her family were sad and worried that she would be going to live so far away, and indeed it caused some ill feeling, to the extent that by the time she left for Africa they were not speaking to each other. Lesley then lost all contact with her family.

To Lesley's dismay, fairly quickly after her arrival her hopes for a bright future were dashed, and her dream of life in the sun turned sour. Lesley found herself feeling alienated and isolated. Her husband's job kept him travelling constantly, and she felt very vulnerable in a strange land. This isolation became acute when she found herself pregnant. When labour was due, she found herself at the hospital alone, her husband yet again far away. All this unhappiness and anxiety cannot have helped her physically, and she felt instinctively that things were going to go wrong.

Labour was indeed complicated, and at one point a drip had to be set up attached to her arm. Soon this felt extremely uncomfortable, and all signs of her condition indicated that something was seriously wrong. At this point Lesley lost consciousness, and the next thing she remembers is seeing an anxious face bending over her – the consultant obstetrician in her nightgown. Finally, with the doctor's help, Lesley gave birth to a beautiful baby girl, much to the relief of everyone.

After resting for most of the day, Lesley began to feel much better, and her baby daughter was obviously healthy and happy. She was delighted to see the doctor again, but was most surprised to hear her version of the night's events. One of a team of gynaecologists, the doctor had been working non-stop at the hospital for forty-eight hours and was completely exhausted. She went to her room, placed a 'do not disturb' notice on the door, locked it, and fell into a deep sleep.

In the early hours of the morning she felt herself being shaken awake, and heard a voice in her ear saying insistently, 'Go at once to room number 6, Mrs Ajao and her baby are dying.' She staggered to her feet grumbling, but found the door still firmly locked from the inside, and no-one in the room. Confused, she reasoned that she must have been dreaming, and went back to bed gratefully sinking back beneath the sheets.

Seconds later, to her astonishment, the same thing occurred again. She was gripped even more firmly by the shoulder, shaken and urged to go to the aid of Mrs Ajao and her baby. This time she was wide awake, and to her disbelief she saw a figure in the room. It was a young woman, dressed all in white and repeating the message over and over. This time she leapt out of bed and ran down the corridor to where Lesley lay. She realised at once that a mistake had been made and the incorrect stimulant was in the liquid drip flowing into Lesley's arm. With great speed she removed the drip not a moment too soon, and Lesley and her baby were safe at last. The doctor's skill and experience then came into play, and the baby was safely delivered.

Lesley and the doctor could only agree and conclude that she had been roused by an angel that night. The doctor told her that she felt sure she and the baby had been saved for some special purpose. Lesley produces to this day the most wonderful artwork, and has had many examples throughout her life of help from a very special source. She will never forget that night however, when the doctor and her guardian angel delivered her a beautiful baby girl.

Angels have very special jobs, mainly they look after babies.

STACEY, 10

60

For as long as she could remember Pamela had suffered from ear, nose and throat infections. Treatment for these conditions and operations almost became a way of life. By the time she had reached the age of thirteen, the problems were very acute and it was clear that she would have to go into hospital for a long spell in an effort to clear these problems once and for all. After a stay of several weeks with Pamela's condition not improving at all, it was suggested that she should have more surgery. The problem at this point was mastoids, which were very painful.

One afternoon the nurses told Pamela that her operation would take place the following morning, but until then she had to endure the severe pain in her ears. The nurses according to their rank wore either a dark blue uniform with a starched frilly cap or a dark green one. During the day they would often receive help from nuns living at a local convent, and they of course wore mainly black.

Evening came with no respite for Pamela. The pain in her ears was so intense that she got out of bed to pace up and down in a futile attempt to take her mind off it. It grew dark, and Pamela could see the nurses in their green and navy uniforms gathered round a lamp in the little room at the end of the ward. The pain was so relentless that in desperation she threw herself to the floor and literally banged her head on it. The smell of the wood and the polish still remains when she closes her eyes and remembers that terrible night and the even worse pain. Distraught and frantic with pain she was at the end of her tether.

It was at this moment that she felt arms go around her and lift her gently from the floor. It was, she says, the strangest of sensations – not like a normal lift, but more like a floating sensation. She realised later that as a thirteen-year-old how difficult it would have been for anyone to lift her like a feather from floor level. She literally floated towards her bed and was gently placed between the sheets.

This was when she saw the figure who had come to her aid. It was dressed completely in white from head to foot. The most amazing thing, however, was that the searing pain in her ears had gone completely. Sinking into bed, Pamela fell immediately into a deep sleep. No memory of what happened next remains with Pamela, until she awoke in bed after the surgery. The operation was complete and successful. Pamela opened her eyes and asked rather hazily 'Am I still in heaven? Are you the angel?' Unamused, a rather crusty old nurse answered a sharp 'No indeed' to both questions and added, 'Go back to sleep girl.'

Over the years Pamela has deliberated the events of that night and reasons that a single nurse would definitely have not been able to lift her in one movement from the floor, so effortlessly. There was not a single member of staff who wore white, all the uniforms being very dark in colour. Who was the mysterious figure in white? Why did the awful pain disappear in an instant? She has come to her own conclusions, but one thing is certain: if ever a child needed help from the angels, Pamela did that night.

Amy's mother exclaimed with frustration, 'It could only happen to us!' Every time they went on holiday, some accident or illness seemed to befall them. This year Amy was the victim. She had been playing cricket on the beach all morning with her parents and two brothers, and worked up a hearty appetite. A picnic lunch had been arranged by their mother, and they sat down to enjoy it. To everyone's surprise, Amy declined any food saying she felt a little sickly and had tummy ache. It was unlike Amy to refuse food, and it was at this point that her mother uttered those words of doom. Seeking directions to the local hospital, they swiftly got Amy to the casualty department. The diagnosis took no time at all; it was very clearly appendicitis, and Amy was admitted. The useless appendage would have to be removed at once.

There was poor Amy not halfway through her holiday, sitting in a hospital ward in a strange town. Gradually she started to feel better but decidedly fed up, since the weather was now improving. At one point, alone in her room, she felt so sad that she started to cry.

At that moment a movement above the door lintel made her glance upwards, lifting her head. There above the lintel were two tiny cherubs, each surrounded by an intense white light. Amy stared captivated, and felt a strong glow of love surround her. They were so beautiful that she was sad when only seconds later they were gone, leaving the little room to its mellow light once more. Amy did not know what to think, but she did know she now felt very happy indeed, and all her misery had completely vanished.

Her family arrived full of chatter and news, but Amy could not bring herself to tell them what had happened to her. It felt very special and private, and she was sure her brothers would simply laugh at her. It was some considerable time later when she and her mother were alone that she plucked up the courage to tell her the story. Her mother smiled and said 'Well, you were very poorly for a while, dear.' Amy felt that her mother believed her to have imagined the whole thing, but she knows deep down that this was not so. It is only now, ten years later, that she feels she can tell her story.

Hospital Angels

In the last chapter, we discussed the link between yellow roses and St Theresa. The following story contains elements of this association in a rather dramatic way.

Holly lay in bed, her face burning, and shivering at the same time. Her throat hurt, and she had not a grain of energy. Jane had never seen her little girl so poorly, and the doctor had to call on a house visit. He was kind and reassuring, and gave Holly something to help reduce her high temperature. It was the early hours of the morning before Holly finally fell asleep, and by that time Jane was exhausted. She could not help but worry despite the doctor's comforting words. She mopped her daughter's brow, for she was still very hot indeed, but at least she was getting some sleep, Jane thought.

Realising that she had not eaten all day Jane went down to the kitchen to prepare a snack and make a cup of tea. Climbing the stairs to check on Holly, and taking her drink with her, she was startled by Holly's voice shouting, 'Mummy!' Dashing to Holly's room, Jane was astonished to see her daughter sitting up in bed smiling. Most amazing of all, Holly pointed to the bedside table. 'Look what the lovely lady gave me,' she said, and there was a single yellow rose!

There seemed to be no logical explanation as to how it got there. The only surety was that Holly was definitely better, and she feels the woman in the long white dress who gave her such a beautiful present must have had something to do with it.

Martin was a happy baby, who filled the house with giggles. Soon it would be his first birthday, an occasion they all looked forward to. Just before his birthday Martin came down with a heavy cold, and Patricia had never seen him look so miserable. He did not improve, and a couple of days later, after trying all the usual child medications, they called the doctor.

The doctor advised a hospital admission, and on arrival a diagnosis of chest infection was announced. Patricia was frightened; her much loved son looked very poorly and seemed to be getting worse. His breathing was laboured, and he could scarcely open his eyes. He was in good hands, however, and was receiving the best treatment available.

Making her way down the hospital corridor to the coffee machine, Patricia felt as if this was all unreal, some bad dream from which she would wake any minute. Her husband had gone home for a few hours' rest and would be back shortly. Walking wearily back to Martin's room, she opened door and was gripped with fear. Standing over the cot was a figure, surrounded by a mist. She could not move, but gradually her fear subsided as the light around the figure increased and she felt a strong feeling of love fill the tiny room.

The figure slowly melted away. Her little boy was still safe and sleeping peacefully. What could it all mean? Martin recovered slowly and steadily, and was eventually allowed home. Patricia told her husband what she had seen, but he dismissed the story, saying Patricia had been overwrought. She will not accept this, however, and says she is certain of what she saw and feels convinced that it was an angel of healing.

Angels fly down from the sky to take care of you when you are poorly.

SAMANTHA, 5

Comfort and Reassurance

Children need all the hugs they can get. A hug is comforting and reassuring, a certain signal that they are loved, often when words are difficult. For adults a hug conjures up times in infancy when one was wrapped in a blanket, had a knee scrape attended to, or was tucked up in bed on a cold winter night. At least as adults we are certain most of the time about the source of our anxieties. This is not always the case for children, who pick up adults' anxieties without any understanding or ability to analyse what is happening.

Laura found herself in this situation one evening. Whilst most adults dread the sound of an ambulance or fire engine, most children find the loud noise and flashing light decidedly exciting. Laura and her brother had always thought so until the night an ambulance was called to their home – and it was no fun at all.

The evening meal was over, and the children were getting ready for bed. Laura's father, who would normally have read a story to the children at this point, declined saying he was not feeling very well. He announced that he would go to bed shortly and have an early night, certain that it would solve his problem and that he would feel right as rain by morning. Laura's mother supervised the bedtime routine, and was about to give the children a drink when her husband complained of feeling much worse. At this point he had developed chest pains and looked very white. Laura's mother acted fast and called for an ambulance. She then called for their grandmother to hold the fort whilst she accompanied her husband to hospital. Laura was picking up her mother's fear, and started to tremble as her grandmother arrived.

Next morning Laura was surprised to see a pale-faced mother making breakfast. 'I have to go back to the hospital soon,' she told them, 'but first I wanted to talk to you and explain what happened.' She told them as simply as possible that their father had suffered a heart attack, he was being looked after by some very special people, and they were not to worry because she felt sure he would be well again soon. Their grandmother had said she would stay as long as she was needed and they were not to worry.

At this point Laura said with a slight tone of exasperation, 'I know Daddy will be well, and I am not worrying because the lady told me not to.' 'Which lady?' her mother asked, confused. 'The lady who kissed me goodnight,' Laura replied. 'Do you mean Grandma?' her mother asked, still deeply puzzled.

'No,' Laura emphasised, 'the pretty lady in the long white dress and a bright light, she told me Daddy would be well.'

Silence fell on the little kitchen. Laura's mother and grandmother exchanged glances, and then her mother came over to Laura and gave her a hug. Her eyes were full of tears, and in truth she did not know what to think. The fact remains, however, that Laura's father did indeed make a full recovery. Now, some fifteen years later, Laura believes she was reassured by her guardian angel.

Carrying a secret and being unable to share it with anyone is a source of anxiety and depression, and for Molly this had been particularly acute.

Lying in bed she heard the car sweep up the gravel drive, its wheels crunching to a halt. The doorbell was pressed with some urgency and irritation. It was to no avail, Molly felt pinned to the bed and no amount of ringing on the doorbell would rouse her. She could almost feel the irritation seeping under the door and picture the cross face. The car sped away, and all was silent again. A huge sigh escaped from deep within Molly, depression hung over her like a fog, and her grief was virtually palpable. The afternoon wore on and still she lay on the bed, motionless and unable to move.

She remembered the time when she was a lively girl of fifteen, living in a tiny village in rural Ireland. The most excitement she had ever known was the day the fair and showband arrived. The fair people were the most glamorous and sparkling individuals she had ever met, and she was captivated by the whole scene. In particular, she was captivated by a bright-eyed youth for the duration of the visit. Soon it was time for the fair to leave, and Molly was felt devastated. Eventually, to her dismay, she discovered she was also pregnant. In rural Ireland all those years ago it was indeed catastrophic, and she felt she could tell no-one. Her parents would have been dismayed and furious, dreading the scandal in the village.

Eventually she plucked up the courage to tell the village priest, the only option, she felt, open to her. He was kind and sympathetic, but urged her to tell no-one until he had time to make arrangements. It was decided that she would go to be cared for by a group of nuns in a convent as far away as possible from her home. When the baby had been delivered, they would try and find her employment. Arrangements were duly made, and Molly left the village for the convent. Family and friends were told that a place had been secured for her in service with a large wealthy family in Dublin. When the baby was born, the nuns did find

Molly a job in service with a family in Dublin who were prepared to take the baby as well.

Time passed, and Molly was settling into her new life well. Life was determined to stretch Molly to the extremes, however. One day when the baby was only just over three months old, Molly went to her cot one morning to find her still and lifeless – the child had died during the night. Molly was distraught and inconsolable, firmly believing that this was punishment for her sin.

She remained in service for many years before she finally returned to her home village, the secret still firmly locked inside her. Eventually she married a farmer, and in time had two more children who grew fit and healthy. They were of course a source of great pleasure, but the guilt and the depression surrounding the events of her dead baby's short life would not go away. The bouts of depression became more frequent and of longer duration, until here she was lying on her bed some thirty years later, still suffering. The room grew dark, and still Molly lay pinned on her bed. This, she thought, is what people mean when they talk about the depth of despair.

From deep within her, and with such a force it frightened her, she yelled at the top of her voice, 'How long, dear God?' In an instant, the room filled with a bright intense light. Molly sat bolt upright in bed. The light filled the whole room by now, and the feeling of love was overpowering. From the centre of this light emerged a large and very beautiful angel. Most amazing of all for Molly was that the angel held a baby in her arms. Both faces radiated a smile towards Molly, sending love and forgiveness. Molly felt the burden of those thirty years lift from her shoulders. She knew she was forgiven and freed from guilt. That day she had peeped into Paradise.

You might think that someone who had experienced angel visitations on a regular basis would have little trouble describing these events to others. Not so for Caroline – her most difficult problem was in fact how to tell her nearest and dearest. From early childhood Caroline knew she possessed psychic gifts. Certain events, mundane or dramatic, would be known to her before they had happened. She would have strong premonitions, and as she grew older they seemed to become more frequent. Many moments in her life have been what one could term angel encounters. These would range from a warm glow to tingling sensations, bright lights, and actual meetings with angels.

Not wishing to frighten her children, Caroline had given them broad hints without going into detail, always giving them the idea that they did indeed have a guardian angel whom they could contact if they should ever feel alone. One day whilst casually chatting, Caroline was delighted when they started to ask specific questions about spiritual matters and angels in particular. She answered as informatively as she knew how, and was pleased by the timing, because she was aware that a well loved aunt was terminally ill. The children would be most distressed when they eventually discovered this, and perhaps this conversation might make things easier.

The aunt died not long after, and Caroline comforted the children by explaining that she felt with certainty that she was happy and in heaven. As she spoke to the children, a tingling sensation filled her entire body and she felt instinctively that this was the aunt communicating and confirming what she had told them.

During the next few months when Caroline thought about her aunt or missed her especially, the warm tingling would often occur. She decided the time was right to tell the girls, and sitting them down one day she explained that she felt certain the aunt was communicating through this tingling sensation. Far from being frightened, the girls were fascinated. One daughter asked her mother if on the next occasion their aunt communicated with her and they were there, would she tell them. 'Certainly,' said Caroline, pleased with their reaction.

Both sisters had their birthday in the same month,

and usually a family outing or special treat would be organised. This year a trip to a musical was arranged. Driving to the theatre the children were very excited but one of them pointed out that normally their aunt would have been with them. As they found their seats she remarked, 'I do wish auntie was here for our birthday treats.' 'I am sure she knows you miss her and are thinking of her today,' Caroline replied. Sitting in their seats they all felt happy anticipation as the orchestra began to play.

At this moment, Caroline felt the familiar tingle spread through her hands, and thought how wonderful that even here in the theatre her aunt was communicating. Remembering her promise to the girls, she suddenly had an idea. Reaching out in the darkness she took a hand of each of her daughters into hers. Their faces lit up, and with eyes like saucers they said they could both feel the tingling. It had been transferred to them. One of the girls whispered to her mother, 'Isn't it wonderful that auntie is here after all!'

The Baker family were going abroad for the first time to stay in a rented French farmhouse. At the end of the first day, their daughter Charlotte said goodnight to her mother and went to bed. Janet and her husband discovered how to open the patio doors, and took their drinks into the garden to enjoy the fresh country air. Turning to her husband, Janet said, 'This is going to be a wonderful holiday.' At this point a wail reached them from upstairs. 'You spoke too soon,' said her husband, and Janet nodded, getting up to go and see what the matter was.

Charlotte was sitting up in bed sobbing. Janet was confused. 'What's the problem?' she asked. 'Where is my lady?' Charlotte said. 'Does she know we're in France?' Her mother had no idea what she was talking about, so she sat down patiently and asked Charlotte to explain. Gradually the story began to unfold, while Janet could only listen wide-eyed. It emerged that some time ago, when Charlotte was back home in England, she had been afraid of the dark. Janet recalls the period and how they had to coax her to bed on several occasions, but also how it had seemed she lost the fear as quickly as it had come.

Charlotte told Janet that one night a lovely lady in a long white dress had stood in the corner of her room and told Charlotte not to be afraid. Every night since, the lady had appeared briefly, and Charlotte would fall asleep at once knowing she would watch over her. Her distress was because now they were in France, she was unsure how her lady would know where she was.

Janet could scarcely believe what she was hearing, but Charlotte's distress was real enough. She held her daughter's hand, and said she was sure that the angel lady (for it seemed to her that was what she was) would certainly know where they were, and watch over her even if she could not be seen. Content with this explanation, the little girl went to sleep. She was never frightened of the dark again, but she also says that she never saw her 'lady' again either.

> *For every soul there is a guardian watching it.*
> THE QUR'AN

It had been a long day for Julia. Her feet ached, and she could feel the beginnings of a migraine. Longing to be home, she locked the door of her florist shop, and jumped into her car. She still had to collect her daughter from a friend's house before she could go home and start the evening meal. She found Alice waiting for her, full of the day's news.

Home at last, Julia parked the car in the drive and opened the front door, wearily switching on the light. Gasping in disbelief, she looked around at the mess which greeted her. Someone had broken in and completely ransacked the tiny flat. Not a great deal had been taken, but the mess was awful – drawers and cupboards emptied all over the floor and lots of broken glass from the window where entry had been gained. Julia tried hard to control her mounting panic for Alice's sake, but it was not easy.

Months passed and although they were more or less back to normal, Julia was still full of fear every time she put her key in the lock. One evening she found the problem quite overwhelming, and sitting at the kitchen table she began to cry. Her daughter was in the lounge watching television, and to Julia's relief had shown no sign of fear herself.

Alice came in and saw her mother crying, and said in a very earnest voice, 'Mummy, you mustn't worry, we shall never have burglars again.' Smiling through her tears, Julia decided to humour her daughter. 'Of course not,' she said, 'I am being silly. The policeman will keep an eye on our flat now.' 'No,' said Alice. 'It's not the policeman that is watching over us, it's the angel.' Julia stared at her daughter. 'What do you mean?' she asked. Alice told her in a very matter-of-fact voice that several weeks ago, not long after the break-in, she had woken up and gone into the kitchen for a drink. Standing in the tiny hallway was an angel, filling the whole area with light. Slowly the angel faded, and Alice knew she had come to watch over them and protect them. No-one would ever break into their home again.

Julia was speechless. Alice had not even mentioned this to her, but had shown no sign of fear at this apparition, only confident acceptance. Puzzled, and yet never doubting her daughter's word, she gave her a big kiss. It is worth noting that five years on they are still safe and secure in their flat.

Protection of the vulnerable is common in angel encounters. There are similarities between the last story and that of Stella, another young mother who feels especially helped.

It had all started so well Stella thought. She and Simon seemed so happy and well-suited that life was very pleasant indeed. Simon worked mainly from home, and one day asked if Stella thought it was a good idea to move out of the city to the country, where life would be more peaceful and less expensive. Stella agreed, and any reservations she might have had melted after the move, as spring turned into a hot summer.

Autumn arrived and with it came the birth of Daniel. Life was smooth and Stella content, believing herself to be a very fortunate woman indeed. Life progressed quickly even at the slower rural pace, and soon it was Daniel's fifth birthday.

Only weeks after Daniel's birthday, Stella's life fell apart. Simon told her he would be leaving permanently. He had formed a relationship with someone else on his increasingly frequent trips to London, and would be moving back to the city. The nagging doubts she had tried to block from her mind were confirmed, but she was still shocked by Simon's announcement.

79

Leafy quiet lanes turned into sinister walkways as the days grew shorter, winter approached and Stella's perspective on her once idyllic home changed dramatically. Loneliness and fear became part of her everyday life, as well as a feeling of sheer helplessness in the isolated cottage. Trying to be cheerful for Daniel's sake was a great strain, but she told herself that she must hide her anxiety from him. Children, of course, are not so easily hoodwinked, and Daniel was only too aware of his mother's fears.

One very dark winter evening Stella and Daniel walked home down the dark lane. It was very frosty, and the dead leaves crunched underfoot. The sound echoed slightly, and Stella became convinced that they were being followed. By the time they reached the house she was shaking, and struggled to get the key in the lock. Switching on all the lights in the house she went into the kitchen to busy herself with the evening meal, trying to control her nerves and appear casual in front of Daniel.

The little boy eyed her intently. 'You mustn't worry, Mummy,' he said. Stella handed him a mug of hot chocolate, astonished to see such a kind, caring expression on the little boy's face. 'I will try not to be so silly,' she said. 'Good,' Daniel replied, 'because you must have seen our angel.' Stella's jaw dropped open. 'Angel?' she repeated. Taking Stella's hand, he dragged her outside. 'Look, there on the roof,' he said, pointing up. 'She is looking after us.'

Stella could see nothing, only the dark roof. 'Are you all right now, Mummy?' Daniel asked in a very grown-up manner. 'Yes, of course I am,' she replied. 'And we will of course be fine.' After all, she thought, if Daniel could see a guardian angel, who was she to disagree.

Angels appear in all sorts of places when one would least expect them, often disguised as normal people in modern-day dress. This is perhaps to ensure that they do not startle the person involved, particularly a child. Our next story is most unusual, and involves an angel obviously concerned with a child's acceptance of the supernatural.

Do sunshine, white sand, palm trees and blue skies make you think of angels? I think not, even though I am sure angels are found all over the world. We are so conditioned to think of angels revealing themselves at night in conjunction with starry skies, that to see one on a hot day in an exotic location seems incongruous.

Melody and her mother were enjoying a much awaited holiday in Australia, and hoped to travel a little further afield whilst on holiday for six weeks. Their story begins in Perth, Western Australia. After some time in this beautiful city they were wondering where to go from there, and several people had suggested Bali. Although Melody's mother was a little nervous at the prospect, she decided to take the plunge. Having booked the flight, she was disconcerted to find that accommodation would be a problem.

They found their way to a local travel agent, but there was nothing he could do. It was the height of the tourist season, and every reasonably priced hotel was full. Melody's mother was at a loss as to what to do next. They had the flights arranged and little idea as to an alternative, even unsure as to their position if they should cancel the proposed trip. This was not a life-threatening situation, but for a mother and her eleven-year-old daughter travelling alone, it was stressful.

However, Melody said to her mother perfectly calmly that she could see a man sitting on the sofa in their apartment. Where he had come from she had no idea, but her mother could see nobody. Her daughter said the man had told her that he had come to help, and they were not to worry. He was dressed in normal, modern-day clothing, and had a calm, reassuring air about him. He told Melody to have faith in him, that all would be well, and that they should not try and cancel their flights. Melody said thank you, and with that he disappeared.

Melody's mother was confused, but found herself also saying thank you, even though she could see nobody. An atmosphere of calm settled in the apartment, and both mother and daughter felt peaceful. What the solution might be, however, was not yet apparent. A little while later, the phone rang, and it was the travel agent. He sounded as surprised as Melody's mother when he told them that a vacancy had arisen, in a lovely, well-positioned hotel, ideal for their needs. It was a most unusual occurrence at that time of the year, he said, but it would be perfect.

A very happy girl and her mother set off for the airport, full of confidence that they had a very special agent of their very own.

Angels don't have legs, they don't need them with such big wings. They fly everywhere around the world helping people.

SAM, 5

Jenny was a dancer of considerable talent, and ballet held a particular fascination for her. At the age of ten she lived to dance, and was determined that this would be her chosen life. She worked hard, and had earned a place in a reputable if small ballet company. Jenny's parents were very supportive, committing themselves financially and time-wise to her interests.

One Christmas the main theatre in Jenny's home town planned to produce a lavish pantomime. Leading parts would be played by well-known TV celebrities, mainly from children's television, and the casting director approached the ballet school to offer roles to their pupils. The entire school was in a state of high excitement, not least Jenny, who fervently hoped to have a substantial part. Rehearsals started, and Jenny found to her delight that she was dancing in a small section with just two other girls, where their talents were sure to be noticed.

Days before the opening night, Jenny's excitement was nearing fever pitch, and she was having to be pushed hard to go to bed and get some sleep. Singing louder than ever one night as she took her bath, she leaped out of the bath, wrapped her towel around her, and pirouetted towards the door. Exactly how it happened she never did come to terms with, but she slipped and fell awkwardly, yelling with pain as she hit the bathroom floor.

Her mother could only weep in sympathy as her father drove them to casualty. Casualty staff, however, told them it was not really as bad as they had feared. Jenny had suffered a bad sprain, but nothing had been broken. Nevertheless, it was the end of her pantomime involvement, and Jenny was near to despair. Back home there was only rest. Her ankle was throbbing and Jenny knew there would be little chance of sleep that night.

After a long time lying down thinking about the events of the evening and trying to cope with the discomfort, Jenny sat up in bed and switched on the bedside lamp. It was a little cold in the bedroom, and that along with the depressing thought of all she would be missing made her shiver. With a start, she realised that she was not alone in the room. At the foot of her bed was the figure of a young girl, much the same age as

84

herself, but surrounded by a bright glow. Her dress appeared to shimmer and was pale blue in colour. A feeling of love and warmth flowed from this figure, and Jenny felt no fear, only elation.

Gradually the figure faded, and Jenny found herself in a state of contentment and very sleepy. Sliding down between the sheets, she slipped into a much needed deep sleep. The next morning her mother came into her room with a drink, and expressed surprise that she had managed to sleep so well. To the surprise of Jenny and her parents, the throbbing pain in her ankle had gone and the swelling was greatly reduced. Over breakfast Jenny told the story of the visit she had had the previous night. It was greeted as these stories so often are with the answer: 'Just a dream; you were overwrought.' Jenny insisted that she had not even been to sleep at that point but had been sitting up in bed with the light on. Her parents did not know how to react and decided to keep their counsel.

Recovery was astonishingly swift, and although Jenny missed the opening night, she was well enough after a check-up at the hospital to join the cast for the rest of the pantomime run. It was some fifteen years ago that this happened, and today Jenny is a successful dancer. She says the memory of that night has never diminished in its clarity, and she feels sure the healing process was speeded by the angel's visit. Since that time a feeling of protection has remained with her and a certain sense of 'what will be, will be.'

Angels to Watch Over Us

Angels have special round things on their heads. They use them to make you better.

LAURA, 5

If a list were compiled of the things children are most afraid of, the dark would definitely be near the top. Through the ages children have demanded light at night to help allay their fears.

Jean and her sister slept together in a huge brass bed. Both sisters were afraid of the dark, and they were allowed a candle placed in a saucer of water on the bedside table. Unfortunately this only made things much worse, because flickering shadows cast on the walls scared them even more.

At about the age of seven, Jean was a bright, sensible child. She and her sister attended Sunday school regularly, and paid attention to all they were told. They decided that when they felt afraid of the dark, they would sing one of the lovely hymns they had learnt at Sunday school. Jean suggested they sing:

> *Lord keep me safe this night*
> *Secure from all my fears*
> *May angels guard me while I sleep*
> *Till morning light appears*

Each night they sang this verse and felt considerably calmer, and then they would go to sleep.

One night after singing this hymn, Jean felt a sudden

86

compulsion to turn her head and look behind her. On the brass rail behind them were the shadows of two angels. They were clearly two young girls, one with long wavy hair, the other with slightly shorter hair. Jean points out here that she and her sister had very short, bobbed hair, so they were obviously not their own shadows. The silhouettes had large wings, spreading wide in a protective gesture.

Jean experienced a sensation of great happiness and security spreading through her. Giving her little sister a shake, she exclaimed 'They have come!' Neither sister showed any surprise, for as Jean said, 'We had asked for angels to guard us, and angels we got!' Knowing finally that there was nothing to fear and feeling perfectly safe, they fell into peaceful sleep.

In telling of their experience, the usual standard reply greeted them: 'Just a dream, dear.' Jean puts forward the following arguments. Firstly she says the angels appeared as shadows to prevent them being afraid, since shadows would be easier to cope with than a full-blown angel. Secondly, the candle was well to the right-hand side of the bed and would not have cast shadows behind their heads. Thirdly, the silhouettes were solid and unwavering, not flickering like other shadows cast by the candle. Had it been a dream, is it likely that both sisters would have had identical ones?

The story has an interesting twist. Many years later Jean became a grandmother, and frequently took photographs of her grandchildren. One night her two granddaughters were ready for bed, and Jean took a photograph. They wore white nightdresses and had long hair, one very long and wavy, the other slightly shorter. When the photograph was developed Jean was struck by the amazing similarity between her own 'angels' in the photograph and the angels who visited the sisters so long ago.

We have all seen on our TV screens and in our newspapers the faces of frightened children who live in a war zone. No matter how distressed we may be by those images, we cannot possibly understand exactly what it must be like for them. There are many people in Britain today, however, who clearly recall being a child in the Second World War and some of the resulting fear. James remembers the period very well indeed. As a twelve-year-old he had a full grasp of the situation. As a London firefighter, James's father was in a highly dangerous position, and his occupation frequently led him into hair-raising situations. There was little time to consider one's personal safety during the Blitz, and a swift reaction was essential.

One night during the early days of the Blitz James and his mother went to stay with a friend. They reasoned that there might be safety in numbers, or at least comfort and company. Trying to sleep in a new bed and a strange house was not easy, and fear was very strong at that moment. It was then that James became aware of what he describes as a presence, which made him sit up sharply in bed. He was wide awake and conscious that the bedroom door was open, and he had a full view of the hall outside, which was bathed in a glowing light. James stared, trying to take in the scene. In the centre of this light he saw a beautiful young woman. Above her head was a luminous halo of light, and in one hand she held what James describes as a beacon. It was the most wonderful sight and lasted some five seconds before dissolving along with the glow, until gradually the hall was dark again.

Mulling over these events for some considerable time afterwards, James tried to collect his thoughts. His fear and anxiety had vanished, and he felt only calmness and peace. He eventually drifted off to sleep feeling extremely happy.

The following day James related the whole encounter to his mother who did not (unusually) tell him it was just a dream. She listened very carefully and then said she would visit the local spiritualists' meeting to see if anyone could give her an explanation. The people at the meeting all agreed that James had been a witness to something very wonderful, and felt sure this was a message of great significance – possibly that they would all be perfectly safe for the duration of the war.

Despite the years of danger that followed and the many frightening events they were subjected to, they did indeed all come through completely unscathed. James is convinced that what he saw that night was a guardian angel. He will never forget how reassuring she was, how comforting and how lovely.

We all need to feel valued, appreciated and loved. If these needs are not met, life is cold and extremely difficult, especially for a child. Karen had felt unloved and isolated as a young girl. She now realises the symptoms provoked by this state were those of depression. She felt totally engulfed by unhappiness, based even at that tender age in the knowledge that she was unloved.

At the age of five Karen needed to visit the dentist. A general anaesthetic was administered, and due to complications she came close to losing her life. However, during this crisis she had the most extraordinary experience.

She recalls with great clarity seeing many angels and communicating with them, and being told that at this point she had a choice to make. Staying with the angels was one option, and since she was surrounded by glowing light radiating pure love (a feeling she had never known), the temptation to say yes instantly was great. The second option was of course to go back to her own life on earth, but this time with the knowledge that there was something else, and that she was loved.

She returned still glowing and convinced that this glow of love would stay with her. Growing older of course meant that external influences became greater, and inevitably the glow diminished until she found the old feelings of depression and anxiety returning. Studying for her exams became difficult, since she felt confused as to which direction she should take and haunted again by feelings of being unloved. For some time she had tried meditation to calm herself and from time to time this proved to be a great help. One day when study was proving to be almost impossible, Karen decided to meditate for a while in order to calm her mind.

Almost at once she was flooded and surrounded with the same intense light she had experienced all those years ago. The warmth and love emanating from that light was, she says, almost beyond description. It was as if the emptiness inside her had been filled to the brim with love. Astonishingly, at the same time she had an overwhelming sense of knowledge. All her strivings for direction and self-awareness were banished, and she knew with clarity which direction she must take.

As the light faded, Karen sat evaluating her life until the answer came to her loud and clear. She had to cease her introspection and look outside herself. She must love others in order to be loved. Giving out love would result in receiving love – a weighty lesson for a fifteen-year-old. Her chosen path was to be nursing. Meditation continues to help Karen, now a happy and contented nurse. Creative writing has also become a vital part of her life. Most importantly, she feels enrichment and fulfilment, and her inner angel shines for all to see.

> *It can in no sense be said that heaven is outside*
> *anyone. It is within.*
> EMANUEL SWEDENBORG

There are books published of people's last words. Some of these are funny, some full of courage and wisdom, but none I believe can surpass the words of my own father. Holding his hand during what were to be his final minutes of consciousness, I was overcome with the awful prospect of losing him. He said I must always remember that the only way one could be separated from a loved one was if you ceased to love them. As long as love was constant, so was the connection. Those words steered me through the grief and have helped others too. They came to me again vividly as I heard Suzanne's story.

As children Suzanne and Mark were inseparable friends. When Mark started school, Suzanne missed him terribly, but a year later she joined him at the local junior school and settled in happily knowing he was there. She was therefore shattered to learn when she was seven years old that Mark would be leaving the area, since his father had been given a promotion that entailed a move to another part of the country. Worse was to come. Shortly after the move, Mark was involved in a road accident on his bicycle and was killed.

Years passed, and inevitably the tragedy faded, but from time to time Suzanne found herself thinking of Mark. She became convinced that on occasions, for a split second, she saw his image out of the corner of her eye, but dismissed it as imagination. Deciding her career would be in teaching, she gained a place at teacher training college, made good friends and had a busy social life.

One day some friends persuaded her to attend a festival of Mind, Body and Spirit. On impulse she sat down before a clairvoyant and listened, fascinated, to her words, as she spoke of many things which would make an impact in the following years. Eventually the woman told her that she had a guardian angel, and asked if she was aware of this. Suzanne looked confused. 'Your angel takes the form of a young boy,' she said. 'He is very close, and I'm getting a picture of him in my mind.' Suzanne could scarcely believe her ears as the description fitted Mark's appearance exactly. 'How wonderful,' she thought. 'We are not separated after all.'

Today women have more choices than ever before, and sometimes this leads to confusion. Career women face a dilemma when motherhood enters the frame. Sally faced this dilemma when at the age of thirty-five and in an important and rewarding job, she and her husband decided that it was now time to have children if they were ever going to. She finally decided that she would take a long break and then return to her career. All went smoothly at first, and they were thrilled to be the parents of a healthy baby boy, but nothing had prepared Sally for the routine and problems of motherhood.

One day was particularly fraught, as the baby cried almost incessantly from early morning until evening. Sally was beside herself. Her husband could not be reached as he was driving home and would not arrive until the early hours. Panic set in. Was the baby seriously ill, or was he simply uncomfortable? Should she ring a doctor? Should she disturb a friend?

Rushing into the kitchen quite at a loss, she poured herself a strong cup of coffee and found herself praying: 'Please God, what should I do? Help me!' In virtually an instant the baby ceased crying. Sally was stunned. Putting her coffee down, she ran to the nursery. There she stopped in her tracks, for the most fantastic sight met her gaze. Beside the little cot stood a huge angel. The light emanating from this figure lit the whole room. It shimmered and appeared almost translucent in appearance.

How long she stood there, trying to take this sight in, she could not guess, but it could only have been minutes at the longest, though it felt like a lifetime. She was so elated and full of awe that she would remember it to her dying day. The angel slowly faded away. Sally was filled with a sense of comfort, knowing she was never alone and most definitely loved. What about the baby whilst all this was taking place? Well, he fell into a deep sleep, of course.

An angel appearance would not be suitable for children of a timid disposition. Andrea was timid, and at times painfully shy, which could be a real problem. It was only with her immediate family that she felt completely relaxed. There were moments when her mother would lose patience with her and came close to exasperation, although she was only too aware that the child had little control over her problem.

The day Mrs Porter moved into the house next door was to be a life-changing day for Andrea. Mrs Porter was not just a very kind elderly lady but a former teacher of children with special needs, and as such possessed an infinite amount of insight and patience. Before long Andrea found she could chat away to her new friend and was completely at ease.

In time Andrea was allowed to call her friend 'Auntie Beatie'. She learnt that Mr Porter had died and that the little house Auntie Beatie had come to live in was to help her make a fresh start after her retirement. Aunt Beatie had never been a mother herself but adored children, particularly Andrea. The years brought all sorts of problems for Andrea, not least homework, and once again Aunt Beatie was a godsend. How everyone had coped without her was a mystery.

It was a dreadful day when Andrea's mother discovered that their friend and neighbour was seriously ill, suffering from malignant and inoperable cancer. Nothing it seemed could be done, save for making her comfortable in the form of care and pain relief. The inevitable eventually happened, and Aunt Beatie died. They all missed her, especially Andrea who felt at this time that most of her self-confidence came directly from Aunt Beatie's support and advice. What she would do from here on without her mentor Andrea had no idea.

That autumn the first day of the new term in a new school arrived. It was not too bad a day all in all, but Andrea was dismayed to find even on the first evening that she would have to get down to homework. Sitting at the desk in her room she felt a gloom descend – it all felt so overpowering. Seriously doubting her ability to cope, she felt tears start to sting her eyes. Virtually at the same instant, she felt the sensation of a hand on her shoulder gently pressing and reassuring. Twisting around in her chair, she fully expected to see her mother standing behind her, having walked in without her knowledge. The door was firmly shut, and save for herself the room completely empty.

There was of course only one possible explanation, she thought – Aunt Beatie is watching over me still. Andrea felt elated and the confidence rushed back into her. I can cope, she thought, and what's more I will. Whether or not the hand on her shoulder was her old friend in the form of an angel, she would never know – but always believed this to be true.

Our last story of reassurance comes from another little girl but one far from shy. Anna was perky, chatty and full of beans, as her mother would tell her. She was adored by her parents and her big brother who was ten years her elder. Often her brother Steven would take her to the park or on shopping trips, during which he would always buy some little treat or other for her.

It was with a wail of grief therefore that Anna greeted the news that Steven was going away. They had an uncle and aunt living in Canada, who had invited Steven to go and stay should he wish to. It would fit into Steven's plans perfectly, since he had always planned to take a year's break between school and university, and if he could find a job he would then have a little financial security. The whole family apart from Anna thought it a wonderful opportunity. Waving goodbye at the airport was quite traumatic for the seven-year-old, since a year sounded like a lifetime to her.

In time postcards arrived, and Anna loved them. Receiving mail was a novelty and a great source of excitement. It certainly helped ease the pain that Steven was so far away. The year rolled on, and soon Steven had been in Canada for eight months. Anna's mother told her it would not be too long before he would be home again.

Lying in bed, Anna looked at all the postcards on her bedroom bulletin board and thought how wonderful they were. Maybe one day I shall go to Canada too, she mused. Gradually she drifted off to sleep, thoughts of adventure and travel filling her head. What made her suddenly wake she had no idea, but wake she did and with great suddenness. At first she wondered where she was, because her bedroom was full of light. She recalls that this was the brightest light she had ever seen and yet quite gentle and comforting to watch.

This light filled the room for several minutes before fading and leaving Anna in darkness once more. Puzzled and confused she went into her parents' bedroom and waking them told them what had happened. Her father was a little grumpy, and pointed out that it was two o'clock in the morning. Anna's mother gently led her back to bed and told her not to worry and go back to sleep.

The following day they received a phone call from the aunt in Canada, saying that they were not to worry but Steven had been involved in a road accident. He had been travelling in a car with some friends, and they had been hit head on by a speeding stolen car. He was in hospital, but his injuries were not life-threatening though they would require a longish spell in the orthopaedic ward.

At the end of this long reassuring conversation, Anna's mother asked when exactly the crash had taken place. The aunt worked out the time difference and answered, 'It would have been about two o'clock in the morning in Britain.' Putting down the receiver, Anna's mother told them what the aunt had said. All three looked at each other for a moment, and then Anna said, 'That explains the light, doesn't it? The angels were telling me Steven would be all right.' Her parents could only nod in agreement.

6

Messages from Beyond the Grave

We have many accounts of angels rescuing children from danger and appearing when they are dangerously ill. Unfortunately, not all children survive serious illness and many families have to face the trauma of losing a child. One of the most distressing aspects of a child dying is that the parents can no longer picture where they are. They will be told time and again that the child has gone to a better place, or more specifically that they are now in heaven. What a blessing it would be if all grieving parents had assurance that this was really the case.

Looking back in history, it is interesting to note that art began to depict cherubs in increasing numbers around the time of the Black Death. There would have been few households at that time that had not lost at least one child to the disease. What a comfort it must have been then to see these cherub paintings and sculptures enabling the parents to imagine their child was now an angel. Similarly in Victorian times when chest ailments and enteritis caused the death of many children, we see depictions of angels everywhere, especially as marble statues in graveyards.

The very words 'children' and 'heaven' in one sentence provoke an emotional reaction. Emanuel Swedenborg teaches that all children go to heaven and in their state of innocence become angels there. He communicated for a period of twenty-five years with angelic sources, and wrote all he was told for others to read. I have received letters and newspaper reports from various parts of the globe stating that children immediately prior to death have discussed heaven, and claimed that they have seen angels.

A family in the USA lost a four-year-old girl to degenerative heart disease. Her mother states that the child would frequently talk about heaven, telling them about visions she had had illustrating the afterlife. How or why, her mother asks, would a little girl make up such stories? Each grieving parent must wish that their child could communicate and tell them they were happy. It may sound like an impossible dream, but this is exactly what happened to the family grieving for their son Michael.

Judy and her family were devastated by the death of

their son. She says she could never have imagined the intensity of the pain. Twelve months on, the pain had not eased one little bit. From an early age Michael had struggled with a chemical imbalance, which in his teens led to mental illness. This became so acute that eventually Michael took his own life.

A particular concern for his family was that Michael should be not only happy in the afterlife but whole in every sense. A series of extraordinary events took place at this point. Firstly Michael's doctor, who had treated him for years, began to have vivid dreams of Michael. Steve, Michael's younger brother, also began to have dreams in which many of the questions they had been asking themselves appeared to be being answered. Judy had prayed long and hard that her son was now at peace, and indications in these dreams seem to point to this being the case. One incredible event then took place that left Judy and her family in no doubt whatsoever that Michael was at peace and happy.

It was very early on a bright summer morning that Steve awoke. He drifted up from sleep slowly and sat up in bed. Rubbing his eyes, he saw to his incredulity his bedroom door slowly open. This happened in a controlled manner and completely unaided. Michael's room was across the hall, and the door of that room was also opened wide. Sitting on the bed was Michael. This was certainly no dream. Steve had had enough dreams of Michael recently to know the difference immediately. Perhaps those dreams had all been to prepare him for this experience.

Michael was dressed all in white and was glowing. Steve describes it as though he was lit from inside by a lamp. His face was pale and smooth, and his features were not as clearly defined as Steve remembered. Staring with fascination and deep intensity so as not to miss any details, Steve was transfixed.

When Steve had come to terms with the sight of his brother, Michael spoke. Softly he said, 'I am here to answer your questions and clarify your dreams.' He went on, 'You may ask anything you wish from me.' Steve remained calm, though feeling excited, and asked many questions. The answers elated and astonished him. Michael tried to explain how different earth and heaven were. Describing the vastness of heaven he said, 'By comparison you could fit the earth on a pinhead.' Music had always been a close bond between the brothers. Both had played guitars together for hours. Michael told his brother that music was now so fantastic in the other world that he could never begin to describe it. You would never hear anything remotely like it on earth, he added.

It was then that Steve asked the question everyone wanted an answer to. Was Michael well and at peace? The reply was emphatic: he was in a perfect state of mind, all illness completely gone. The peace was wonderful and a complete release. With this answered, Michael was gone, and Steve was left so elated that he could scarcely contain his joy.

Leaping out of bed, he rushed into Judy's room trying to tell her everything at once and no doubt not making much sense at first. Pulling his mother from the bedroom, he led her down the hall to Michael's room and to the exact spot where his brother had been. He had spoken to Steve with such calmness and clarity that they could only marvel and rejoice, remembering the dreadful state he had been in. Judy was elated as Steve struggled to communicate how happy his brother was. Finally he said, 'He is happy beyond anything we can feel on earth.' He had come to the conclusion that Michael had become a higher being, perhaps even an angel. His weak, sick brother was no more, having become strong, intelligent and free from all suffering. Steve could not emphasise enough that he was wide awake during this wonderful time, and there was absolutely no possibility that he had been dreaming.

Even though Michael had gone from the room, Steve and his mother could still feel his presence. All sense of guilt had gone. They now knew for certain that Michael loved them, and that he had, as Judy put it, given them 'soul growth'.

M aeve's story took place in the 1940s when tremendous changes were occurring in Britain. The Second World War was finally over, and the enormous task of rebuilding was underway. Manchester had its share of rebuilding and associated problems, and everyone was trying to get back to normal. The practical problems were compounded, however, by waves of childhood ailments. Gastroenteritis had reached almost epidemic proportions, and children were succumbing daily to it. Osteomyelitis was another problem at this time, when penicillin was only just becoming available.

Maeve thinks she was approximately four years of age at the time. Her family were soon touched by the tragedy of gastroenteritis like so many others around them. Maeve's little sister, only thirteen months old, was taken into hospital suffering from this distressing complaint and soon died. The whole family was devastated, and Maeve's mother was quite beside herself when suddenly Maeve too became seriously ill with measles. The doctor advised that she should go to hospital, but her mother would on no account allow her to go having only just lost one child in hospital. She nursed her herself, and would virtually not let her out of her sight.

Scarcely able to comprehend the events surrounding her, Maeve nevertheless recalls this time vividly. For comfort, warmth and convenience Maeve's bed was brought downstairs and erected in the living room. A large coal fire flickered in the hearth, and soon she was well enough to sit up in bed. It was at this point that for the first time Maeve noticed a large box in the corner of the room, placed on stilts. It was in those days the custom to bring the deceased into the house to await the day of the funeral. Maeve had no understanding of this or of what the large box contained, but she was told to try and remain quiet. She was comfortable and happy enough except at night, since she usually shared a room with her older sister. She requested a small bedside lamp which along with the glow from the fire would prevent the room from becoming too dark. This was arranged, and that night she felt considerably happier.

Fascinated by the coal fire, Maeve sat up in bed watching the glow of the embers and feeling warm and much better. Suddenly, to her surprise, she saw only a few feet away her little sister floating. She was close to ceiling height and dressed in a long white gown, and Maeve is certain she had wings because they moved as she hovered above her. It was then she asked Maeve, 'Do you want to come to heaven with me?' 'No,' answered Maeve, and at once the tiny angel faded away.

The incident is etched on Maeve's mind, and several factors puzzle her. How had her sister communicated, since at the time of her death she had not been able to speak? Maybe it was through transference, for Maeve is certain that this was not a dream, so clear is the memory. The coffin was taken away, and Maeve fully recovered. The events of that night will stay with Maeve forever, and she is more than certain that children who lose their lives go straight to heaven and become angels.

When a child dies, an angel comes down from heaven, takes the child in its arms and spreading out its large white wings visits all the places that had been particularly dear to the child. From the best loved place the angel gathers a handful of flowers, flying up again to heaven with them. Here they bloom more beautiful than on earth, but the flower which is most loved receives a voice so that it can join the song of the chorus of bliss.

HANS CHRISTIAN ANDERSEN

A trip to the park was the highlight of Nancy's week. In the summer Nancy's mother would often take sandwiches and fruit and they would have a picnic on the grass. Recently these trips had been tinged with sadness, for Nancy's friend Fiona had died that spring, and it did not seem quite the same without her. So many hours had been spent together in the park, and the little girl's infectious giggle was sorely missed. No-one could have guessed that the birthday party they had held for Fiona in the park only a few months ago would be her last.

It was going to be a hot day, so Nancy's mother said they would have a picnic in the park. She packed some of Nancy's favourite treats, and despite everything they walked happily to the park. After lunch Nancy decided to go to the area where the swings were, which was deserted. Sitting on her chosen swing, Nancy listlessly swung to and fro. Maybe she would like a good push, her mother reasoned. Putting down the book she had been reading, she stood up, intending to go across to her daughter. The sound of laughter made her look sharply towards the swing. Nancy was jumping off and running towards her in a state of some excitement.

With shining eyes, Nancy declared that everything would be all right now, for Fiona had come back from heaven. Apparently as she had been swinging sadly on her swing, she had been thinking about Fiona and wishing she could be there. Then the little girl's distinctive laugh had made Nancy turn round. A little distance behind her was Fiona! She was wearing a long white dress, and her hair was all sparkly. 'She must have come back, Mummy.'

Nancy's mother told her to sit down on the grass, and she then told her very gently what she thought had happened. She said that she too had heard the little girl's laughter, but she could not see her. She had not returned from heaven, but had been aware that Nancy was unhappy and had come back in the form of an angel to tell her that she was very happy and wanted her little friend to be happy also. Nancy perked up at that idea, and said Fiona must have found a wonderful park in heaven.

On the face of it our next story is one of heartbreak, but when Diane got in touch with me her message was clearly that eventually a rainbow follows the storm. Hope is the key she offers to others in a similar situation. She feels that the telling of her story will inspire others to hold on, and I believe she is right.

When Diane lost her three-day-old son Darren, she felt a dramatic change in her life would help her to overcome the grief. It was decided that they should move house, so that a new area and new people might help them face the future more positively. The move did seem to help, and before too much time had elapsed Diane found herself pregnant again. Diane was full of optimism, and the pregnancy went smoothly. At last the day arrived, and Diane held in her arms a beautiful, healthy little girl.

The baby was christened Elaine, but at only three months old problems arose for her. Her initial good health started to deteriorate, and she was constantly sickly. Doctors assured Diane that all would eventually be well, but Diane had a terrible feeling inside that this would not be the case. All her instincts told her that this was more than an infant feeding problem.

One day Elaine was so poorly that an ambulance was

called, and the hospital decided to keep her as an in-
patient to try and find out once and for all what the
problem might be. Confusingly, all the tests proved
negative. This only served to worry Diane and her
husband more than ever. A pattern began of sending
the child home, the child deteriorating, her returning
to hospital, and yet more tests which always proved
negative. It was like living in a nightmare. Each bout of
illness left her weaker than before, and eventually the
hospital admitted her for a very long stay to ensure
everything possible would be investigated. This was
intended to last for two months, but eventually it was
discovered that Elaine had a very rare condition called
orithine trancaromylase deficiency (ODT). This was to
be treated by a special diet, and would mean a long
road back to full recovery. At last a ray of hope!

Years went by, and Elaine started school. It was discovered there that she was wise beyond her years. She
was a loving, kind girl, loved by everyone. Shortly after
starting secondary school, Elaine became seriously ill
again. All through her school life there had been long
periods when she could not attend school, and had to
pay numerous visits to the hospital. This time, however,
it was clear a long stay was ahead, which was particularly depressing as she had a birthday approaching. The
hospital staff produced a birthday cake, and they all sang
to Elaine trying to make her day special. All the time
doctors and nurses were telling Diane not to worry, but
the icy cold feeling inside would not go away.

Finally, one beautiful summer's day, Elaine had deteriorated yet again and, whilst she slept, Diane slipped out into the grounds of the hospital for some much needed fresh air and to be alone for a while. Looking up at the window of her daughter's room she saw her pale face appear at the window. At once she rushed back to be with her. 'Who was the lady with you on the grass?' Elaine asked. 'I was alone, darling,' her mother replied. 'I saw her very clearly, Mummy,' she said. 'She was wearing a beautifully coloured dress full of flowers.' Elaine explained that she had just woken from a lovely dream. She had been in a very special place where she was no longer sick and did not have to take any medicine or pills, and she was very happy there. 'I want to go back there, Mummy,' she said. 'It was beautiful. I want to die.'

Diane was stunned to hear her daughter say these things, and stared in disbelief. All she could do to cope was to change the subject completely. Soon after this, Elaine grew very weary and leaning back in her pillows looked very frail. She opened her eyes and said, 'I love you, Mummy' and these proved to be her last words. The life-support machine was switched off, and Diane felt the very depth of despair.

One of the consequences of all this heartache and stress was the break-up of Diane's marriage and Diane then felt completely alone.

The years have rolled by. Diane in time married again and is extremely happy in her marriage. Over the years she has had angelic communication from both her children, and she says they are now definitely free from sickness and pain and extremely happy. She feels without a shadow of doubt that they will all be reunited one day in the spiritual world. She adds that she is living proof that even the depths of despair can be overcome, and there truly is light at the end of the tunnel.

> *Silently one by one, in the infinite meadows of heaven blossom the lovely stars, the forget-me-nots of angels.*
> HENRY WORDSWORTH LONGFELLOW

Harry was a thoroughly nice, kind, decent man, much loved by family and friends. So his daughter-in-law said, and it was she who told me this amazing story. Carol instantly liked Harry from the first moment they met. In time she grew to love him as a father, and Harry loved her along with his son and grandchildren. The children were aware that they had a very special grandfather. He would tell Carol she was the daughter he had always wanted, and he helped cement together a very happy extended family.

One night Harry began to feel unwell. A pain in his chest made him go to bed early, but he decided a good night's sleep was all he needed to get him back to normal. During the night Harry died. The entire family was devastated, but for Carol there was an extra pain. The birth of her third child was imminent, and she had so wanted Harry to see his new grandchild. More distressing still was that Carol gave birth during the time of Harry's funeral. Unable to attend, she felt keenly that she had been unable to say goodbye. Gazing down at her new-born son, she felt joy and grief in equal measures.

Several days elapsed, and Carol carried on the normal care of her new-born son in a bit of a daze. He was a good baby, and people remarked that he looked a little like Harry. How Carol wished he had seen him. Sleep would not come for her this particular night, even though the baby was sleeping soundly. Carol was sitting up in bed awaiting her husband who was unavoidably late. The bedside clock showed the time as just after midnight, and she was wide awake, looking forward to her husband getting home.

Presently she became aware of something strange happening in the room; there was a definite feeling of a presence in the altered atmosphere. At the foot of the bed a glow started to build until it became a bright light. Carol stared transfixed as slowly emerging from the light came the figure of Harry. He smiled as he spoke. He told her that he had come to see the new baby and to say goodbye, although she must not forget that he would never be far away.

Slowly the vision faded, until the room was once more in darkness save for a tiny lamp.

Carol had not felt a trace of fear, only calmness and a tremendous sense of comfort. She looked at her sleeping new-born son and for the first time she could distinctly see the likeness to his grandfather. A noise from the next room startled her; both her daughters were crying. Quickly slipping out of bed, she rushed to the girls bedroom. 'Whatever is the matter?' she asked. Her elder daughter, still a toddler but bright and articulate, said, 'Grandpa just said goodbye. Where has he gone?' Gathering her little girls in her arms, Carol told them that he would never be far away and would always watch over them. The fact was that he had gone to be an angel in heaven.

North Wales is an area of great natural beauty. Jennifer and Clare were very excited as they had been to Wales several times before, and loved all it had to offer. Like all children they thought the beach essential, and spent many hours paddling in rock pools and building sand castles. This year they were staying in a familiar little seaside town, and renting a lovely seaside cottage.

Early one evening after spending the whole day on the beach, the family arrived back at the cottage to prepare the evening meal. The girls were still full of energy, running in and out of the house and through the garden, chasing each other and squealing with delight. Climbing up to the breakfast bar, the girls were still giddy, so their mother asked them to calm down and eat their evening meal a little less noisily. At that moment Jennifer reached across to give Clare a mischievous poke in the ribs. What happened next changed their lives for ever. Jennifer overturned her stool losing her balance, and fell backwards with great force into the patio doors. Her parents saw it all happen as if in slow motion, horrified but helpless to prevent the impact.

To everyone's disbelief Jennifer was declared dead on arrival at the hospital. Her neck had been broken in the fall, since she had hit the doors with great force and at a dangerous angle. A happy family holiday had turned into a nightmare in one split second. Clare was in such a state of despair that no-one knew how to console her. She missed her sister very much, and most nights would cry herself to sleep. The one thing that worried Clare above all others was where Jennifer was and if she felt pain. She talked incessantly about heaven and wanted to know what it was like. Was Jennifer there, and was she lonely without them?

Several months went by, and the situation was no easier. Clare would lie awake fretting. Soon it would be the day of Jennifer's birthday, and everyone was dreading it. At nine years old she was old enough to understand the pain of loss, but too young to be able to cope with it.

Sitting up in bed with the sheet pulled up to her

chin, she switched on the bedside light to try and read a book, but she had no heart for it. Suddenly another light appeared at the foot of her bed, and in the centre of this light she saw Jennifer. She had on a dress of pure white, and light appeared to dance around her head. She was smiling the broad, happy smile Clare remembered so well. She raised a hand towards Clare as if in greeting, and then she was gone as quickly as she had appeared. The only light was now from the little bedside lamp, and the room seemed very dark. Clare's worst fear and greatest nagging question had been dealt with. Her sister had wanted her to know she was happy and perfectly all right, and there was no need for Clare to worry about her.

Clare has never forgotten her sister of course, and would never want to. She misses her still, almost ten years later. Inside, however, is a warm glow of knowledge emanating from the assurance that she has a little sister among the angels.

Jason considered owning a motorbike to be the pinnacle of happiness and could not wait until he was old enough to own one. Close friends of the family had an eighteen-year-old son, Jeremy, who would ride his large shiny bike past Jason's house. Whenever Jason was in earshot, Jason would plead with him to let him ride on the pillion.

At last, after months of pleading, Jeremy finally agreed that he would take Jason for a very short ride. This, he reasoned, might at least keep him quiet for a little time. He handed him a helmet and said it would be no more than a trip around the block. Jason was beside himself with excitement as he climbed on the huge shiny bike.

It is uncertain just what sequence of events took place, but one thing is clear. They found themselves unable to avoid hitting a car in front of them, which in turn had ploughed into the car in front. Inevitably traffic behind hit them, and there was a pile-up of crashed vehicles.

The boys were taken to hospital and then surgery, and it became clear that Jason's injuries were very serious indeed. Despite intensive surgery and life-support systems, Jason only lived for a day after surgery. He never regained consciousness. His parents could hardly believe the events of the past twenty-four hours, and sat by their son's bedside in deep distress.

A family friend happened to be a nurse at the hospital and on duty at this tragic time. It was a help to know a close friend had been there, looking after Jason and comforting them. This friend had stayed with them in Jason's room, and used all her professional skills.

The parents wished to be alone for a while with Jason, so their friend left. As she closed the door behind her, she noticed a man across the corridor struggling with a pair of crutches. She went across to his bedside to help him stand straight on his crutches. 'Has the young boy died?' he asked. With a surprised look she answered, 'Yes,' wondering how he knew since the door to Jason's room had been closed at all times. 'A few minutes ago I saw an angel standing in the corridor outside the room,' he said. 'It was only for a split second, but I was convinced he had taken the young boy with him.'

In the stories of this chapter we have seen the courage of parents facing the loss of a much loved child. I have been approached by many parents asking me to include their particular story in the hope that it would help and comfort others. I sincerely hope so too. Many of the accounts are harrowing, and the pain these people face is hard to imagine, but the longing to help others shines through.

This is certainly true of Lisa, who firmly believes that children have an inherent link with angels and the spiritual world. She feels this is the only explanation for the events surrounding the death of her young son.

Lisa's son was suffering from leukaemia and losing the battle. He grew very weak, and they all knew the end was not too far away. He became so weak that speech was impossible, and Lisa was extremely distressed. The family was not religious and had never expressed any views on the afterlife. With startling suddenness, her son opened his eyes and said that he could quite distinctly see two angels standing at the foot of his bed. She is sure no-one had ever mentioned angels, and there was certainly no literature around the house on the subject. Everyone was astonished.

The statement her son made as he lay dying has been the most wonderful comfort to Lisa. She believes it was deeply significant that he could find the strength to talk to them and tell them that wonderful things were happening for him. She thought it was proof positive that he would be cared for and happy in another life.

For a child to grasp what happens when someone dies is clearly very difficult. Some children, however, seem to have everything worked out very well. I would like to end this chapter with an amusing but inspiring story. During a children's angel workshop I chatted to Thomas. He was five years old, and his father had died when he was only a baby. He sat at the table listening to other children talk about angels, and then spoke up with great authority. 'Here is what happens,' he said. 'First of all you are poorly, then you are very poorly indeed, and then you die. It is then that you have go into a big box called a coffin, but it's all right because that's when the angels come. The angels' special job is to take you to heaven, and there you will be very happy.' With that cleared up for everyone, he went back to his drawing. I thought again as I had during several children's workshops: where does all their wisdom come from? Thank you, Thomas Lloyd, for your very valuable input.

Thomas has remarkable insight, but sometimes these matters can confuse. One child attending a memorial service for a classmate, asked his teacher why had she told him that his little friend was in heaven. The teacher answered the child positively, saying that the classmate was now an angel. 'Why is she standing behind the candles then?' he asked. The child's forthright and matter-of-fact question brought great comfort to the grieving mother.

I recall being told about a young boy sent upstairs to tell his grandfather that lunch was about to be served. The boy came down again and said, 'Grandpa is talking to the angels,' totally at ease with the scene. His parents discovered that the grandfather was dead in his chair. How wonderful to be so accepting and unafraid in these circumstances.

Mystery Angels

In recent years there have been an increasing number of television programmes devoted to mysteries. It seems we are fascinated by things that cannot be explained, such as stories of extraterrestrial activity, crop circles and earth mysteries. Angels certainly have a great air of mystery attached to them. Encounters that do not appear to have a reason have mystified the people concerned. People not in immediate danger, seriously ill or depressed are delighted but confused as to why the event took place.

The most extraordinary event can arise out of the most mundane situation. Rosemary, for instance, believed it to be a very ordinary day as she sat in her garden one summer. Fudge bounded across the lawn in only a few strides. He was growing larger by the day and still only a puppy. Fudge was most definitely a kind of therapy; his presence was very soothing, and she was forced to take some exercise at least once a day. The fresh air and brisk walk always lifted her spirits considerably. Several years had elapsed since the death of her young daughter at six months old. Rosemary and her husband had hoped that in time they might become parents again, but so far this had not happened.

The day was wonderful, and Rosemary made a pot of tea and sat down at the garden table. Fudge settled at her feet, and she decided that when the evening came and with it cooler air she would take him for a very long walk. Suddenly, from the bottom of the garden, there was a rustle in the flower bushes. Fudge sat upright and pricked up his ears. Slowly and purposefully a little girl stepped out into the sunshine and full view. She had a halo of blonde curls and a broad smile directed straight at Rosemary.

Taken by surprise, Rosemary took a second or so to respond. 'Hello, where did you come from?' she asked. There was no reply. Confused, Rosemary approached the child. 'Are you lost?' she asked, bending low towards the child. The child had a certain mesmerising quality, but still she did not answer. Leaning forward, the little girl kissed Rosemary on the cheek, and then walked on past the house and down the side path leading to the front gate.

With a sensation of being released from a spell and suddenly galvanised into action, Rosemary ran down the side path to catch up with the child. She was nowhere to be seen, even though only seconds had elapsed. The garden, the quiet road – all empty. The front garden path was quite long, and to the side of the house was an empty flat field. She could not have been in that field without being seen. Several metres of lawn separated their front garden from the house next door, so again she would have been seen clearly had she walked in that direction.

Some time later, climbing the stairs in her house, Rosemary found herself wandering into the nursery. Gazing out across the lawn, she thought again of her lovely baby. The question came into her head like a bolt from the blue: how old would her child have been now? She placed a hand on her cheek where the little girl had kissed it. I wonder, thought Rosemary, I wonder . . .

> *We trust in plumed procession*
> *for such the angels go*
> *Rank after rank, with even feet*
> *and uniforms of snow.*
> EMILY DICKINSON

Ian had had a scientific education, but was still on a spiritual journey. He was interested in learning about all aspects of spirituality, and his spiritual horizons were expanding.

It was late one night, and he was soundly asleep one

minute and then wide awake the next with no idea why or how he had suddenly been roused from sleep. Sitting up in bed, he was suddenly aware of a presence in the room, even though the bedroom door was firmly shut. In front of the door there then appeared a figure, glowing and golden, radiating light. Although he knew for certain he was wide awake, to make sure he turned away and touched the bedroom wall. It was solid and real, and no dream. As he looked again towards the door, the figure was still there in full view and so clear that every detail is etched in Ian's memory. It remained for some considerable time, and did not vanish in seconds like so many accounts relate. The figure was physically very beautiful and dressed in a long glowing robe which had the appearance of being composed of pure energy. It was male and very tall.

There is no question in Ian's mind that this was real. It was not a dream and certainly not a projection of his own imagination. Eventually the figure gave Ian the most wonderful smile before slowly vanishing. Ian had the distinct impression that he was checking on his spiritual progress and journey.

Ian had often reflected on the inner spiritual ability, which he now sees as corresponding to Swedenborg's description of the angel within. He found himself some time later in a position to use this inner angel. Sitting in a comfortable armchair, he was contentedly reading and feeling quite relaxed. The peace was soon disturbed, however, by the insistent crying of a baby on the other side of the wall. This baby was obviously in the flat next door and clearly distressed. The crying persisted, and no-one appeared to be attending to the child. The decibel level and the distress increased, and it was then that with an almost reflex action Ian stretched out his arm towards the wall.

He projected a flow of golden light and energy towards the infant, spontaneously and without prior thought. Instantly the baby stopped crying and became peaceful. How often do we read about the golden light radiating peace and love accompanying an angel? It is clearly a quality within us all. We can all try harder to reach out and project love through our own particular walls.

Occasionally a story reaches me where the child visited by an angel can think of no obvious reason at all why it should do so. In the case of Natasha I can only think that the child was so happy and full of joy that the angels wanted to join in! Natasha was the youngest of a family of four children, loved by all her siblings and parents. They were a well-off family, and the home was large and well appointed. Every child had a room of his or her own, and Natasha loved her spacious bedroom in the large

Victorian house. Of all her toys Natasha loved her magnificent dolls' house the most, and would spend hours in her room absorbed in the make-believe world it promoted. When she had extra money she would often go and buy tiny furniture for the dolls' house.

Autumn was approaching, and the evenings were darkening rapidly. It was a Saturday and the whole family had decided to go to a new shopping mall not too far away. They were to have lunch there, and everyone looked forward with pleasure to the proposed trip. Natasha bought a couple of items for her dolls' house and was very happy.

At supper time they all chatted happily about the new shopping mall. Before bedtime Natasha decided she would go upstairs a little early in order to place the new items of furniture in her house before it was time to go to sleep. Gazing around her bedroom she smiled to herself with delight at the memory of the lovely day. She felt cosy, loved and very fortunate.

The next moment she was surprised when without warning the room was suddenly filled with glowing spheres of light slightly bigger than a tennis ball. Natasha described them as appearing to be lit from inside with a brilliant light radiating in all directions as they whirled through the air. The feeling they gave her was one of love and happiness, which complemented her own feelings exactly. The room had its heavy curtains drawn, and Natasha is certain the lights could not have been reflections from an outside source. They were, she insists, far more than just spheres of light; they positively glowed and filled her with joy.

As an adult Natasha has often tried to explain the events of that night. She has never experienced anything similar since. She has concluded that the lights were some sort of angelic manifestation. It was as if they were sharing in her happiness and rejoicing in the fact that one so young could fully appreciate all she had. The idea of angels playing with a child and giving and receiving love is very beautiful.

> *All God's angels come to us disguised.*
> JAMES RUSSELL LOWELL

There is no such thing as a 'normal' angel story; they are innately special and unique to the person involved. Certain characteristics or common denominators can be detected, but each one has its own heavenly insight. The following story, however, is particularly unusual. On the surface the story is about a cheerful little boy with a cheeky smile, but it also has a mystical dimension.

The story happened in India in 1910, where Fozia's grandfather grew up. It was the most extraordinary event in her grandfather's childhood, and is etched on his memory. He attended a religious school which was quite strict, and encouraged the boys to study hard. Fozia's grandfather was a diligent student and was most inspired by his learned 'ustad' or teacher, a very learned, wise and discreet old man. One day a new boy arrived at the school, and everyone was intrigued by him. He was a mystery; no-one was quite sure where he had come from or who his family was. The wise ustad said nothing to the other boys, and told them simply to get on with their work and not to be intrusive.

No matter how much they questioned him, the new boy was very vague in his answers about his background, and would cleverly field any penetrating questions. In all other respects he appeared normal. He was cheerful and popular except for the fact that he won all physical games hands down with an apparent ease that irritated his classmates. It was suspected by many at the school that the old ustad knew a great deal more about the boy than he let on, but he always kept his counsel. The boy was treated exactly the same as anyone else, firmly but fairly.

One day a group of boys were walking outside the school and were passing a house under construction. The workmen were struggling to lift a large heavy wooden beam into place. Curiosity rooted the boys to the spot, as they wondered how on earth they would manage this monster of a beam. More men were called to help, but time after time they were defeated. After resting for a moment, several men decided to have one more try, but to no avail. They shook their heads in despair.

At this moment the new boy stepped forward, and whilst everyone stared open-mouthed he lifted the enormous beam single-handed, and placed it into position as if lifting a feather. He had, in short, performed the impossible. Fozia's grandfather ran like the wind back to school to tell the ustad what had happened. He was told to be discreet and not to broadcast the incident, as people would not understand.

When the boys were gathered together, the ustad spoke to them. They could scarcely believe their ears when this wise old man told them that this child was an angel sent to earth in human form to help and guide wherever he was needed.

The amazing child moved on as quickly as he had come, mysteriously telling no-one where he was going and leaving no address or any other trace. Fozia's grandfather told the story so often that it was clear that many years later he was still puzzled about the boy and the dramatic events of that day so long ago. India is truly a land of mystery.

Dusk was falling on the village of Tythegston in Glamorgan, Wales, as Wendy set out on an errand. The village was too small to have a shop, but Mr Durston kept a store of essential things in his own house and would sell them from there. It was to his house that Wendy was sent.

At the age of eight Wendy was a sensitive and religious girl, who attended the village church. It was a very pleasing shape, and she enjoyed attending and singing the hymns. The light was beginning to fade as she passed the old church, but she noticed a faint flickering in the church window. The window was a large arched one and faced the lane. Mrs Maggie Mathews took care of the church, and Wendy assumed that she was inside busy with some task. Drawing level with the window, Wendy looked up, totally unprepared for the sight that met her. In silhouette against the lighted window was a huge angel. It reminded her of the Renaissance paintings she had seen. Long heavy wings reached from the top of the figure to the toes. Standing still as a statue, she was spellbound, as she watched the wings move and settle in the way a bird's would. There was a bright glow surrounding the angel, whilst in the background the more gentle light continued to flicker, producing an effect similar to a gas or oil lamp.

Wanting others to see this spectacular sight, she suddenly found her feet and ran as fast as she could to Mr Durston's house, a short distance away. Knocking urgently on his door, she exclaimed with a sharp intake of breath that there was an angel in the church. The kindly gentleman smiled in bemusement and said, 'It must be Mrs Mathews, dear.' He did, though, accompany her to the church as quickly as possible. Alas, the church was now in total darkness, and Wendy could

have cried with disappointment. They elicited, however, that Mrs Mathews had not been anywhere near
the church that evening, and no-one else had. Wendy
knew that she had not been mistaken, and had definitely seen an angel in the church window.

Now an adult, she visits the village from time to time.
It has changed little and is still unspoilt and beautiful. She
regards herself as very fortunate indeed to have seen
such a sight. Gazing up at the window on her infrequent
visits, she always feels a 'tingle in the spine' as the
memory of that summer evening floods back.

Many children, it would seem, momentarily
glimpse an angel. Like Wendy, they will not
be in need of rescue or seriously ill, but they
do grow with a strong sense of the spiritual world.

On reflection, a graveyard might be a likely place to
see an angel and several stories have reached me about
such a location. Children, accompanying mothers
placing flowers on a grave, have wandered off and seen
angels. One young girl reports seeing two huge, trans-
parent angels, which she insists were definitely not the
stone carvings. Often the vision lasts for just a second,
and frequently the adults involved dismiss the incident
as mere fantasy.

Angelic intervention, however, is often a clear warning and maybe comes in guises we least expect. Every mother will tell you how impossible it is to keep her children within sight twenty-four hours a day. No matter how careful and diligent a mother you are, there will always be the odd occasion when you are distracted and a child will face danger.

In the summer of 1998 Pam and her children were outdoors enjoying the sunshine. Alex was two-and-a-half years old and his sister Ebony only one. Their older sister, Alycia, was at playgroup, so Pam thought they could spend the morning playing in the garden in the sunshine. The house had a long garden; at the top was a flagged patio and at the bottom a large sandpit. The patio was attached to a conservatory, which led to the kitchen. Shortly after lunch Pam went indoors to wash the dishes, leaving the children on the patio area playing.

Staring into the soapy water, Pam was suddenly startled by a strong odour, which seemed to literally hit her in the face. The smell reminded Pam of dirt or earth, as if someone had thrown dirt into her face. It was a most unusual occurence, and startled Pam into looking up from the kitchen sink.

Through the window she saw that the children had moved from the patio area to the bottom of the garden and were in the sandpit. Alex was throwing sand into the baby's face. Going cold at the thought of the damage to eyes, nose and mouth this could cause, Pam rushed outside and rescued Ebony. It was only after the incident, when Ebony was washed clean of sand, that Pam realised what a clear warning she had received. She believes she was alerted by a guardian angel to prevent a potentially dangerous incident.

Velvet was a handsome, black, cocker spaniel, much loved by the Grindall family in general and Ray in particular. His outstanding characteristic was fearlessness; he would happily engage in combat with dogs twice his size and quite ferocious.

One evening when Ray was in his early teens, he sat by the fire with a book in the company of his father. They were keeping a respectful silence because Ray's grandmother who lived with the family was dangerously ill. Upstairs Ray's mother was sitting by the old lady's bedside and Velvet lay at the side of the bed, aware that all was not normal. Ray's grandmother had lived with them for three years, since the death of her much loved husband, George. He had been missed very much, especially by his wife.

Slipping into a coma, Ray's grandmother seemed to be fading. Her daughter held her hand in concern, and Velvet watched with large patient eyes. Suddenly Ray and his father were startled by the noise of Velvet thudding down the stairs, whimpering and howling intermittently. They were astonished to see Velvet hurl himself into the room visibly shaking and with the hair on his back standing on end.

They rushed upstairs to the bedroom to try and see what the matter could be. Calmly, Ray's mother related the events of the past few minutes. Grandma had sunk deeper into a coma and was not responding to her daughter at all. Without warning, however, she suddenly woke, lifted her head from the pillow and stared at a point in the corner of the room. Showing no sign of frailty at this moment, she broke out into the most brilliant smile and said, 'Hello, George,' before sinking back and dying peacefully. Simultaneously Velvet had jumped up, stared at the very same spot in the room, let out a yelp of fright, backed out of the room with his hair on end, and hurled himself down the stairs yelping.

Ray is quite certain that his grandfather had appeared in angel form to take his grandmother to heaven, and that Velvet had seen him too. He adds that nothing of this world would ever frighten that fearless dog.

Picture the scene of a school Nativity play with dozens of infants dressed in angel costumes. Paul was six years old, and although he did not have a speaking part in this extravaganza he was enjoying taking part. Swept along the corridor to the stage, he tumbled out and found his place right at the front of the stage where he had to sit throughout. He was quite happy with this arrangement, because he could see all the action and everyone coming and going.

A tall woman entered the stage from the corridor. She carried a small baby in her arms and was accompanied by a little girl of about ten years of age. They wore long white dresses and walked slowly to the back of the stage where the woman sat on a chair. The girl knelt beside her and placed her hands together, appearing to pray.

Paul stared in fascination, since he had never seen them before. He was intrigued by the fact that they had bare feet. The most captivating feature, however, was the huge beautiful pair of wings the woman had. Paul can remember vividly being able to see each feather clearly. The contrast with the children's cellophane and sellotaped wings was dramatic. Paul says it is a sight he will never forget.

Paul nudged the boy sitting next to him and pointed the little trio out to him. The boy gave a vague shrug and appeared to be totally uninterested. Paul slowly realised that no-one could see these figures. It was years later that he realised that these figures were not actors in the entertainment but real angels – and he was the only person to have seen them.

Angels to Watch Over Us

ANGEL WINGS

The children giggle as they straggle across a makeshift stage
Some shy, some uncertain, some keen to figure in the play
Besides the homespun stable, the splendour of kings
What fascinates me most are the angels wings
How best to represent this unearthly elegance
Wire threaded tinsel, foil on cardboard or nets of gossamer
*   pretence?*
Should they be heart shaped, modest as infants
Or broad and sweeping as those of stone on Faxman's tombs?
Children have their spilling innocence to give them wings
But how do ours grow to lofty fulfilment in our being?
Glorious dreams need nurture, but repay the cradling
Of our heart's desire, so that each angel finds a place where
*   wings*
Touch others and give unvaunted uplifting power with
*   surprise*
At how they may bless these earthly lives.

DAVID LOMAX

Mirrors have always held a great fascination. For Rita, one Sunday afternoon, a glance into a mirror brought more than the reflection she had expected. About to leave home and visit friends, she was ready for a well earned break from home decorating. She had worked hard on her house, filling it with bright, warm colours to replace the dark interior. The crowning glory was the large antique mirror she had bought for the hall. It had cost a great deal more than she had intended, but

136

it looked beautiful and reflected the light exactly as she wanted.

Picking up her gloves and handbag, she had a last look in the mirror to check her hair. Raising a hair-brush halfway to her head, Rita froze in mid-action. Staring into her eyes from behind her shoulder was a little girl. Rita knew for certain she was alone in the house and the mirror faced a blank wall. The hall had only one door and that was at the far end away from the mirror. The girl was smiling at Rita through the mirror and her face positively radiated light. She also seemed to be surrounded by a bright glow.

Once the shock had worn off, Rita found this vision lovely and captivating, and she could scarcely move. Eventually spurred into action, she twisted around quickly, but there was nothing behind her – no trace of the little girl. Glancing back into the mirror she saw only her own reflection. Thinking about that day, she realised that it been the first time had looked into the mirror. She lives alone and feels now that this little child was a guardian angel.

Everyone must be familiar with the phenomenon of hearing some fascinating fact for the first time and then in a short space of time coming across it again in some form or other. It happened to me while researching this book. I heard an angel story unlike any I had ever heard before, and whilst I was pondering on it another one of startling similarity came to my notice. Three thousand miles separate the children involved, so I find it even more remarkable.

The first account comes from Philadelphia, USA, and involves a young girl sitting by a swimming pool momentarily alone. On the other side of the pool a man appeared dressed in a white suit and standing next to a poolside table. As she watched, the man slowly faded away. The child got up from her chair and walked around the pool to the spot where he had stood. To her astonishment there was a note on the table warning her not to go into the pool. On a second separate occasion the child again found a warning note, and this time it was signed with a name. Her family firmly believes the notes were left by her guardian angel.

The second story takes place in Cumbria, England, in the heart of the beautiful Lake District. Josh was ten years old and on holiday with his extended family. Josh and his cousins were passionate fishermen, and it was to be a fishing-orientated break.

The three cousins set out on their first day in the Lakes, carrying all their tackle and a bag full of sandwiches and drinks. The day grew very hot, and the boys thought the lake might be the perfect place to cool off. They had been warned, however, not to swim in the lakes, which are deceptively deep and always cold even in the hottest weather. Ignoring the warning, they decided to go ahead and have a swim. Removing their clothes and placing them in a pile beside the fishing gear, they headed towards the water's edge.

Just as they were about to take the plunge, something made Josh turn around. He saw a man standing beside their clothes dressed in a white suit. Before Josh's startled eyes, this man slowly faded away.

Letting out a yell of surprise, he ran towards their belongings, swiftly followed by his two cousins. There on top of the clothes was a note written on a large piece of paper which read: 'You must not go into the water.' The boys hurriedly dressed and ran back to the cottage. It was Josh's mother who told me that no-one could ever doubt their sincerity, since they were so shocked and had the note for all to see.

Sue grew up with a view of London's rooftops from her bedroom window. She found the view endlessly fascinating, and would sit by her window admiring the different levels and varying types of roof tiles. At night there was the extra bonus of seeing an uninterrupted view of the stars, and on bright moonlit nights all the rooftops were floodlit.

One particularly clear starry night is etched in Sue's memory forever. It was cold and clear, and the stars were very bright. Knowing that she would have a lovely view of the stars, she went to her favourite window-seat to look out. The most surprising thing ever to have happened to Sue then took place. There, directly in front of her window, standing on a flat rooftop in full view, was an angel!

Although only four years old at the time, every detail remains as fresh as if it were yesterday. The figure was immense, dressed in long, white, glistening robes. The wings almost defied description, they were so large, starting well above the head of the angel and reaching right down to the ground. Each feather was clearly defined. In the moonlight she could clearly see the face and described it as humanlike but with no defining male or female features.

Why, she now wonders, would a child so young see

an angel outside her bedroom window? There was no obvious danger, and the incident puzzled Sue for many years. As an adult, however, further spiritual experiences have occurred at difficult times in her life, and she feels that the angel prepared the way. She was able to 'open up' and receive such help without fear. Whatever the reason, it certainly was a night to remember.

Angels always appear in a bright light. They have to be able to see where they are going.

LUCY, 5

Jessica's older sister Rosie was howling with pain. She had rushed from the garden to chat with a friend on the footpath and had trodden on a piece of glass. Her foot was bleeding profusely, and her mother knew a trip to casualty would be necessary.

Casualty was full to bursting, and they realised they would have to endure a long wait. Time wore on, and no matter how many patients were attended to, the hall never seemed to get less full. Jessica started to wander around with boredom, and at that moment Rosie was asked to go into the treatment room. Picking up the baby and momentarily disctracted, Jessica's mother ushered Rosie in to see the doctor.

Seconds later, Jessica realised they had gone. She rushed down the corridor where she had seen others go as they left the main hall. The corridor was full of blue doors on either side, and there was no way of knowing which one her family had gone through. Pressing on down the busy corridor, she found herself turning left and then right, and then she was hopelessly lost.

She then noticed a door leading outside and thought maybe her mother and sisters had gone out to the car. Pushing the doors, she found herself in a huge car park. Wandering down endless rows of cars, she began to cry. There was no sign of her mother's car or her mother and sisters, and panic was rising inside her.

At that moment a tall woman stepped out from behind a row of cars, smiling, and took hold of Jessica's hand. Silently she led her through the door back inside the hospital. With absolute surety she went down the hospital corridors until they came to the one with all the blue doors. Stopping outside one, she pushed it open and there sitting on a chair with the baby in her lap was Jessica's mother. Rosie was on a table having her foot attended to, and Jessica rushed towards them with relief.

Jessica's mother asked where she had been, since there were people outside looking for her. 'I was lost and went outside by mistake,' Jessica answered, 'but the lady brought me back.' 'Which one?' her mother asked. 'The one who opened the door for me just now,' Jessica replied. 'You were alone when you came through that door,' her mother said.

Jessica insisted that she had been brought back by

the tall lady. As they left the treatment room, her mother asked a woman waiting outside on a chair if she had seen the little girl come down the corridor. 'Yes,' she answered, 'she came all the way down this long corridor and straight into the treatment room.' 'Did you see the lady with her?' she asked. 'The little girl was alone,' said the woman. 'I saw her go through the door by herself.'

'I think you must have a guardian angel,' her mother said, and Jessica could see she was not joking.

> *Angels come to earth to help people and then they disappear.*
>
> KIRSTY, 10

The breakfast porridge was almost ready. Karen had given her daughter a tangerine to eat whilst waiting. Handing the fruit to her casually, she hoped she would eat it without question, since fruit was the only food Karen had difficulty getting her daughter to eat.

It was a rather strange sensation making breakfast in her mother's house. She could not believe that she would not come into the room, busy and cheerful. It was three years since her mother had died, and Karen's daughter Catherine had been born around the same time. She would never know her grandmother, and that was a great sadness for Karen. Lost in her own thoughts, Karen stirred the porridge only vaguely aware that Catherine was chatting away. She had decided that Catherine could perhaps see her aunt through the kitchen door and was talking to her. Turning to face her daughter, she saw the kitchen was still empty and that no-one was occupying the adjoining room. No-one else was out of bed, it appeared. Who, then, was Catherine talking to?

'I was talking to your mummy,' Catherine said. Taken aback, Karen asked where she had been. 'Up there,' said Catherine, pointing to a spot on the ceiling. 'She told me that I must eat my fruit because it was very good for me.' Karen was dumbfounded.

Soon it was bedtime for Catherine. She was tucked up in bed, and everyone in turn kissed her goodnight. She appeared to settle down happily enough. A short time later, Karen's father came downstairs and said to her 'Catherine is chatting away upstairs. I don't know what it's all about.'

Dashing up the stairs as quickly and quietly as she could, Karen stood behind the bedroom door. Sure enough, Catherine was chatting animatedly. Slowly Karen put her head around the door. Her daughter was staring up at the ceiling, smiling and talking away. Pushing the door open, Karen asked if she was all right. 'Yes,' came the reply. 'I was talking to your mummy again.' This time she added, 'She looked so pretty in her long pink dress with flowers in her hand.'

Stunned, Karen could scarcely take this in, because her mother had been buried in a long pink dress. She loved roses and always had some near. Entering the room at this point to see what was going on, Karen's sister remarked on the overpowering scent of roses. She too was astonished to find that there were no flowers of any kind in the room and the windows were firmly shut.

Catherine never saw her grandmother again. It was as if she had come to say goodbye from the angelic realms. But to this day, from time to time, the house is full of the scent of roses.

Three short stories reached me with an unusual common feature. No angels were seen, heard or felt, and yet each person is convinced the incidents were of an angelic nature.

Paula was sitting in the garden on a very hot day in summer reading a book. She had the house and garden to herself, and she was enjoying the peace. Like so many teenagers at this time of the year she was studying for her GCSE examinations. All sorts of little things distracted her – bees, the drone of an aeroplane – but mostly she was dwelling on the long summer break ahead.

Almost dozing, she was surprised to be suddenly blasted by very cold air – bizarre on such a hot day. It seemed to swirl around her before stopping just as quickly. She glanced around, but the garden was perfectly still, and the kitchen door was firmly closed. Where could such an icy cold blast have come from on a hot, still afternoon? Putting down her book, she decided to go indoors for a drink, and glancing at her watch noticed it was exactly three o'clock.

At five o'clock Paula gave up on study, and decided to go indoors and start the evening meal for her mother. Washing the salad, she heard the car pull up into the drive. Her mother came into the kitchen looking pale and upset. 'What's wrong?' her daughter asked. She had gone to Paula's grandmother's to have a chat and a cup of tea, only to find her dead in her garden chair. It was a terrible shock, and she could not yet accept it. Paula put her arms around her mother and said, 'Tell me all about it while I make a drink for you. Firstly, what time did it happen? 'Three o'clock,' her mother replied. For the second time that afternoon Paula went cold.

Peter was twelve when his father died. It was no surprise to anyone, for he had battled with cancer for almost two years. Although the family was relieved for him, they were also bereft. It took many months before Peter could come to terms with the fact that his father was no longer there.

Two years passed, and late one night Peter was sitting in the lounge reading a magazine. Once more he found himself thinking about his father and wishing he was still there with him. Behind his chair a cold draft wafted past, and felt almost like fingers on his neck. Peter did not look round to see where it had come from or ponder for a second about what it meant. 'No question about it,' he says, 'that was my father.'

Our third story on this theme is from Diane. She too was in her garden on a hot day when the air was very still. Suddenly, from nowhere a strong breeze shook the willow tree violently. This lasted for just a minute, and then everything was still again. That day her grandmother was attending the funeral of a relative. Diane's mother believes the gust of wind was the spirit of their relative on the way to heaven.

Jean and her son David were about to embark on a complicated trip, which involved travelling down to London, then changing for a journey to East Anglia. Jean was nervous as she was unused to travel, and to add to the concern David had just recently been diagnosed as a diabetic. They had been invited to spend Easter with a group of friends, and they had been looking forward to it immensely. Jean decided that she would not let her anxiety spoil the holiday. Jean's father drove them to the station and helped them with their luggage. The first part was fairly straightforward, and they settled back into their seats until they came to Euston, London.

The bustle of the huge station brought a rising panic to Jean's outwardly calm exterior. She had only the name of their destination and not a clue as to where they should catch the train. Eventually she asked a railway employee, and he took her by the hand, seized the suitcase and told them to follow him quickly. The train they required was just about to leave, and there would not be another one for several hours.

Dashing down the platform, they almost fell into the train with their suitcase hurled in behind them. The train started to leave immediately, and the man shouted instructions as to where they should change, but his voice was lost in the noise and confusion and Jean could not hear. She now found herself worrying not about which train to get on, but when to get off. David said he felt sure the man had said the train would split at one point, but he had no idea which section they had to be on. At this point Jean could scarcely remember the name of their final destination, she was in such a state.

Looking up, she was astonished to see a man sitting opposite them. She could have sworn the carriage was empty when they had scrambled in, or they would have trampled over him in the rush. How on earth had he avoided the suitcase being hurled at their feet after them? It was all very strange. The man smiled and exuded calmness as he said, 'Please do not worry, I will help.' Jean felt instantly relaxed.

The train passed through some very beautiful countryside and Jean, who was passionately fond of trees, found herself thinking how lovely they were. The man smiled at her and said, 'Yes, they are lovely aren't they,' as if answering a question, although Jean had not spoken her thought.

Thirty minutes after leaving Euston, the man put his newspaper down and said, 'You must get off at the next stop and join the front half of the train.' He then told them the name of the final destination where they should alight. Unquestioningly, Jean stepped from the train at the next stop. Taking their suitcase, the man followed them down the platform. They seemed to be in the middle of nowhere, Jean thought, not a station at all – just an open platform with fields on either side. The platform was quite long, and it was a fair walk to the front of the long train.

Seeing them safely onto the train, the man

reminded Jean of the name of the station where she should alight. The thought went through Jean's head that how on earth did he know where they were going when she did not herself? Closing the door behind them, Jean turned to say thank you to the kind man. She put her head through the window, but to her amazement there was no-one there. The long platform was empty, yet there was nowhere he could possibly have gone in only seconds, with no buildings in sight.

Jean and David stared at each other and slowly added up the events. They were certain the man had not been in the train carriage when they had got in. Where had he come from? He seemed to have the ability to read Jean's thoughts. How? He knew without being told where they must change and where they were going. What on earth had happened? Safely reaching their final destination, they were relieved to find their friends waiting for them. Jean was asked by her friends if something had happened, because they both had such a glow about them. Jean answered, 'It's no wonder we're glowing. We've just met an angel.'

Our final mystery takes place in Northumberland and centres around Henrietta. For forty years Henrietta had lived in a very large old house. It had belonged to her husband's family and they had moved in the week they had been married. Children had been born and grown up there, and eventually flown the nest. When Henrietta's husband died, she knew sooner or later she would have to make a painful decision. It was all too obvious that she could not live in the large old house alone. It was far too big for one person to manage from a practical and financial point of view, and the only logical solution was to move somewhere smaller. After much searching, a manageable cottage was found. It was, if anything, older than Henrietta's house, built of solid grey stone, with a little garden and a view of the hills. Once she had sorted everything out, she knew she would be fine.

Abandoning her large amounts of furniture was heart-rending but necessary. Eventually all was ready, and the day of the move dawned. Her family rallied round and jollied her along as the removal van was filled. The move would be a distance of only ten miles or so, and she thought it would be an easy matter to visit old neighbours. The family working party soon had everything safely installed in the cottage. There was a sprinkling of snow on the hills, and the view was breathtaking. Spring would bring surprises of discovering what appeared in the garden, and it would be marvellous to see the cherry tree bloom.

It was getting late, and at last her family said goodnight. The bed was ready in the bedroom, but Henrietta was so tired she felt she could have fallen asleep on the floor. She had a sound night's sleep, and thought that a good omen. The following morning, taking a shower and dressing, she told herself that she was very lucky, but deep down she realised she was whistling in the dark. There was a real sense of loss that she was trying to ignore, and a rising fear that she would regret her actions.

By the time she was ready to descend the stairs, she felt all optimism drain away and a gloom descend. Close to tears, she slowly made her way downstairs. Stepping from the last step, she looked up and was startled to see a young boy standing in the hall. She guessed him to be about ten years old, and he appeared to be dressed in a large, white, Victorian nightshirt. There was an inner glow coming from this child, and he beamed broadly at Henrietta.

She could not move, but stood rooted to the spot, staring in incredulity. In the blink of an eye he was gone, but he had left an atmosphere of such happiness and love that Henrietta wanted to cry with joy. What could this mean? Who was this child? Finally Henrietta decided that he was an angel, reassuring her that all would be well and that happiness would surround her in her new home.

She has not seen the boy again, but she was absolutely right about the reassurance. She is most definitely extremely happy in her lovely old cottage.

Epilogue

In this book we have seen a great variety of angelic appearances and manifestations. Although angels often appear in the form of a traditional 'church angel' with long white robe and wings, surrounded by an aura or glow of light, they may also be very small in size or wear contemporary dress, sometimes even without wings. Quite often they appear in the form of a dead friend or relative, especially when their purpose is to offer reassurance that the deceased is now safe, happy, whole – and still connected to the person who has been left behind. Angels have always been associated with beauty, and are often accompanied by heavenly music or exquisite scents. Sometimes a waft of roses – when there are no flowers in the room – may be the only sign of their presence.

Angels have many roles. They visit us to comfort us in our loneliness, suffering, sickness and bereavement. Guardian angels may even rescue their charges from near-certain death when humans are helpless to intervene. They aid the sick and tend the suffering through the healing process, sometimes helping them towards miraculous recoveries when doctors and nurses had given up hope. They are there to offer strength in our final hours and to comfort the bereaved. They can refresh faith and replenish hope with their angelic communications.

Angels often act in mysterious ways, and there is no telling who will be graced by a visitation. As we have sometimes seen, they do not visit only in emergencies, but can appear at any moment in our lives, sometimes out of the blue and for no apparent reason at all. They seem to be attracted by abounding joy almost as much as by fear. Whenever they occur, angelic visitations always create an impact.

Why do the angels visit us? There are many theories, and nobody knows for sure. What does seem certain, from these and other stories, is that angels always have a positive and inspirational purpose. An angelic visit is clearly remembered for a lifetime, even when it took place in early childhood and the person concerned has reached old age. They give us comfort, consolation, and the courage to continue a life that may be hard, painful and full of challenge. As we have seen, they also often give us a sense of purpose in our lives, which can last a lifetime. This purpose often seems connected with creative expression or helping and inspiring others in some way.

Angelic manifestations can help us make sense of certain puzzling, perhaps half-forgotten, experiences in our lives, when we may have felt touched by an inexplicably unseen presence. They can also reassure us that we are not alone in a cold, hostile universe. We all have guardian angels who watch over us and protect us, and who may well make themselves known to us at the right moment.

If you have had an angel experience and wish to share it with the author, please contact her care of Rider Books, Editorial Department, Random House, 20 Vauxhall Bridge Road, London SW1V 2SA.

AN ANGEL AT MY SHOULDER
True Stories of Angelic Experiences
Glennyce S. Eckersley

An Angel At My Shoulder shows angels are returning – and being acknowledged – once again. Here are true stories of countless ordinary people being rescued by angels, being comforted and healed by them, feeling their presence in the face of death – and often appearing to little children. These tales are drawn from such countries as Britain, Australia, Ireland and the United States – showing angels can be found all round the globe: helping others, often changing their lives completely.

Warm and uplifting, *An Angel At My Shoulder* suggests it is more than time to reconsider our view of angels, to let them back into our hectic, mechanised world and to realise we are never alone . . .

'If you believe in angels Glennyce S. Eckersley's extraordinary true stories about angelic encounters will affirm your belief that angels are truly watching over us. If you don't believe in angels, you may find your non-belief wavering . . . This book touches the soul and opens the doors to the realm where heaven and earth meet and love abounds.'

DENISE LINN, **author of** *Sacred Space*

ANGELS AND MIRACLES
Extraordinary stories that cannot be easily explained
Glennyce S. Eckersley

This book is about coincidences and modern-day miracles: the seemingly random acts that may well turn out to be not so random after all. How do they happen? – why? – and to whom?

Only in recent times have we felt so alone and isolated in our universe. For centuries men and women fervently believed in the intervention of a higher power in their lives. Today, as more of us search for greater spiritual fulfilment, we wonder once again whether such events might mean we live, not in a purely chaotic world, but rather in one of harmony, meaning and order at a deeper level, one in which there may be angelic and even divine intervention.

The extraordinary true stories in this book suggest that the many different things that happen to us must be fundamentally interconnected and meaningful, even if they seem like unexpected miracles.

Killer Ball at Honeychurch Hall

Hannah Dennison

CONSTABLE • LONDON

CONSTABLE

First published in the United States by Minotaur Books,
an imprint of St Martin's Publishing Group, 2016

This edition published in Great Britain in 2016 by Constable

A CIP catalogue record for this book
is available from the British Library.

ISBN: 978-1-47212-378-7 (paperback)

Printed and bound in Great Britain by
CPI Group (UK) Ltd, Croydon CR0 4YY

Papers used by Constable are from well-managed forests
and other responsible sources

MIX
Paper from
responsible sources
FSC® C104740

Constable
is an imprint of
Little, Brown Book Group
Carmelite House
50 Victoria Embankment
London EC4Y 0DZ

An Hachette UK Company
www.hachette.co.uk

www.littlebrown.com

For my beautiful sister, Lesley –
Your sunny disposition always brightens my day

Acknowledgments

I've always had a fascination for historic houses and have lived in a few myself—two specifically dated back to the sixteenth century and one definitely had a ghost. I know that because I saw him and so did my poor cat. I truly believe that bricks and mortar absorb the essence of those who have lived in them throughout the years, along with their secrets, hopes and dreams.

Writing the Honeychurch Hall series is a glorious excuse to indulge in this passion of mine. It also has the added benefit of necessitating a lot of research. I'd like to thank esteemed historian Dr. Claire Gapper, who opened my eyes to the intricacies of Elizabethan plasterwork, and Paul Langley, whose knowledge of the English Civil War in the seventeenth century is—quite simply—brilliant.

I must thank my dear friend Leonard Lassalle, who hired me to work in his antique shop in Tunbridge Wells, Kent, so many decades ago. Thank you for continuing to be my go-to expert in the antique world.

I'd like to thank Jane Wynne, who owns the Carriage House upon which my fictional character, Iris Stanford, lives on the Honeychurch Hall estate. Your generosity in allowing me to roam around will not be forgotten—not to mention your delicious lemon drizzle cake.

A special thank-you to my wonderful agent, Dominick Abel; my amazing editor, Marcia Markland—who always knows exactly how to make my stories better; the super-efficient Quressa Robinson; my publicist, Shailyn Tavella—who happily embraced my quirky publicity ideas, and to the fabulous Talia Sherer. I'm certain that without your enthusiasm for my work, Honeychurch Hall may not be available in so many libraries. I'm also thrilled that Mary Ann Lasher continues to create the most exquisite covers for the series. They really are a work of art. And a big thank-you to Pourio Lee, for his talented, elegant design work that has made my website so spectacular.

As always, I couldn't do any of this without the support of my daughter, Sarah, my family, my long-suffering boss, Mark Davis, and my talented comrades in the trenches—Elizabeth Duncan, Clare Langley-Hawthorne, Daryl Wood Gerber, Kate Carlisle and Mark Durel.

And, last but by no means least, my husband, Jason, who, with every book, willingly takes on the roles of nursemaid, drill sergeant, cheerleader, therapist, cook, launderer and man Friday. Without whose love and support, none of this would be possible. You are a superstar and I'm so lucky to have you in my life.

Earl of Grenville

Created by Henry V in 1414, the title of Earl of Grenville has been passed down the male Honeychurch line and still exists today.

EARL of GRENVILLE

8TH EARL OF GRENVILLE
Rupert James
Honeychurch
B: 1800 D: 1880

Edward Rupert
9TH EARL OF GRENVILLE
B: 1835 D: 1899
Fought in Crimean War (1853–56). Decorated soldier, brought back mummified hawk.

Gerald James
B: 1840 D: 1912
Married American heiress—moved to New York. *Died in 1912 in the Arctic. He was a Polar explorer.

Elizabeth Edith
B: 1864 D: 1895
Never married. No children. *Fell from horse and broke her neck out hunting.

Harold Rupert
10TH EARL OF GRENVILLE
B: 1865 D: 1912
Fought in the Boer War (1899–1902). *Died on *Titanic*.

James Rupert
B: 1873 D: 1950
Married showgirl. Ran a Turkish harem in London, fond of Burlesque & ran with Edward VII set.

Cassandra Mary
B: 1872 D: 1965
Never married. Lived in desert with a sheik, drove ambulances in WWI, war office WW2.

Max James
11TH EARL OF GRENVILLE
B: 1887 D: 1916
No children. *Fighter pilot shot down over France in WWI.

Harold Edward
12TH EARL OF GRENVILLE
Edith's father.
B: 1900 D: 1940
*Died in London Blitz with wife.

Gerald Rupert
B: 1903 D: 1932
Lived in New York. Lost everything in the Wall Street Crash and committed suicide.

Rose Anne
B: 1907 D: 1988
Married German POW at end of war, moved to Germany. Huge scandal! Had 3 children.

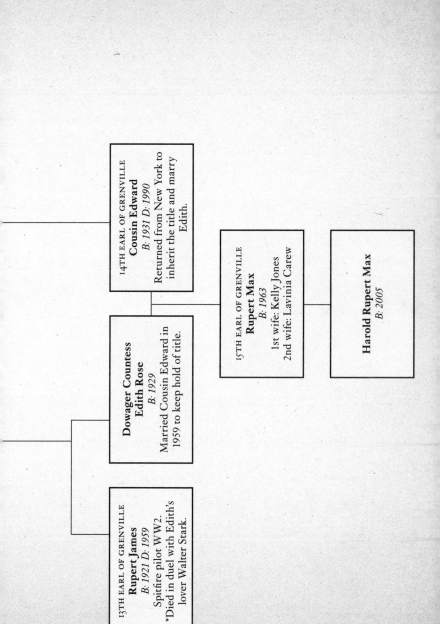

13TH EARL OF GRENVILLE
Rupert James
B: 1921 D: 1959
Spitfire pilot WW2.
*Died in duel with Edith's
lover Walter Stark.

**Dowager Countess
Edith Rose**
B: 1929
Married Cousin Edward in
1959 to keep hold of title.

14TH EARL OF GRENVILLE
Cousin Edward
B: 1931 D: 1990
Returned from New York to
inherit the title and marry
Edith.

15TH EARL OF GRENVILLE
Rupert Max
B: 1963
1st wife: Kelly Jones
2nd wife: Lavinia Carew

Harold Rupert Max
B: 2005

Killer Ball
at
Honeychurch
Hall

Chapter One

"You are absolutely not selling William Dobson, Rupert!"
The dowager countess, Lady Edith Honeychurch, was furious.
Even Mr. Chips, her tan-and-white Jack Russell, seemed to
bristle with indignation.

Edith's son looked pained. "Do we have to go through this
again, Mother?"

For emphasis, Edith slapped her riding crop against the
side of her leather boot. "As long as I am alive, this is still my
house!"

"Mother," Rupert hissed and gestured to where Mum and
I were standing in the doorway. "Not in front of..."

"The servants?" Mum chimed in cheerfully. "Don't mind
us. We're always arguing—aren't we, Kat?"

I gave a polite smile, but Rupert looked even more uncomfortable.

"Why don't we come back later?" I said and grabbed Mum's
arm but she stood her ground and pulled her secondhand mink
coat even closer. It really was freezing cold.

"Who is William Dobson?" Mum asked. "Is he for hire?
Maybe he can help Kat hang her bathroom cabinet?"

"I think Edith is referring to the seventeenth-century artist, William Dobson—"

"An artist who painted one of our ancestors who saved the Hall from being razed to the ground in the English Civil War," Edith said angrily. "And now Rupert wants to sell it and he's asked *you*, Katherine, to take it off for auction, so I hear!"

"No," Rupert lied. "I just wanted to show Katherine and Iris the damaged ceiling."

"Nonsense. You thought you could sneak them in through the Tudor courtyard without my knowing but you seem to forget that Cropper never misses a trick."

Cropper, of course, was the old butler. Although he rarely spoke he seemed to have an uncanny gift of being everywhere at once.

The truth was, I'd also thought it odd that Rupert had arranged to meet us at the end of the half-mile-long pergola walk on the far southwest corner of the Hall. Covered in ancient wisteria with roots as big as my arm, I'd never noticed the old wooden gate that led to a narrow passageway. At the end, a pretty archway opened into a small cobbled courtyard. Mullioned casement windows took up three sides and on the fourth were two doors. It was there that Edith had been waiting.

Edith raised a quizzical eyebrow at me. "Why are you holding those padded blankets, Katherine? And what is in that canvas bag?"

I'd brought the padded blankets to wrap up the painting and my canvas bag was full of my tools.

Mum and I both looked to Rupert for the answer.

"*Did* he ask you to value the Dobson, Katherine?" Edith demanded.

Of course he had! Rupert had phoned that morning to say

that something "catastrophic" had happened in the Tudor wing and that they needed to sell a painting.

I was only too happy to oblige. I was still trying to get my antiques business going. Despite having moved all my stock into the two gatehouses that flanked the main entrance, Kat's Collectibles & Valuation Services was slow in getting off the ground.

"You're right," said Rupert defiantly. "I did. Katherine told me that the last Dobson sold for around three hundred and fifty thousand pounds. Luxton's of Newton Abbot has a sale of old masters and British paintings coming up—"

"I knew it!" Edith exclaimed.

"Mother!" Rupert ran his fingers through his thinning hair, clearly exasperated. "We have to do something and unless you can think of a way to raise thousands and thousands of pounds at the drop of a hat, I'm all ears."

"But surely it can't be that bad," said Mum.

"The plasterwork ceiling is Elizabethan and very rare," Edith said. "There is only one other like it in Devon at Holcombe Rogus."

"Presumably you're going to apply for a grant?" I said to Rupert. "The Historic Houses Association runs all kinds of maintenance and restoration programs. I have a contact there."

"Alfred is very good at decorating," Mum said suddenly.

It was true. Mum's stepbrother had helped paint the Carriage House.

"Repairing a plasterwork ceiling needs specific materials that can only be applied by skilled craftsmen," I said gently.

"That wouldn't faze my Alfred. He's got a real gift for making a copy look like the real thing." And of course, she was right. This so-called gift of Alfred's had sent him to prison more times than I could count.

Edith smiled. "Very kind of you to offer, Iris. But I'm sure that Alfred is far too busy overseeing the horses."

"Perhaps there is something else that might be worth selling?" I said, anxious to change the subject.

"I'm not sure if you remember, your ladyship," said Mum, "but if there's one person who knows what sells well it's my Katherine. She was the TV host of *Fakes & Treasures*."

"And I can assure you that there is nothing *fake* in this house," Edith said frostily.

"Perhaps you could sell your snuff box collection?" said Rupert with a hint of malice. To be honest, the thought had crossed my mind as well. Edith had more snuff boxes than I could shake a stick at and many were extremely valuable.

"Never!" Edith declared. "I will decide what needs to be sold. And may I remind you, Rupert, you are not the one who makes the decisions around here."

"I *know*!" said Rupert.

Mum started humming to herself. It was a peculiar habit she'd picked up when she was feeling embarrassed. I gave her a discreet nudge and she stopped.

"Really, we can come back another day," I said.

"Repairs need to be started right away," said Rupert. "Katherine says that this sale is one of the best in the country. But naturally, whatever you feel is best, Mother."

"Very well." Edith turned to me. "Rupert, take Katherine to the King's Parlor. Show her the Hollar drawings of Honeychurch Hall. They might do—oh!" Suddenly, Edith switched her gaze onto my mother. "What on earth are you wearing, Iris?"

Mum reddened. "It's a mink coat, m'lady."

"I can see that."

Ever since Mum had bought the old coat at the Chillingford Court sale, she'd worn it everywhere regardless of the occasion or whether we were inside or out. Apparently, it had been one of her dreams to own one and she hated to let it out of her sight. I teased her and called it Truly Scrumptious in honor of my mother's fictional Pekinese dog that was splashed over her website. I still found it hard to believe that my mother was the international best-selling romance writer, Krystalle Storm.

Edith stepped closer. I got a whiff of horse and lavender water that always surrounded her like an atmosphere. "Turn around," she commanded.

After a moment's hesitation, Mum gave a twirl. Although I detested fur coats of any description, I had to admit this was quite magnificent despite the all-pervasive smell of mothballs.

"I thought so," said Edith. "That coat belonged to my friend, Alice."

Mum's face lit up. "Yes! That's right. Princess Alice, the Countess of Athlone. How did you know?"

"I recognized the red paint on the back of the collar," said Edith.

"Oh." Mum seemed annoyed. "I didn't think anyone could see it." Needless to say, I had pointed the stain out to her before the coat went under the hammer but Mum's mind was made up. She had to have it.

"Activists, no doubt," said Edith. "Rabbit fur is much safer. So extraordinary to want to wear someone's castoffs."

"It's not that obvious," I whispered to Mum who looked utterly crestfallen.

"But speaking of paint, Katherine, how are you getting on at Jane's Cottage? I would have thought you would have moved in by now."

"The painting is all done, and most of the curtains and

blinds are up," I said. "I just need a few mirrors hung and new shelves in the kitchen pantry . . ."

"She put an ad in the post office for someone to do a spot of D-I-Y," Mum put in.

"The wood burner stove goes in next week."

"Central heating? Whatever for?" Edith exclaimed. "Well, I'm sure that's all very interesting. Rupert, show Katherine the Hollar drawings but I repeat, do *not* do anything without talking to me first." And, with a snap of her fingers, she called Mr. Chips to heel and the pair headed off.

For a moment, Rupert just stood there. The fifteenth Earl of Grenville appeared years older than his fifty-two. Dark smudges lay beneath red-rimmed eyes and even his neat, military mustache had lost its crispness. Rupert wasn't even wearing his customary tie, choosing a pair of uncharacteristically scruffy jeans and an old moth-eaten sweater. For the first time, I realized just how much pressure he was under to keep the Hall afloat. Edith may rule the roost but it fell to him to manage the day-to-day running of the estate and handle all the bills.

A blast of cold air and the slam of an outside door brought Rupert to his senses. Mum shivered and pulled her mink coat closer. "It's like the arctic in here," she said. "I'm so happy I'm wearing my mink."

"As you gathered, Mother doesn't believe in central heating. If she had, perhaps the pipes wouldn't have burst and brought down the ceiling and we wouldn't be having this problem. Please, after you." Rupert ushered us ahead. "Down the passage and through the door at the end."

"I remember when the whole house was open," Mum said. "How many rooms are there, m'lord? One hundred? Two, perhaps?"

"I've never counted," said Rupert.

"How did you find out about the burst pipes?" Mum asked.

"Fortunately Harry's room shares a wall with the original house." Rupert cracked his first smile. "He was convinced the Germans had dropped a bomb."

Knowing Harry's obsession with Squadron Leader James Bigglesworth, the famous World War I flying ace, it was just the sort of thing he'd say. "And I bet he told you which kind."

"Yes." Rupert grinned. "Harry said it was a *minenwerfer*."

"A what?" Mum frowned.

"A high-power trench mortar shell that apparently makes no noise coming through the air."

"So if Harry had been away at boarding school," Mum said pointedly. "You would never have known."

Rupert scowled. "I'd rather have burst pipes."

"Thanks Mum," I muttered. It was common knowledge that none of the Honeychurches had been happy about Harry breaking the family tradition and going to the local school—and it had been my idea.

Rupert threw open the end door and ushered us into a screens passage. We passed through the first of two archways and into the Great Hall.

"Oh!" Mum gasped. "I know exactly where we are. Good heavens! I haven't been here for years!"

Chapter Two

"My father closed off this part of the house before I was born," said Rupert.

"Yes, I remember it all," said Mum. "My brothers and I loved to go exploring."

I made a note to ask her about this so-called *exploring*. Mum was prone to change her version of events to suit the occasion. She'd often told me that "her kind" was never allowed inside the main house and that the closest she got was the servants' quarters and kitchens.

Like many medieval houses, as years passed and architectural fashions changed, the spirit of the house evolved, too. I was reminded of Charles Ryder, in Evelyn Waugh's novel *Brideshead Revisited*, who summed up my feelings perfectly by saying how much he *"loved buildings that grew silently with the centuries, catching and keeping the best of each generation."*

It was exactly what made the destruction of such magnificent houses so tragic. Each loss was a loss to history. I couldn't help wondering if Harry, as the future heir, would fight hard to keep the Hall going.

The Great Hall wasn't large by the standard of other great

houses in England. The long rectangular room was typical of its time with a spectacular hammer beam roof. On one side were floor to ceiling stained glass windows showing knights in battle. On the other, an enormous stone fireplace bore an elaborate overmantel decorated with the Grenville coat of arms and the family motto: *ad perseverate est ad triumphum*—"To Endure is to Triumph."

Above the screens passage behind us was a minstrels' gallery. At the far end was a long oak refectory table atop a dais that spanned the width of the room. Two beautiful paneled back chairs with scrolled cresting and earpieces stood behind.

Covering the stone walls that flanked the fireplace was an impressive collection of weapons dating from the English Civil War. There were a variety of polearms and halberds; muskets, vicious stiletto knives, rapiers and basket-hilted two-edged mortuary swords.

"Yes." Mum nodded again. "I remember all this."

"Wow," I exclaimed. "What a collection! Have you ever considered . . . ?"

"These are not for sale," said Rupert as if reading my mind. "As you know, most of the suits of armor were moved into the modern wing. That is, if you can call our nineteenth-century façade modern."

"Have you ever thought about opening the Hall to the public?" I suggested. "It doesn't have to be like the National Trust or British Heritage, but the Historic Houses Association conducts open houses to private homes."

"Can you imagine my mother playing the gracious hostess?" said Rupert.

"Not really," I admitted.

"Every summer there was a bit of a do on midsummer night

for her ladyship's birthday," said Mum, who was clearly walking down memory lane. "Her brother—that would be your
uncle, m'lord, the thirteenth Earl of Grenville—would host a
costume ball. Beautiful costumes, they were. And the games!
Lots of games! People running all over the house playing cha-
rades and squashed sardines."

"What on earth are squashed sardines?" Rupert asked.

"It's a form of hide-and-seek," Mum enthused. "Only it's
the other way around. One person hides and the others must
find him and hide with him and the last person to find *them*
must pay a forfeit."

"Oh, you mean *Smee*," said Rupert. "That's what *we* call it."

I hated it when Rupert pulled his upper-class card. He
seemed to deliberately want to put Mum in her place.

"Wasn't there a ghost story called *Smee*?" I said.

"You know it?" Rupert sounded surprised. "It was written
by A. M. Burrage. Nanny used to read it to me at night and
frighten me half to death."

"The hiding places get incredibly cramped and as you can
imagine," Mum went on, oblivious, "there was quite a lot of
hanky-panky going on." She turned to the minstrels' gallery.
"And a band played up there."

"For someone who wasn't invited to the ball," I said, "you
seem to know a lot of details."

"Alfred, Billy and I used to sneak in," Mum continued.
"There was one of those peephole things where we could watch
everything." She laughed. "Oh, begging your pardon, m'lord."

"I'm sure you did," said Rupert dryly.

"What these walls must have seen," said Mum. "How exciting to know your ancestors lived here, m'lord. To be able to
trace your lineage all the way back to when Henry V created
the first Earl of Grenville—that's just wonderful."

"Good heavens, you've been looking at all that?" Rupert exclaimed.

"I'm becoming quite an expert on your family history."

Rupert gave a polite smile. "I can't imagine why."

I suppose for him, it was normal but Mum had really gotten involved in studying the family trees of both those who resided upstairs, and down. I felt a twinge of something that felt like inferiority! Maybe that was why the English aristocracy carried a sense of entitlement and assurance. They knew their roots. Portraits of their ancestors lined the walls of countless country estates. But for me, an only child, I'd never met my father's parents—in fact, they were a bit of a mystery. Mum's background was just plain murky. She claimed to have been adopted by a traveling fairground and spent her life on the road. Perhaps I did regard the "toffs" as Mum liked to call them, as different from us, after all.

It also brought up feelings about this new life I was embarking upon. Much as I disliked the fame that my celebrity status had brought me, it had given me a sense of identity. Even being the girlfriend of David Wynne, an international art investigator, had reinforced that. Now that I was starting over, I felt a little lost and unsure of myself.

"Why the long face?" said Mum, bringing me out of my thoughts.

"I was just thinking about the Dobson painting," I lied. "Wasn't he the principal painter to King Charles I after van Dyck died?"

"She's a walking encyclopedia of knowledge, is my Katherine," said Mum proudly.

"I'm sure she is." Rupert turned us back into the screens passage and toward the open oak door at the end. "The King's Parlor is through here."

"Oh! I must write this down." Mum withdrew a block of Post-it Notes from her mink coat pocket and a pen. "So King Charles actually stayed here? How thrilling!"

"One of my ancestors was commissioned under the great Seal of England to mint coins for King Charles. The Royalists needed the money to raise troops for the king."

"They made coins here?" Mum said.

Rupert nodded. "Yes. The Honeychurch mint."

"Fancy being able to make your own money," said Mum. "Alfred would have been in his element."

We entered the King's Parlor and I couldn't hide my dismay. "Harry was right when he said he thought someone had dropped a bomb."

Water from the burst pipe above had brought down a quarter of the ornamental plasterwork ceiling. Chunks of plaster had been swept into the corner with a broom and an attempt had been made to save the Aubusson rug by pushing it away from the sludge that still covered half of the floor.

Although the rest of the ceiling was intact, the water had bled into the strapwork plasterwork leaving ugly brown rings. It was a huge restoration job and would take more than the sale of one or two paintings to cover the cost of the damage.

"You're right," said Mum. "I think Alfred would be a bit out of his league."

Mum pointed to where a tarpaulin bulged from the gaping hole above. "What's up there?"

"I have no idea," said Rupert. "Another bedroom I suppose."

"How long had the water been running?" I asked.

"Harry woke me the moment he heard the bang," said Rupert. "I was up most of the night mopping up the damage."

"What on earth are you going to do with that beautiful carpet?" Mum said.

"We'll drag it out with a tractor." Rupert pointed to a heavy velvet curtain. "Behind there is a door to another passage that opens into the Tudor courtyard. It was built so that the king could leave privately if he so wished."

I dragged my attention back to the King's Parlor. It was a pretty room and had all the features expected of its Tudor beginnings. The rich oak linenfold paneling was decorated with symbols of the Tudor rose, thistle and fleur-de-lis as was the fireplace and overmantel. Multipaned casement windows bore the Grenville coat of arms and motto. There were very few pieces of furniture—a gate-leg table, love seat, joint stool and a four-poster bed minus the mattress and hangings. Flanking the fireplace were the Hollar drawings on one side bearing little gold plaques, WENCESLAUS HOLLAR 1601–1677, and a series of miniatures on the other, but pride of place was the Dobson painting. It was beautiful and I could quite understand why Edith refused to sell it.

The painting depicted three men in cavalier dress seated at a gate-leg table. They were drinking a flagon of wine and had glasses raised in a toast. A white standard poodle sat obediently at one of the cavalier's feet.

"That's my ancestor with Prince Rupert of the Rhine and his brother, Prince Maurice."

"The same Maurice who has the haunted chair at the Hare & Hounds pub?" Mum asked.

"So we're led to believe," said Rupert.

"And were you named after Prince Rupert of the Rhine?" I asked.

"Yes. As was my mother's brother—the thirteenth earl."

Mum shivered. "I feel as if someone has just walked over my grave. It reminds me of that headstone I saw once. Let me see, how does the verse go—

"Stop traveler and cast an eye,
As you are now so once was I,
Prepare in time make no delay
For youth and time will pass away!"

"That's cheery," I said.

Mum studied the painting. "Why the poodle?"

"That's Boy," said Rupert. "He belonged to Prince Rupert who took him everywhere. Even in battle. In fact, the Parliamentarians used to think he was Prince Rupert's familiar."

"I rather like that idea," I said.

"They were a superstitious lot back in the seventeenth century," Rupert went on. "Anyone could spread any rumor and be believed. We've got a few original pamphlets from that time in the Museum Room warning the locals that Cromwell's New Model Army would be spiking babies on spits and turning mothers into serpents."

Mum thought for a moment. "What happened to the dog?"

"Sadly, Boy was shot by a Roundhead," said Rupert. "As I'm sure Harry has told you many times, the Royalists sought refuge here when they were retreating."

"I'm surprised Cromwell's army didn't burn the Hall down when they came after them," I said.

"We're rather clever at switching sides," said Rupert wryly. "Family legend has it that the Honeychurch fortunes and the Hall were saved by the quick thinking of the estate steward and the warrener. They hid anything and everything that hinted of Royalist sympathies—the minting tools and supposedly, the silver coins."

"Wait!" said Mum who had been scribbling furiously on her Post-it Notes. "Do we know the names of the estate steward and the warrener?"

"I've no idea," said Rupert.

"Don't worry." Mum beamed. "I'll find out."

"If you're really interested," Rupert went on, "you should talk to Lavinia's brother Piers. He's the president of the local English Civil War Society."

"I might do just that," said Mum. "Oh—I meant to ask, speaking about dogs. How is your English setter? I don't see him around so much these days."

At this, Rupert's face softened. "Poor old Cromwell. He's stone deaf now and riddled with arthritis. Spends all his time sleeping in front of the log fire in the library." Rupert smiled. "Thank you for asking, Iris."

Mum flushed with pleasure. "And how is Lady Lavinia?"

"I have no idea."

"*Really?* You have *no* idea?" Mum shot me a knowing look and mouthed something unintelligible. I hadn't a clue what she was trying to convey and promptly ignored her.

"May I take a look at the Hollar drawings?"

"Isn't that why you're here?" said Rupert.

Topographical drawings were not my strong point but I did know a little about them and found it fascinating how artists were commissioned to visually record land and properties hundreds of years before photography was invented.

The drawings were of a much earlier Honeychurch Hall and had been done in red, black and white chalk, and black ink. They showed two different views of the main house and surrounding parkland and looked nothing like the Hall we knew today. There was no Palladian front, Georgian wing or Victorian addition.

Set to the right of the Hall and on top of a knoll, was a semifortified, four square, two-story building with a walkway on top next to a huge oak tree. Beside it was a large mound peppered with burrows with rabbits scampering about. It was utterly charming.

Mum joined me. "What's the funny little building on the hill behind the Hall? I don't recognize that."

"That was Warren Lodge," said Rupert. "When Cromwell's army came through, they burned that down. Only the oak tree remains. Jane's Cottage was built on the original site in the 1800s as a summer house."

"Jane's Cottage!" Mum exclaimed. "I'd never have guessed."

"And now it's surrounded by trees," I said. "I suspected the oak was hundreds of years old. The trunk is enormous."

"So who was this Jane who had a cottage named in her honor?" Mum asked, brandishing a fresh Post-it.

"I really have *no* idea, Iris." Rupert sounded exasperated. "Now, if you'll excuse me, I'll leave you to it—oh, and when you see Eric, perhaps you could give him some help moving that carpet."

And with that, Rupert left the room.

"I think I annoyed his lordship with all my questions," said Mum.

"I think it was the question about Lavinia that did it. What were you trying to tell me?"

"That it's *true*!"

"What's true?"

"It's true about the upper-classes preferring their dogs to their wives," she said. "Did you see how his expression went all squishy when he talked about Cromwell?"

"You're incorrigible." I laughed. "Come on, Mother. Here. Take these." I gave her the padded blankets and directed Mum to the gate-leg table. Once I'd removed the drawings off the wall, we'd wrap them and I'd take them back to my new workshop.

I put my canvas tool bag on the floor and withdrew a pair of white cotton gloves.

I then turned my attention to the first Hollar drawing. It really was very pretty and I felt sad about sending it off to auction. I had been used to seeing this kind of thing—stately homeowners auctioning off their possessions to keep their homes afloat and it never used to bother me. But now it did.

When I first moved to Devon, I couldn't wait to go back to London and civilization. But as the weeks turned into months, I found the six-hundred-year-old country estate had gotten under my skin. I felt fiercely protective of Honeychurch Hall and everything about it.

I grabbed the joint stool, set it up under the painting and took off my shoes.

"Mind you don't slip in those socks," said Mum. "You know how accident-prone you can be."

I gently lifted the frame a fraction of an inch away from the wall to see the chain behind. It should have been easy to remove but for some reason the chain kept getting stuck.

"Mini Maglite, please," I said.

Mum delved into my canvas bag. "Mini Maglite."

Placing my cheek flat against the wall I held the frame in one hand and the flashlight in the other. Sure enough I could see a small nub sticking out of the linenfold paneling.

I gave Mum the flashlight back. "Screwdriver please."

"Screwdriver, doctor."

"I just need to see what this thing is." Gently, I slid the screwdriver behind the frame and prodded the nub.

"How nice to be able to sell a painting for thousands of pounds—oh!" Mum gave a cry of surprise. "Oh! Kat, look!" On the left-hand side of the fireplace, part of the linenfold paneling had popped out of the wall. "The paneling! I bet it's a secret cupboard or something."

In a few quick strides she had opened the panel. "Yes! I'm right. It is! Come and see."

Together we peered into a small, low recess that couldn't have been more than five feet wide, four feet high and four feet deep. A raised lip ran along the bottom of the linenfold paneling. On the back wall were three bookshelves.

"Do you think it was one of those hidey-hole things for naughty priests?" Mum said.

"Catholic priests fleeing persecution, you mean?" I said. "I think you're right. No one would ever be able to tell that it was here."

"You'd have to be very short, curl up in a ball almost," said Mum. "I wouldn't fancy being stuck here for days on end. But why have the bookshelves?"

I pointed to a lone book that lay in the corner, splayed open with the spine up. It was covered in red shiny paper decorated with vegetables. Next to it was a grubby white mesh purse.

"How about . . . for books?"

Mum suddenly went very still. "Oh."

"I hate it when books are left like that," I said but as I stepped forward over the lip to pick it up, Mum sprang into action.

"Don't!" she cried and roughly elbowed me aside. I lost my balance and thrust both hands out to save my fall but fell heavily onto the top shelf.

There was a whoosh of air and I felt myself falling, falling, a sharp pain, a deafening crash and then—darkness.

Chapter Three

It was pitch black and deathly quiet. The air felt thick and smelled stale.

I knew I'd fallen quite a few feet into some kind of cellar. I'd really hurt my shoulder and for a few moments just lay there trying to find my bearings.

I'd heard of double-hides, secret rooms behind secret rooms. Anne Frank's house in Amsterdam had one very similar where a bookcase had a false back that swung up and away from the wall to reveal another room beyond.

Everything was going to be okay, I told myself. Mum knew where I was. In fact, I was certain that she had already gone for help. I had obviously triggered a catch to a priest hole and now I'd fallen into a second one. There was no point screaming for help. The walls were three feet thick. All I needed to do was wait.

Gingerly, I reached overhead to get some sense of the area I'd fallen into. My hands found nothing but air. I could stretch my left arm out but my right brushed rough brick that I assumed had to be the chimney breast. As my eyes adjusted to the gloom I realized that the area was quite spacious and began to edge slowly forward.

Suddenly, light flared behind and above me. I spun round to see Mum's anxious face peering down. "Kat? Are you alive?"

"Just about."

I had fallen about six or seven feet. Not far enough to break anything, but too far to be able to climb out without help.

"I had to find Eric," said Mum.

Eric Pugsley's face joined my mother's. He seemed excited.

"Bloody hell! It's another secret room!" he exclaimed. "Bloody hell! Does his lordship know?"

"I came straight to get you," said Mum. "I thought Kat had fallen into a black hole."

"Anything down there?" Eric demanded.

"No. Just me," I said. "And I'd quite like to come out. My feet are cold. I'm only wearing socks."

"It was most extraordinary," Mum declared. "One moment you were there, and the next . . . this wooden flap shot out and you plunged in and then it crashed back into place again. Can you imagine what would have happened if I hadn't been here to save you?"

Eric must have picked up my flashlight and turned it full into my face.

"Eric!" I exclaimed, shielding my eyes. "You're blinding me. Go and get a ladder or something."

There was a shriek from Mum. "Oh my God, oh my God!"

"Bloody hell!" Eric cried again.

"What?" My stomach gave a lurch. "What's the matter?"

"Now don't panic," said Mum clearly panicking. "And *don't move!*"

"Bloody hell," said Eric yet again.

I began to get the chills. "What's the matter? What have you seen?"

"Nothing, nothing at all," Mum sang cheerfully. "Just stay there. Eric will get the ladder but whatever you do, *don't* turn around!"

I turned around.

"Oh God!" I gasped.

There, in the flare of the flashlight, lying at the base of the chimney breast were the remains of a woman wrapped in a shroud of golden cloth. She was on her back with her arms splayed. It was utterly horrible.

"Is it a dead priest?" Mum exclaimed. "Did he starve?"

"No," I whispered. "It's a woman."

"I bet she fell in there just like Kat did," I heard Mum say to Eric. But I was too freaked out as the full horror of discovering a body hit me for the first time.

"I'm coming down!" Eric thrust the flashlight at Mum who promptly bungled the catch and dropped it. It fell into the chamber, struck the chimney breast and rolled across the floor casting strobes of eerie light.

The flashlight hit the body, illuminating a heart-shaped pendant around a broken neck. What little remained of her hair was packed closely to the skull in peculiar round whorls secured by bobby pins. Wasted arms lay on the floor encircled by heavy bangles. Behind her head lay strands of beads, threaded into an elaborate black wig.

I was so horrified I couldn't move. Eric scrambled down and came to my side. I caught the usual stench of axle grease that clung to his clothes from his constant tinkering in the scrapyard behind Mum's Carriage House.

"You okay?" he said gruffly but didn't wait for my reply. He snatched up the flashlight giving me a glimpse of thick, bushy eyebrows that seemed particularly menacing this afternoon— and just stepped over the body.

"Where is he going?" called Mum from above as Eric moved deeper into the room.

I heard excited cries of, "Bloody hell!" and "Blimey!"

"Quickly!" Mum exclaimed. "I bet he's found another body. Go and see!"

I must have still been in shock because I did as I was told.

Farther in, Eric had found a small oak chest set close to the outer brick wall. "Hold the flashlight. This is it! We've found it!"

The lid came up easily. "Hold the flashlight!" Eric said again.

"What is it?"

"Hang on." Eric knelt down and leaned inside. Almost reverently, he brought out a shallow oval bowl that contained small punches and dies. He went back in and retrieved several pairs of shears, tongs and a hammer but then got up, clearly disappointed. "It's not here. Damn. Damn. *Damn!*"

"What isn't there?" I asked.

"What's going on?" I heard Mum call out. "Is anyone back there? Anyone alive?"

"I'm certain that these are some of the tools that were used for the Honeychurch mint," said Eric. "See these stamps? The lions? The fleur-de-lis? But where are the bloody coins?"

"Do you think someone got here before we did?" I asked.

"What do you mean?" said Eric. "Someone got here before we did?"

Was he dense? "There's a dead woman down here."

"How would I know?" Eric seemed angry.

"There's no need to be rude," I exclaimed as he pushed past me.

Mum was almost expiring with curiosity and had managed to squeeze the joint stool through the first chamber and was attempting to lower it into the second.

Eric took it from her, stepped up and clambered out. "I'll get his lordship and call the police."

"I see the age of chivalry is dead," said Mum. "Let me help you out, Katherine, since Eric isn't going to."

"And don't you go saying anything to anyone," Eric said. "We'll want to keep this quiet."

"Quiet?" Mum exclaimed. "Are you mad?"

"The dowager countess doesn't like scandal." I caught a tinge of bitterness in Eric's voice that was hardly surprising. Just a few months ago he'd been made a scapegoat for one of Lady Lavinia's massive errors of judgment.

Mum hauled me up and out and I filled her in on what was down there. "That's absolutely horrible!" she said with a shiver. "I wonder who on earth she was? I wonder what happened?"

"Me, too."

"Do you think she was put there deliberately?"

"I think it's more a question of who knew about the double-hide."

Mum's jaw dropped. "So you think the culprit must be connected to the *Hall*? Someone who lived here?"

"I don't know, Mum," I said.

"We should study my family trees," Mum declared. "You never know. They may give us a clue."

One hour later, Detective Inspector Shawn Cropper stepped out of the double-hide. His hazel-flecked eyes were dancing with excitement. Even his drab trench coat that he insisted on wearing seemed crisp and unusually clean.

"A word, Eric?" He drew Eric aside whilst Mum and I watched the pair of them whispering animatedly. I caught the words, "Honeychurch mint" and "mechanical press."

Rupert burst into the King's Parlor. "Well?" he demanded. "Is it true?"

"Yes, sir," said Shawn. "I'm afraid there is a body—"

"But no silver coins, m'lord," Eric chipped in. "They're gone."

"Are you certain?" Rupert strode to the open panel. "Did you search everywhere?"

Shawn stepped in front of him. "That won't be possible, m'lord." He withdrew a roll of blue crime scene tape.

"Good heavens, Shawn," said Mum. "Do you always keep that in your pocket?"

Shawn ignored her. "We're taking every precaution not to contaminate the scene, m'lord."

"Contaminate the scene? I don't understand." Rupert frowned. "What does it matter? The woman has been dead for years."

"I'm sorry to say it's officially a cold case and must be treated as such," said Shawn somewhat pompously. "I've already put a call in to the ME. He'll want to do isotopic testing, radiocarbon and that sort of thing. And notifying the next of kin—should there be one."

"I'm afraid we can't do that," said Rupert. "Got to keep this under wraps, Shawn. You know what Mother is like. It's probably someone who lived on the estate. We'll handle it."

"How many people knew about the existence of the double-hide?" Shawn asked.

"I have no idea," said Rupert. "The secret location is traditionally passed down from father to son but obviously, I didn't know it was here."

"And the man who built it," said Mum, who, I noticed, was holding onto the book we'd found as if her life depended upon it. "He'd know."

"Quite," said Rupert.

"What will happen to the body—to her?" Mum said.

"The pathologist will want to look at her in situ—as they say—and then she'll be taken away."

"Can I at least take those drawings?" I said. "Otherwise they won't make next Thursday's sale. As it is they won't be in the catalog."

"And I'd like to look at the minting tools," Rupert declared.

"Not until we've got the all-clear," said Shawn. "Until then, this room is out of bounds."

WPC Roxy Cairns raced into the King's Parlor. She seemed out of breath. "Sorry, sir! I just heard from Muriel at the post office that Kat and Eric found a skeleton in a priest hole!"

"The post office?" Mum exclaimed. "Bad news travels fast."

"Mrs. Cropper told her," said Roxy. "You really need to tell your grandmother to be more discreet, Shawn."

Shawn's jaw tightened. So much for keeping news under wraps!

Fortunately Rupert and Eric didn't seem to have heard. They were talking in whispers in the corner of the room and then, without saying a word, just left.

"Well, at least you're here now," said Shawn dryly.

"I had to cover for our desk sergeant," Roxy protested. "Malcolm had a doctor's appointment and he got held up at the surgery."

"By gunpoint?" Mum muttered.

"Then I had to buy stamps," said Roxy. "We're running low."

The local police were always short-staffed. The satellite station at Little Dipperton was only open from Monday to Friday and kept strict business hours.

"We won't know how old the deceased is until we've run some tests," said Shawn.

Roxy's eyes widened. "You mean—it's not a priest? I bet it

was some poor servant the toffs didn't like and wanted to get rid of."

Mum got out her Post-its. "Like whom? I'm working on a below-stairs family tree."

"Roxy!" Shawn said sharply. "That's enough!"

The little redheaded policewoman made no secret of just how much she despised the "toffs" as she called them, too.

Shawn checked his watch. "I'll be back in a couple of hours. I've got to go and pick up Ned and Jasper from school."

"Don't worry, Shawn," said Roxy. "I'll stand guard here and wait for Dick and co."

"Kat's being used as a free babysitter at the moment," Mum said suddenly. "She's got to pick up Harry. Maybe she can pick up the boys, too?"

"I'd be happy to," I said.

"They've got dental appointments," said Shawn. "But I appreciate the offer."

"You're such a wonderful father." Mum gave me a pointed look and mouthed, "Already trained." I ignored it but it was true, he certainly seemed to be. Having tragically lost his wife to cancer, Shawn was bringing up twin boys of five on his own and doing a good job, too.

"I was surprised to see Harry at Little Dipperton Primary School," Shawn went on.

"It's better for him there than those stuffy boarding schools," Roxy said boldly. "Look how those kids turn out!"

"Roxy!" Shawn said again. "Keep your opinions to yourself. Now, if you'll excuse me. I'll be back as soon as I can. Officer Cairns will take over from here."

And with that, Shawn hurried away.

Roxy got out her notebook. "Can you tell me exactly what happened?"

"*Again?*" said Mum.

"Again," Roxy said.

As we trooped over to the entrance to the double-hide, I told the story again.

Roxy took out her flashlight and swept the beam across the bottom of the floor. "So you say you were in here and tripped?"

"That's right and—"

"She fell onto the bookshelves," said Mum helpfully.

"Did you trip over that little purse, I wonder?" Roxy stuck the flashlight between her teeth, pulled out a pair of disposable latex gloves and put them on. She stooped down to pick up the grubby purse.

"We haven't touched anything," Mum lied. "Come on, Katherine, we'd better go."

"No, wait," I said. "That's vintage. Can I take a look? You never know. Maybe it belonged to that poor woman."

"You're the expert." Roxy snapped open the clasp and showed me the inside. Sewn on the fabric of a small pouch was the logo WHITING & DAVIS, MADE IN THE USA. There was also a powder compact, lipstick and a packet of Lucky Strike cigarettes.

"I'd date that somewhere in the fifties," I said.

"Lucky Strikes." Roxy frowned. "Those are American cigarettes. I watched *Mad Men* on TV. Everyone smoked Lucky Strikes over there." Roxy frowned again. "I bet these belonged to old Edith."

"Don't you mean, her ladyship?" Mum said pointedly. "And how do you know she smoked?"

"They all did back then." Roxy thought for a moment. "I wonder where she got those cigarettes from?"

"America?" Mum stated the obvious. "I suppose everyone went to America back then."

"Well, if she didn't, then I bet she knew who did," said Roxy. "I bet this purse belonged to the dead woman."

"Really? We never thought of that, did we, Katherine?" Mum's voice was dripping with sarcasm. I knew she didn't care much for Roxy.

"Maybe she fell in there, just like you did, Ms. Stanford?" Roxy went on. "Or she was pushed. *Pushed* so she'd keep quiet about some scandal or other that this lot like to keep hushed up." Roxy seemed pleased with her theory. "And we'll get the DNA from the lipstick. This was the deceased's purse alright, I'm sure of it."

"What about the book?" I said.

"What book?" Roxy said sharply.

"One has nothing to do with the other," said Mum, glowering at me. I saw then that she no longer had it.

"Let me be the judge of that," Roxy said. "Where is this book?"

"Mum? What have you done with it?"

"Me?" Mum exclaimed. "Nothing. It was you."

I caught a flash of red peeping out from behind a velvet curtain on the windowsill. "Well I certainly didn't put it over there."

Roxy marched over to the windowsill but as she picked it up a flyer fluttered to the floor. Mum lunged forward but Roxy was too fast.

"Well, well, well," she said. "What do we have here?"

"Has anyone ever said you sound like a policeman?" said Mum nervously.

"It's a flyer for a summer fair at the Hall in 1958." Roxy skimmed the contents and laughed. "Bushman's Fair and Traveling Boxing Emporium."

In the foreground was a boxing ring showing two bare-chested men, gloved and looking ready to fight. A list of side-shows included Professor Jon's Flea Circus, the Dance of the Seven Veils and Madame Z's Psychic Touch.

On the right was a brand-new attraction. A young woman in a short blue dress with angulated shoulder pads is pictured with her finger stuck into an electrical wall outlet. Her hair—obviously a wig—stands up on end and her eyes look wild. The caption read, ELECTRA! THE 27,000 VOLTS GIRL: NO HOME SHOULD BE WITHOUT THIS WONDER OF TECHNOLOGY.

"*'With Electra you will see these household chores disappear in a flash!'*" Roxy read aloud. "*'Put the spark back into your relationship!'* This is hysterical!"

"How funny." I looked over at Mum who suddenly seemed to find her mink coat far more interesting.

"Why does the name Bushman mean something to me?" Roxy turned to my mother. "Wasn't this your lot, Iris?"

"Those flyers were left all over the country," Mum said defensively. "Not just here."

Roxy stuck the flyer carefully back inside the book, then her eyes widened. "Golly!" She burst out laughing again.

"What's so amusing?" I asked.

"This is only *Lady* bloody *Chatterley's Lover*!" Roxy grinned.

I looked again at my mother who was now engrossed in stroking the sleeve of her mink coat.

Roxy took a peek inside the book. "This is pretty tame stuff," she said. "I wonder why it's covered in this awful paper? What kind of paper is this anyway?"

"Can I take a look?" I asked.

"Not without gloves," said Roxy. "It could be evidence."

I retrieved my white cotton gloves. "Satisfied?"

Although the end boards had been completely covered both inside and out with the garish kitchen paper, the title page and verso showed this book to be a first edition that had been printed in Italy.

"This is a rare book," I exclaimed excitedly. "To begin with it was only printed in Italy. It was banned in England up until 1959. Perhaps that was why it was covered? To hide the title?"

Roxy seemed impressed. "And if it belonged to our dead girl—along with the purse and cigarettes—that might give us a time frame. Maybe she traveled a lot?"

"So, not a servant girl, after all," said Mum. "Can we go now?"

I handed the book back to Roxy.

She sat down on the joint stool and cracked it open. "Yeah. We'll keep you posted."

"We'll leave you to your reading then," said Mum.

I took Mum's arm and propelled her out of the room. I knew she was hiding something. I could tell.

"Why are you holding my arm like that?" Mum grumbled and yanked hers free.

"Because you and I are going to have a little chat," I said. "And for a change, I want the absolute truth."

Chapter Four

"Well?" I demanded, as Mum and I returned to her MINI for the short drive back to the Carriage House. The weather was appalling with the rain coming down in sheets and a gale-force wind. "Aren't you going to tell me what's going on? I know that book has something to do with you. And you were at the Hall in the fifties. I know you were."

"That book does not belong to me," Mum said hotly. "Cross my heart and hope to die. Anyway, where would I get hold of a book like that? I've never been to Italy."

"You'd find a way," I said darkly.

A black Fiat 500 barreled toward us. As we pulled onto the grass verge to let it pass by the engine promptly stalled. I recognized the earnest face of Dick, the forensic scientist, at the wheel. He gave us a cheery wave as he sailed on by.

I glanced over at the fuel gauge. It was just as I thought. "You're nearly empty."

"Stop nagging," said Mum. "I hardly drive anywhere."

We set off once again.

"I wonder if there is a connection to the book, the purse and that poor woman," I mused. "I suppose Shawn will check any missing person reports for that time period."

"Roxy watches too much television," Mum grumbled.

"It's a great idea to take a look at your family trees."

"Not today." Mum suddenly seemed to change her tune. "I'm working on my publicity campaign for *Forbidden*—it comes out in just a couple of weeks—and then my publisher wants an outline for the next in the series."

"Well, can't I look at them? You don't have to be there—oh? There's Ginny."

Parked in front of the Carriage House stood a new black Peugeot with a PRESS placard on the dashboard. Ginny Riley got out of the car and flashed us a brilliant smile.

"Surely that's not the young girl from the *Dipperton Deal?*" Mum exclaimed as we drove through the open double-doors and into the carriageway itself. Alfred had spent two full weeks cleaning the interior where at one time, there had been room for four carriages. Now, we used it to park our cars. A door at the far end conveniently led directly into the living quarters, which was just as well. It was a cold, wet and windy February.

"I hardly recognized her," Mum went on. "I can see those dazzling veneers from here!"

Just a few months ago, twenty-something Ginny Riley had been a sweet and earnest trainee reporter for our weekly newspaper. But that had all changed with her exposé of a nasty scam from which the village of Little Dipperton had still not fully recovered. Although the scam's ringleader had been a former boyfriend of Lady Lavinia's, the Honeychurches had managed to keep that fact secret. Instead, Eric Pugsley had agreed to take the fall. Maybe Roxy had a point. Perhaps the body in the double-hide had been hushed up, after all.

Naturally, Ginny's front-page scoop had propelled her up the career ladder. She had abandoned the *Dipperton Deal* and went off to work for the prestigious *Western Times* in the city of Plymouth, about forty-five minutes away.

Ginny had changed. Gone was the fresh-faced girl with her brown hair pulled back into a ponytail. She wore it short in a pixie cut. She'd also exchanged her jeans, sweatshirt and trainers for a tailored suit, high-heeled shoes and heavy makeup that made her seem far older than her years.

"I'll let you deal with the newspapers, dear," said Mum. "I must get back to my book."

Mum gave Ginny a polite wave and went into the house.

Ginny strode over toward me. "Is it true that you found a dead body in a priest hole?" she asked, thrusting her iPhone under my nose. I noticed that it was switched to record.

"And hello to you, too!" I said deliberately into the iPhone. "How are you, Ginny?"

"Fine, thanks."

"You found out pretty quickly," I said.

Ginny grinned. "Any thoughts on who it might be?"

"You should talk to the police about that."

"They won't speak to me until they've notified the family," said Ginny. "That means it must be recent. Not some old priest that has been rotting there for hundreds of years."

"I don't know."

"Come on, Kat," said Ginny. "At least confirm it was a woman? At least give me that."

"Can't. Sorry." I gestured to her Peugeot. "Nice new car. Congratulations. You seem to be doing very well."

"Thanks. The *Times* definitely pays better than the *Deal* and sometimes my stories get picked up by nationals." Ginny smiled. "You told me I could be anything I wanted to be, remember? You said the world was my oyster and you were right!"

I did remember our conversation all those months ago and for a moment, I softened toward the young woman. I didn't blame her ambition and an urge to escape the monotony of reporting dreary funerals and dog shows, but the new Ginny worried me.

At one time I had begun to regard her as a younger sister. We occasionally met for coffee and talked about her love life and other things that women have to deal with these days. But as time passed, she became far more interested in my personal life and her questions became more intrusive. I began to avoid her phone calls and eventually, they petered out altogether. Mum said I was being paranoid, especially now I no longer had my TV show, but I had learned the hard way about having my private life dragged into the newspapers and how easy it was for an innocent comment to be taken out of context.

"Please give me a quote," said Ginny. "Just one. That's all I'm asking."

"Honestly, I'd rather not."

"Why? Are you scared of what the old bag will say?"

I was taken aback. "Old bag?"

"The dowager countess," said Ginny. "I know she freaks out at the first whiff of scandal."

I'd never heard Ginny be so disrespectful. In the past she had always spoken highly of Lady Edith Honeychurch.

"Oh don't look so shocked." Ginny grinned. "Everyone knows the Honeychurches close ranks and hush stuff up. I'll just focus on the double-hide in the sealed-off wing."

"I didn't say anything about it being a double-hide," I said sharply. "Nor about the wing being sealed off."

"Who saw the body first?" Ginny persisted. "You or Eric Pugsley?"

"Why don't you ask him?" I knew that Eric would never talk to Ginny again.

She gave a snort of disdain. "Yeah, right. He refuses to speak to me."

"That doesn't surprise me." Ginny's article on the scam had left Eric practically shunned by the village. Although I still couldn't understand why he had agreed to be the scapegoat in the first place.

"Come on, Kat, give me something!" she pleaded. "It's my first murder story."

"Who said anything about it being a murder?"

"Don't you wonder *why* the wing was sealed off?" said Ginny. I didn't answer. "How about 'Murder, Mischief and Mayhem at Honeychurch Hall.' Pretty good headline, eh?"

"There is a rare plasterwork ceiling in the King's Parlor," I said suddenly.

"So?"

"If you want a story, there it is. It was damaged when a water pipe burst on the floor above. How about that for an exclusive—the plight of the country house."

"So *that's* where you found the body?" said Ginny. "In the King's Parlor?"

"No comment."

"I'll find out one way or another," she said.

"I'm sure you will but it won't be from me." I smiled. "Good luck with your story."

"Thanks," said Ginny. "I'll be back!"

I watched Ginny return to her car. She took off her high-heels and exchanged them for flats. Then she put the shoes into a cloth bag on the rear passenger seat before setting off. They were expensive shoes and reminded me of Eric's wife, Vera, who had had a vast shoe collection. The Honeychurch family had managed to hush up that tragedy, too. Even the prison sentence imposed on William Bushman—the former stable manager—was barely mentioned in the *Dipperton Deal* and since the newspaper had used his real name of Ralph Jackson, there was no connection to Honeychurch Hall at all. Maybe Ginny had a point.

I checked my watch. It was time to pick up Harry from school.

As I headed out of the main gates I realized Harry would have to be told *something*. The problem was that the Honeychurch clan seemed to use a code for anything "unpleasant." Hence William Bushman aka Ralph Jackson was not serving time in prison but had merely gone on a climbing expedition to the Himalayas. I didn't agree with lying to children even if it was to protect them.

I resolved to stay out of it. After several escapes from the "prisoner-of-war camp," as Harry referred to his former boarding school, I was already in the proverbial doghouse for planting the idea into Harry's head about switching to the local primary school—an idea that had been met with horror for "breaking with tradition" and "mixing with the hoi polloi." Unfortunately, my well-intentioned plan seemed to have backfired. Harry was teased about his "posh" accent and seemed even unhappier than before.

I pulled up outside Little Dipperton Primary School, parked my Golf and went to join the throng of mothers hovering around the school gates with their strollers. Here, the children didn't have to wear a school uniform. I had to admit that most looked very scruffy in their anoraks, jeans and trainers and nothing like the smart blazer, flannel trousers and cap that Harry had worn when he was boarding at Blundell's.

I used to feel a pang of envy seeing mothers with their

children. With the end of my relationship with David came the end of my hopes of having a family with him, too. I knew I wasn't quite past my biological sell-by date yet, but I would be forty in a few weeks and even if I met someone—which I wasn't ready to do quite yet—and immediately fell pregnant, I'd be forty-one. That would make me nearly fifty picking up a seven-year old from the local school. Maybe I should just get a cat.

"Kat?" a voice shouted, breaking my thoughts. I looked over to find a pretty young woman with her blond hair swept up into an untidy coil on top of her head. With her ankle-length rain-coat, a mass of swirling scarves and Edwardian button-boots, she somehow managed to make disheveled look stylish.

I waved to my new friend, Pippa Carmichael. At first, the other mothers had given me a wide berth as if I were an alien from another planet. I used to find that happened a lot when I was at the height of my so-called *Fakes & Treasures* fame. People seemed either too nervous to talk to me or felt they knew me intimately and offered the most astonishingly personal advice.

I had found that making new friends in a new place was harder than I expected especially in a community like Little Dipperton. The brief friendship I'd known with a fellow an-tique dealer in Dartmouth ended when she returned to France with her husband. She'd warned me that it would take at least forty years to become accepted as a "local" and it would seem that she was right!

Pippa had been different.

For a start, she had lived in Putney—a stone's throw from Tooting—where I'd been born. Just knowing someone who knew a familiar shop or a restaurant had helped a lot.

Pippa had moved from London with her son Max following

a nasty divorce and started a catering business. The two of us had struck up an easy rapport.

Max and Harry had been "school holiday" friends, which was one of the reasons I thought sending Harry to Max's school would have been so perfect. I had wrongly assumed their friendship would have continued.

Far from greeting me with a smile, Pippa looked worried. "I've been wanting to talk to you." She pulled me gently aside and out of the earshot of the other women.

"What's the matter?" I said.

She gave a heavy sigh. "I've tried to talk to Harry's mother but she never gets out of that Range Rover when she comes to pick him up." Pippa paused. "God. This is so awkward."

"Is this about Harry?" I asked.

"I know it's not your problem, but ..." She hesitated. "Perhaps you would talk to him."

"Is something wrong?" I said, feeling a horrible tightness in my chest. "Has he done something?"

Pippa paused again. "The thing is, Max says that Harry wants to hang out with him and his friends all the time."

"I thought they *were* friends." I was surprised at the surge of protective feelings that suddenly consumed me.

"I know, I know ... but, school holiday friends aren't real friends, are they?" Pippa looked miserable and I knew that she desperately wanted me to agree. "Harry needs to make his own friends."

My heart went out to poor Harry. "Maybe Max needs to tell him that."

"He's tried." Pippa stole a look at three women who were standing in a cluster next to her white Vauxhall Astra. I caught encouraging nods and guessed that she had been coerced into being the spokeswoman for all of them.

"Pippa, I can't do that," I said. "If Max won't tell Harry then you have to talk to Lavinia."

"She's such a cold fish," said Pippa with unexpected feeling. "How Rupert ever married her is beyond me."

"Then talk to Rupert."

Pippa reddened. "I . . . I don't know why I said that. I hardly know him."

"And you're wrong about Lavinia," I said. "She's just shy."

Pippa looked over to the women again. "Our kids have all been friends since nursery school. They don't like newcomers."

"Well, I can definitely identify with that feeling!" I said wryly. "And I suspect you can, too."

An awkward silence fell between us as we both tried to find something to say. I genuinely liked Pippa and suspected she was being forced to do this.

"Okay, I'll phone Lavinia," Pippa said grudgingly. "Do I have to call her your ladyship?"

"Yes. You'll get Cropper, the butler," I said. "And he will summon her to the phone."

"Seems funny in this day and age." Pippa laughed. "When are you starting your antique business?"

"I'm almost set up at the gatehouses for Kat's Collectibles. I'll be offering a mobile valuation service as well," I said, "but I've still got no central heating at Jane's Cottage. I'm also looking for someone who is good at D-I-Y."

"You should put an ad in the post office," said Pippa.

"I did."

"A good handyman is hard to find." Pippa gestured to her white Vauxhall that had a huge dent in the rear passenger door. "I'm still trying to find someone to repair that without paying a fortune."

The clang of the school bell stopped all further conversation and moments later the playground was filled with the chatter of schoolchildren released from captivity for the day.

I recognized towheaded Max sauntering across the playground with four friends, all laughing and playing the fool. Harry trailed behind them, a solitary figure in new jeans, black lace-up shoes and a child's navy Barbour that immediately set him apart. He seemed so different from the confident young boy I'd first met dressed as Squadron Leader James Bigglesworth in his World War I flying helmet, goggles and white scarf.

"How was your day?" I asked him as we got into my car.

"Okay, I suppose." Harry dumped his rucksack onto the passenger side floor and gave a heavy sigh. I caught him giving a longing glance at Max as Pippa herded the boys into her car.

"Do you have much homework?" I asked.

"A bit."

"Well, at least it's the weekend," I said.

"Max, Jed, Emerson, Ronan and Callum are going to see Exeter City play Portsmouth tomorrow," he said glumly.

"I thought we were going riding together tomorrow."

Harry bit his lip. "I asked Max if I could go with them," he went on, "but Max said there weren't any tickets left but then Callum came up and asked if *he* could go and Max said yes."

I felt my heart contract with pain for Harry. "I thought you didn't like soccer," I said lightly.

"Yes I do!" Harry shouted. "I *love* it. But Father doesn't. He says soccer is full of hooligans and that rugby is a gentleman's sport—and cricket, of course."

"Oh dear."

"And then they're all going back to Jed's place and having pizza and playing with his Xbox."

"I think Squadron Leader Bigglesworth should have them court-martialed for unsporting behavior," I said, attempting a joke.

"Biggles doesn't exist," Harry said angrily. "He never did!"

"Of course he did."

"Max says it's all made up."

"Didn't you tell him that you'd been to the RAF Museum in London and actually saw his combat report?"

Harry's eyes widened with delight. "No! I didn't!"

"There you are then," I said. "You can tell Max on Monday." I reached over to ruffle his hair.

"Ouch." Harry winced. To my alarm I saw the faint mark of a purple bruise on his temple.

"What happened to you?"

"I fell over," he mumbled.

"How?" I demanded.

"I don't want to talk about it." Harry turned away from me and stared out of the window. We continued the rest of the journey in silence whilst I agonized over what had happened. Had Harry really fallen over or were Max and his friends bullying him? I just had to speak to Lavinia.

We turned into the grand main entrance to Honeychurch Hall and passed the eighteenth-century gatehouses that were now the new home for Kat's Collectibles. With the scaffolding up—I was in the process of repairing the gutters—the place looked dilapidated.

"Why do we have to live in a house that falls down?" Harry suddenly cried. "Why can't we live in a normal house like my friends where all their houses are the same? Why can't I be like everyone else?"

"Ah," I said. "But I bet your friends don't have secret rooms and stories of hidden treasure."

"Treasure?" Harry gasped. "Secret *rooms*? What treasure? What secret rooms?"

I probably should have let his parents tell him, but the words just came out. I wanted desperately to distract him and it had worked.

As I filled Harry in on the day's discoveries—making sure not to mention the corpse—he almost seemed back to his old self.

"But you didn't exactly *find* any treasure," said Harry.

"No, but there was definitely evidence that the coins had been made at the Hall."

"Wicked!" he said.

"So if you hadn't heard the pipes explode in the night—"

"Surely you mean the *minenwerfer*, Stanford," said Harry, returning to his alter ego.

"Of course, sir. So if wasn't for that, no one would have ever found the double-hide."

"Can we go and see it now?"

"I'm sure your father would want to show you himself," I said hastily. "Obviously the double-hide is of great historical importance so experts will need to look at it first."

"Maybe we can find the treasure by next week and then Father can bring it to show-and-tell at school," he said hopefully. "Ronan's grandfather is letting him take his glass eye. When he was born, the doctor poked the real one out by accident with a fork."

"I think you meant forceps," I said. "But that's a horrible story."

"Ronan says he likes to frighten his grandmother. He told me that whenever she says, 'Keep an eye on this for me, will you, luv?' he pops it out and leaves it on the table."

"Oh dear!"

"And Callum says he's going to bring in a live snake. A python. He says it's so big it could eat a horse—oh! Look, there's Roxy!"

Roxy's panda car slowed down to let us pass by. She opened her window.

"Afternoon, Master Harry," she said, giving him a big smile. "How was school?"

"I hate school." Harry scowled and then brightened. "But Kat's told me all about *nearly* finding the treasure in the secret chamber."

"Yes, isn't it exciting?" said Roxy. "And perhaps tomorrow you'll be able to go in there."

"Wicked!"

"I was just on my way to see Iris actually," said Roxy. "Is she home?"

"She should be. Why?"

I glanced over to her passenger seat and saw a telltale plastic shopping bag with very little inside. A peculiar feeling swept over me—and one I was becoming quite familiar with whenever I saw such a bag with a police officer. I knew from experience that whatever was in it was never good news.

"Just a few questions," said Roxy.

"I'll be ten minutes," I said. "Why don't you wait for me and we can see her together?"

"Why?" said Roxy slyly. "Does Iris need someone to hold her hand?"

"Not at all," I said. "I'm sure she'll be only too happy to make you a cup of tea."

"Somehow," said Roxy cryptically, "I doubt it."

Chapter Five

There was silence in the kitchen when I walked in. Roxy stood with her back to the oak dresser that was full of Mum's coronation china. She was clasping the plastic shopping bag to her chest. Mum feigned boredom but I could tell she was worried by the way she kept sighing. "Shall we have some tea?" I suggested.

"Not for me, thanks," said Roxy. "I don't drink on duty."

"We're waiting for Shawn," Mum said. *"Apparently."*

"He took the twins to the dentist and now he's dropping them off with his grandmother."

"Mrs. Cropper?" Mum seemed surprised.

"No, Helen's mum," said Roxy. "She helps Shawn out after school."

"He needs an au pair—or a new wife." Mum looked pointedly at me.

"It's not been two years since Helen died," Roxy said sharply. "She was the love of his life. He'll never marry again."

"Oh, I am sorry, dear," said Mum sweetly. "That must be so hard for you. As I was saying to Officer Cairns, Kat, I'm not sure how I can help." Mum looked daggers at the plastic shopping bag. I could tell the suspense was killing her. "Do you want to put that down somewhere?"

Roxy clasped it closer. "No, thanks."

Mum looked over at the singing bird clock above the kitchen door. It wasn't quite five. "Is it too early for something stronger?"

"You might need to keep your wits about you," Roxy declared.

I wasn't sure if she was joking. "Tea, in that case." I marched over to the kettle and switched it on.

"Can I use your loo?" said Roxy.

"Use the one downstairs just off the carriageway," said Mum. "Through the door and take the first one on the left. The bowl is Victorian and very pretty. It's decorated with horse heads and flowers so do take a look before you sit down—shall I hold your shopping?"

"No, thanks." Roxy clasped the plastic shopping bag even closer and scurried off.

"Are you thinking what I'm thinking?" Mum whispered urgently.

"The plastic shopping bag?"

"Shawn's show-and-tell," said Mum. "It's pathetic."

"We'll soon find out." I handed Mum a china mug of tea with a splash of milk.

"She's so childish."

"Speaking of children," I said and went on to tell Mum how concerned I was about Harry. "And what's more, he has a nasty bruise on his forehead. I think he's being bullied."

"Don't worry. I'll get Alfred to give him a few boxing lessons."

"Don't you dare!" I exclaimed.

"Harry's got to show them who is boss," said Mum. "Alfred taught me, you know. I've still got a very good left hook."

The doorbell sounded. "I'll get it," I said. "I expect it will be Shawn."

But it wasn't. It was a man in his early seventies. He reminded me of a slimmer version of an aging Marlon Brando with deep-set eyes, fleshy lips and a strong jaw.

"Can I help you?" I said.

"Bryan—with a *y*—Laney," he said and offered his hand. "You advertised for someone to do a spot of D-I-Y?"

"Oh. Yes. I did." I took in his appearance. With his dark green corduroy trousers and a sports jacket he had an almost military bearing—someone I'd never have taken for a handyman. But then my father had been a tax collector and no one ever believed he was good at D-I-Y, either. Dad had always done our decorating, loved woodwork and was always puttering in the garage making this and that.

"Muriel at the post office told me," Bryan said. "I used to live around here. I'm in the process of moving back. Need a bit of work, that kind of thing." He smiled. "Retirement doesn't suit me."

"Okay," I said. "Why don't we meet tomorrow morning so I can show you what needs to be done and then you can give me an estimate."

"O-nine-hundred hours suit you?" he said.

"Perfect. Do you have a mobile?"

Bryan handed me a scrap of paper with his phone number on it. He'd obviously been prepared. "By the way, I always enjoyed your show. Pity you retired. I don't think the new host is much good—she's not got your class."

"Oh, thanks," I said, secretly pleased.

"Don't ever cut your hair, Rapunzel," he said with a wink. "It's beautiful. Good afternoon."

I could easily imagine that Bryan had been a bit of a ladies' man back in the day. I returned to the kitchen and found that Shawn must have slipped in through the carriageway entrance.

"It's all over the news," I heard Shawn say. "I heard it on the radio on my drive over."

"Ah, here she is," said Mum. "What were you doing?"

"I'll tell you later," I said. "What's on the news?"

"Sounds like Ginny's been busy spreading the word." Mum pulled out a chair and sat down at the kitchen table.

"Just that a double-hide has been found at Honeychurch Hall along with some remains," Shawn said.

"Her ladyship is going to love that," Roxy muttered.

"No other details yet, of course, and that's the way we want it to stay—at least for the time being."

"Apparently, they've identified the body," Mum blurted out.

"Already?" I exclaimed. "Who?"

"We got in touch with Interpol and we're ninety-nine percent certain that the woman's name is Pandora Haslam-Grimley," said Shawn. "She was an American heiress. The DNA results from the lipstick should confirm it."

"I told you she was American," Roxy put in. "The Lucky Strikes gave it away."

"The last time anyone saw Ms. Haslam-Grimley alive was at the Honeychurch annual midsummer ball in 1958."

I looked to Mum who just shrugged. "Never heard of her."

"According to our sources, Ms. Haslam-Grimley was a bit of a free spirit," said Shawn. "After her visit at Honeychurch she had made plans to go on a cruise. It was a full month before anyone realized something was wrong."

"No one reported it?" I was stunned. "Not even her friends? Surely someone like Pandora would have attracted a lot of media attention?"

Shawn cleared his throat. "Actually, it was overshadowed by a far more tragic event," he said. "The dowager countess's brother Rupert died in a freak shooting accident."

My eyes flew to my mother's and I saw she'd turned pale. Of course we knew the real story behind the "freak shooting accident." It had been the subject of *Forbidden*, my mother's soon-to-be-published second book in her Star-Crossed Lovers series. But I wasn't sure if Shawn was aware of the details. So much was kept under wraps in this household. It was hard to tell.

As if reading my mind, Roxy said, "Another Honeychurch hush-up."

Shawn ignored her. "So that narrows the date down to mid-June in 1958. The police did retrace Pandora's steps and someone did say they saw her getting on the train at Dipperton Halt, but they were unable to verify it."

"Who was the investigating officer at the time?" I asked.

"He died in 2003," said Shawn. "And although my father became a police officer, he was just a kid back then."

"How convenient," said Mum.

"We'll be working with Interpol on this," Shawn went on. "But we wanted to get a head start, so to speak."

"But we *will* be reporting our findings, Shawn," Roxy reminded him. "So we're starting with anyone who was here at the Hall in June of 1958—Iris?"

"I can hardly remember what I had for breakfast this morning let alone where I was in 1958!"

Roxy put down the plastic shopping bag to pull on her disposable latex gloves.

"Here we go," Mum muttered.

With a crackle and flourish, Roxy withdrew the Bushman's Fair and Traveling Boxing Emporium flyer. "Well, we can confirm that you *were* here in June of 1958."

Mum rolled her eyes. "Look, dear, I don't want to state the obvious, but we camped here in the park every summer. There were dozens of us. We were never invited to the Hall and we certainly didn't socialize with any of the toffs—and besides, I only found out about the priest-hole thingy this morning. I was just as shocked as everyone."

Although my mother was a notorious fibber, I honestly didn't think she'd known about the double-hide. Even so, I knew she was holding something back. I could tell by the way she sat back in her chair with her arms folded.

"My grandfather told me that only three people ever knew the locations of the priest holes," said Shawn thoughtfully. "The person who built it, the master of the house and the estate steward. The secret was passed down from father to son."

"That's what Rupert told us," I said.

"Yeah, well...someone *else* knew where it was." Roxy looked directly at my mother. "Someone who was, perhaps, jealous of Pandora Haslam-Grimley and everything she stood for. Someone who watched on the outside, wishing for a different life. Someone like *you*, Iris."

"Roxy!" Shawn warned.

"Or maybe you're covering up for someone else?" said Roxy. "Someone in your troupe—or tribe or whatever you call it?"

Mum's jaw tightened. "Don't be ridiculous. I told you, the only part of Honeychurch we were allowed into was the servants' wing."

And that was a definite lie. Mum had made a comment just mere hours earlier when we had first entered the Great Hall.

She'd pointed up to the minstrel's gallery and told Rupert how she and her brothers used to watch the summer balls and spy on the guests.

"We're only asking if you remember anything about that particular ball, that's all," said Shawn. "It was a costume ball."

"They were all costume balls," said Mum. "From what I can remember. I was only fifteen."

"That would explain the unusual dress that Pandora was wearing," Shawn said to Roxy. "You see, Iris—you are helping us with our inquiries, after all."

Roxy continued to stare at my mother. "And let's not forget the heart-shaped necklace with the fake diamond."

"I don't know why you keep staring at me," said Mum.

Shawn and Roxy exchanged meaningful glances. He gave her a nod and she retrieved *Lady Chatterley's Lover* from the plastic shopping bag.

"Do you recognize this book, Iris?" said Roxy.

"I saw it earlier. Yes. I recognize this book."

"So *today* was the first time that you'd seen this book?"

"Cross my heart and hope to die."

Roxy put the book on the table and opened it. The end board was completely covered with the shelf-liner paper—right up to the inner hinge where it had been slit open. Roxy withdrew a small penknife from her pocket.

"Careful!" I exclaimed. "That book is a first edition and very valuable."

With painstaking precision, Roxy gently removed the paper. There was no dust jacket underneath. She showed Mum and me her handiwork. "Recognize this?"

There, written in ink on the end board itself were the damning words, *This book belongs to Iris Bushman.*

"Mum?" I gasped.

"That's not my handwriting," Mum exclaimed. "I've been framed."

"If I had a pound for every time I heard that," Roxy said, "I'd be able to live at Honeychurch Hall myself!"

"Anyway, you can't prove anything," said Mum.

"How do you explain the Bushman flyer being inside the book?"

"When you're being *framed*, it's hard to explain anything. That's what being *framed* means."

"There's no way my mother could have bought this book. As you know it was printed in Italy." I thought for a moment. "Maybe it belonged to Pandora? I can't think how else it would have gotten into the country and as you said, Shawn, she was quite the traveler."

Chuffah-chuffah-chuffah-chuffah erupted from Shawn's pocket. The chuffing sound grew louder drowning out all further speculation as Shawn fumbled in his pocket and took out his iPhone.

Shawn hit the answer button and barked, "Cropper," and turned away to take the call.

"Saved by the Scarborough Spa Express from Wakefield Westgate to Ardsley Tunnel," Mum declared, shooting Roxy a mutinous look.

There was an awkward silence as we waited for Shawn to hang up.

"Right, Dick and his photographer have finished," Shawn said to Roxy. "They'll be removing the body tomorrow. But the Yard are sending their own forensic anthropologist over and we've already had phone calls from the local historical society."

"Does that mean I can go and take the paintings?" I asked.

Roxy looked puzzled.

"I've been asked to do a valuation," I said. "For the auction."

"Kat is helping the dowager countess raise money to repair the ceiling," said Mum.

"Tomorrow should be fine," said Shawn. "But we'll be holding onto the tools just in case."

"Of what?" Mum demanded.

"We're still not clear on exactly how Ms. Pandora Haslam-Grimley died."

"I thought her neck was broken," I said.

"As I said, when we're sure, we'll let you know." Shawn gave a nod to Roxy who put the book and the flyer back into her plastic shopping bag. "Thank you for your time. We'll see ourselves out."

Roxy paused at the kitchen door. "Don't go anywhere, Iris," she said darkly. "We'll be back."

"Well?" I said to Mum, the moment we heard the front door slam. "What have you got to say for yourself?"

"Of course I remember Pandora Haslam-Grimley," Mum exclaimed. "She was a horrible, horrible girl, nasty, vindictive and a complete tramp. I'm glad she's dead!"

"Oh, Mum!" I wailed. "Please don't tell me you had something to do with this."

"I can't believe you would think such a thing!" Mum was indignant. "If my own daughter thinks I'm guilty, it's no wonder that the police have practically got me mounting the scaffold."

"And the book, *Lady Chatterley*—is it yours?"

"Not exactly," said Mum sheepishly.

"Oh my God, it *is* yours!"

"Let's have a gin and tonic and then I can explain everything."

Chapter Six

"You *stole* it?" I gasped. "From who?"

"Whom, you mean. From *whom*. And I didn't steal it, I borrowed it. Completely different."

"And you covered it in that funny paper."

"It's shelf liner," said Mum. "But no. It was already like that."

"But your name is inside."

"That's not my handwriting," said Mum. "And anyway, I'd hardly go to the trouble of covering it with shelf liner and then promptly writing my name inside. Surely you're not that dense."

"You would if you didn't want anyone to see what you were reading."

"Do you want to hear what I have to say or not?"

"Sorry. You're right," I said. "You talk and I'll listen."

"I found the book in the hayloft—"

"Hayloft? What, here? At the Carriage House? What were you doing in the hayloft?"

"I thought you were going to let me speak?"

"Sorry."

"When we left the park that summer—for the last time, I may add—I put it back. End of story."

"So... are you saying that the book belonged to someone else? Someone below stairs?"

"I don't know."

"Maybe we should ask Alfred to do a bit of channeling?" I joked. "He's good at communicating with the dead."

"You leave Alfred out of this," said Mum quickly.

A peculiar feeling came over me. "Is this something to do with Alfred? Are you protecting him?"

"No," Mum exclaimed. "What a notion!"

Much as I'd grown to like Mum's stepbrother, I still wasn't sure what to make of him. With a prison record as long as my arm that covered a wide variety of offenses ranging from armed robbery to fraud, it wouldn't surprise me if he was somehow involved.

"That must have been pretty racy stuff for you to read at age fifteen," I said.

"*You* did."

"I studied D. H. Lawrence for my A levels," I said. "And to be honest, I didn't really understand it."

"Well, nor did I. I just wanted it for some ideas."

"What kind of ideas?"

"Oh nothing like that," she said quickly. "No prancing around naked in the rain or threading flowers through the hair on a man's chest—no, I had already started writing stories and wanted to put in a bit of hanky-panky but hadn't a clue where to begin."

"I trust you found it informative." I knew I was being sarcastic but Mum didn't seem to notice.

"Oh yes," she said dreamily. "I think that's when I realized I wanted to be a romance writer. The way that D. H. Lawrence describes his love scenes..." She gave a shiver. "*Yet the passion licked round her, consuming and when the sensual flame of it pressed through her bowels—"*

"Stop right there!" I exclaimed. "I get the picture."

"I had to read the book in secret in case Aunt June caught me," Mum went on. "It was very cramped in our caravan. There were five of us, you know. I don't remember when the ban was lifted, do you?"

"In 1959," I said.

"Isn't it funny how things change," Mum mused. "Only last week I was in the hairdresser's in Dartmouth and I overheard two young women chatting quite openly about bondage in *Fifty Shades of Grey*."

"Weren't you curious as to how a banned book happened to end up in Little Dipperton? It's hardly something you'd pick up at the post office and general store."

"Sometimes," said Mum. "At one point I thought it belonged to Mrs. Cropper."

"The cook?" I laughed. It was hard to imagine the somewhat dour Mrs. Cropper as someone who devoured racy books in secret.

"Don't look like that. We were all young once," said Mum. "The summer nights were long and hot. Hormones were raging. It was marvelous!" Mum thought for a moment. "Why don't we see who else might have been around in the summer of 1958?"

"Well—yes, on the estate," I said. "But what if one of the guests decided to get rid of Pandora?"

"Just humor me," said Mum. "Come on. I'll top up our drinks. You find some nibbles."

Moments later we were in Mum's office upstairs and she was wheeling her office chair over to where two family trees labeled Above-Stairs and Below-Stairs were spread across the far wall.

My mother's office seemed more chaotic than usual with her new rolltop desk—a Christmas present I'd bought her to take the place of the old dining room table—covered in scrunched-up balls of paper that also littered the floor.

"Slaughtering a few trees today, are we?" I said dryly. "I wish you'd at least try to use a computer."

"I'm perfectly happy with Daddy's Olivetti, thank you. Besides, it's brought me a lot of luck. Oh—" Mum gave a sigh. "I wonder what *he* would have made of all this. Do you think he would have been proud of me?"

Given that Dad never knew about my mother's secret writing life and all her undisclosed earnings that were being squirreled away in an offshore account, somehow I doubted it.

Mum unearthed two coasters for our drinks in one of the pigeonholes.

"How *is* the new book coming along?" I asked.

"I'm still fiddling about with the story," said Mum. "But thanks to Pandora—oh, don't look like that—her discovery has given me a brilliant idea. In fact, it's reminded me of something I'd forgotten about. Something I'd buried."

"*Buried?* Not a body, I hope."

"Don't be silly. I'm quite excited actually."

"What is it?"

"Oh—I can't tell you." Mum beamed. "Now, pull up that stool, bring over the round table, put the peanuts down *there* and let's take a look at my trees."

I did as I was told.

"Wow!" I was impressed. "You've filled in a lot of blanks. You should get Rupert to pay you for your services!"

Over the last few months, the branches of both family trees

had been steadily spreading. As various details came to light, Mum added her Post-it Notes.

"I can start the English Civil War now." Mum passed me a notepad and a pen. "Seeing that Dobson oil painting was very helpful."

"The problem is, how do we know that whoever did Pandora in, lived or worked at the Hall?"

"Because whoever put her into the double-hide had to have known where it was," said Mum. "Maybe it was Edith's brother? As the thirteenth Earl of Grenville, he *must* have known about the location."

"Maybe," I said. "But that's no use to us now, is it, considering—"

"He's dead."

"I wonder how the purse and book came to be left in the first hide," I said. "When did Rupert say the Tudor wing was sealed off?"

"Before he was born. That would be ..." Mum traced her pencil down the line to Rupert's square. "In 1963. Plenty of time for evidence to be planted."

Mum took a huge gulp of her gin and tonic. I snatched up a handful of peanuts.

We fell into a comfortable silence as we both studied the family trees of both above and below stairs. Mum had given each family below stairs their own color. A series of interconnecting lines showed that there had been a lot of intermarrying going on.

"Isn't it illegal to marry first cousins?" I said.

"Oh, it's just to avoid birth defects," said Mum airily. "Anyway, our queen and the Duke of Edinburgh are both great-great-great-grandchildren of Queen Victoria so they're related. And Queen Victoria and Prince Albert were first cousins."

"Well, don't go marrying Alfred," I said.

"Very funny. You should be a comedienne."

"You've done a really great job with these family trees—especially below stairs." I pointed to a list in the margin labeled "Servant Hierarchy."

"Obviously they don't have all those people below stairs now," said Mum.

I read:

SERVED, BUT NOT CONSIDERED SERVANTS—CHAMBERLAIN, LAND STEWARD, HOUSE STEWARD; SENIOR SERVANTS—GOVERNESS, NURSE, COACHMAN, HEAD GARDENER, GAMEKEEPER; UPPER SERVANTS—BUTLER, HOUSEKEEPER, VALET, LADY'S MAID, COOK; LOWER SERVANTS—FOOTMAN (IST AND 2ND), UNDER BUTLER, GROOM, STABLE BOY, BOOT BOY, HALL BOY, GROUNDSKEEPER, PARLORMAID, CHAMBERMAID, UPPER LAUNDRY MAID, STILL-ROOM MAID, MAIDS-OF-ALL-WORK ("BETWEEN MAIDS"), UNDER COOK, KITCHEN MAID, SCULLERY MAID; UNCLASSIFIED SERVANT—GATEKEEPER.

Mum had begun to pencil in the positions held by each of the five main families—Pugsley, Banks, Stark, Cropper, Laney, and Jones—who served below stairs.

"I've only gone as far back as the 1800s," said Mum. "It's very time consuming."

"You could save yourself a lot of trouble by using the Internet," I pointed out.

Mum ignored me. "Do you see how each family kept within its own station within the servant hierarchy?"

I studied the diagram again. "So from top to bottom in order of importance would be Laney, Cropper, Stark, Banks, Jones and then Pugsley?"

Mum nodded.

"Poor Eric Pugsley is at the bottom of the heap so when he married Vera, it was above his station," I said. "Vera was Joan Stark's daughter. Joan must have been around in the fifties, Mum."

"She was, but we may as well forget about her," said Mum. "She's got Alzheimer's, remember?"

I did remember. Joan Stark was living in a residential care home called Sunny Hill Lodge. "What about this thread—Land Steward. You've just written in Laney."

"He's her ladyship's land agent now," said Mum. "That's who I dealt with when I bought the Carriage House."

"What about his forebears? It's just blank."

"I can't trace everyone, Katherine," Mum grumbled. "And really that job is obsolete. I mean, believe it or not there is no chamberlain or boot boy here at the Hall anymore, either."

"Laney—wait—you won't believe this." I told Mum about my visitor. "Bryan Laney told me he used to live around here. What's more, he's in his seventies. I bet he was in Little Dipperton in the fifties."

"Possibly," said Mum slowly.

"You should put his name on the board."

"I suppose I could." Mum hesitated.

"He has to be connected to the Hall. We should tell Shawn. Don't you think it's odd that he should suddenly turn up out of the blue?"

"I suppose so."

"By the way Bryan is spelled with a *y*."

"You're so bossy." Mum duly wrote Bryan Laney on a Post-it and stuck it on the board. "And you say he's going to do a bit of D-I-Y for you?"

"Do a spot of tiling, hang a few mirrors and redo the shelves in the pantry—that kind of thing."

Mum's eyes filled with tears. "I wish Daddy were alive. He would have loved to have hung your mirrors."

I reached over and gave her shoulder a squeeze. "I know, Mum."

"Oh, this is hopeless!" Mum threw her pencil across the room. "Let the police do their job is what I say. I've got a book to write and you've got a business to run!"

I reached for another handful of peanuts and shoveled them in.

Mum regarded me with what looked like pity and gave a heavy sigh.

"What?" I said.

"Do be careful, darling," she said.

"About what?"

"You don't want to let yourself go."

"They're just peanuts."

"You've put on a little bit of weight and you know what they say?"

"No."

"A minute in your mouth and a month on your hips."

"I'm enjoying eating what I like if you don't mind," I said. "I've had to starve myself for years to compensate for those ten pounds everyone gains on camera."

"And you've stopped wearing makeup."

It was true. I had gotten lazy. "It's because I'm with the horses a lot and I don't think they care."

"Are you in mourning?"

"For what?"

"David."

"I'm over him, Mum." It had been months since David and I had officially broken up. I'd come to realize that I wasn't so much missing the man as missing the dream of what our future together would have been.

"Good," said Mum. "Well, I suppose you'll find out sooner or later."

To my dismay, my stomach gave a lurch. "Find out what?"

Mum stood up and retrieved a newspaper from behind a cushion on the wingback chair. It was the dreaded *Daily Post* and was folded to Star Stalkers, a celebrity column written by David's estranged wife and my nemesis, Trudy. A photo of Trudy accompanied her byline.

"She really should do something about her hair," said Mum. "She always looks like she's going to kill off a few puppies."

I had to agree. With her sharp chin and black bob with a white streak, Trudy resembled the Disney character Cruella de Vil from *101 Dalmatians*.

"I'm really not interested in what Trudy has to say, Mum."

"But you are over David," Mum insisted.

Despite my earlier protestations that I was, my heart began to hammer in my chest. "Is this *about* David?"

So David had gotten divorced after all. Charming, sophisticated, wealthy, and as one of the world's leading art investigators, I knew he wouldn't remain single for long.

Mum patted my knee as she passed me the newspaper. "I am so sorry, dear."

I stared at the headline in disbelief:

RENEWING OUR VOWS UNDER THE HAWAIIAN SUN

A color photograph showed David and Trudy standing arm in arm on a sandy beach with the ocean crashing behind them. They were wreathed in flower garlands. Trudy wore a sheer white dress and David was in white shorts and a Hawaiian shirt. On either side of them stood their two teenagers—Chloe and Sam—also dressed in white. They were one big happy family.

I was so shocked I couldn't say a word. After all the years of promising his heart to me, he had stayed with Trudy, after all. It was a double blow.

"I do think his legs aren't his strong point," said Mum. "They're like a chicken's."

I handed the newspaper back in silence, went over to the window and stared blindly out.

Mum joined me and put her arm around my shoulders.

"I'm fine," I whispered. And in a strange way, I was. Whatever feelings I had left for him had died right there. For good. Forever.

"I know you are," she said gently.

We stood looking out at Cromwell Meadows where frost glittered under an inky night sky full of stars—something I never saw in London. To my left a roped-off square marked the entrance to the underground tunnel; to my right stood Eric's scrapyard. A pyramid of tires and discarded pieces of farm machinery joined the many "end-of-life" vehicles that littered the field, coated in crystals. The car crusher machine, a forklift truck and a stack of pulverized cars stood next to the battered caravan that Eric called his "office."

A light shone in the window. Eric's Massey Ferguson tractor, his old Land Rover and an unfamiliar green-and-white VW camper van were parked outside nose to nose.

"What on earth is Eric doing working so late?" said Mum. "Looks like he has company."

"I think I'm going to go and talk to him," I said suddenly.

"Whatever for?" Mum exclaimed. "You won't make David jealous now by throwing yourself at those eyebrows."

"You don't think so?" I smiled. "No, I just want to ask him something."

"Maybe he's entertaining a lady friend."

"Maybe," I said. "I'll knock before I enter."

"But why do you want to talk to him?" Mum persisted.

I wracked my brain. "I'm just curious about his mother-in-law and her Alzheimer's. You never know. Maybe Joan might remember something."

"I doubt it," said Mum.

"But isn't it true that sometimes people who suffer from the disease remember the past far more clearly than the present?"

"Maybe." My mother gave a mock sigh. "So I assume that means I'll be cooking tonight?"

"Yes. Love you, Mum." I kissed her cheek and left the room.

Chapter Seven

I pulled on a warm coat, woolen hat and gloves and grabbed a flashlight. Of course I hadn't wanted to talk to Eric. I just needed to be alone with my thoughts. I knew the day would come when David would meet another woman but never in my wildest imaginings did I think he would reconcile with Trudy.

I cut across the courtyard and dragged open the corrugated iron gate to Eric's scrapyard. The warning TRESPASSERS WILL BE PROSECUTED: POACHERS WILL BE SHOT flared in the beam of my flashlight. I wondered when was the last time someone was shot for poaching a rabbit.

As I strode across the crisp grass I turned back to see if Mum was still at the window. If she wasn't, I planned to take a walk through the woods and circle back to the Carriage House. Unfortunately, I saw her silhouette watching me. She waved. I waved back. Now I'd have to visit Eric.

I knew she was worried about me. I knew that she tried hard to distract me by making silly jokes or asking for my help with her stories. She was happy here and I knew I would be, too. Eventually.

Despite Mum insisting she could read the tea leaves, she

always said that no one knew what was around the corner. If someone had told me a year ago that I would be living in the middle of nowhere without David or the paparazzi, dressed in jodhpurs with my hair crushed under a hairnet, I would have laughed.

Yet, Honeychurch Hall meant something to my mother. For a childhood spent on the road, it was the one place that remained constant and now she was back for good. I imagined how her summers must have been. Magical, I suspected, as all summers are when looked back through rose-tinted spectacles.

I reached Eric's old caravan and heard the murmur of male voices. At least Eric wasn't "entertaining."

For a moment I hesitated, then rapped smartly on the caravan door.

The talking ceased immediately, then, "Were you expecting someone?" I heard a voice say.

"No." There was a twitch from a grubby net curtain and Eric's face pressed against the glass. To my surprise he smiled. "It's Kat. I forgot she was coming over tonight."

It was obviously untrue but definitely piqued my curiosity.

Eric threw open the caravan door. "Come on in."

I stepped up into the living area of the cramped office and was instantly assaulted by the smell of stale cigarettes and alcohol along with the usual musty aroma that was peculiar to caravans.

"Rapunzel!" Bryan waved from one of the two red banquettes. He raised a plastic tumbler in a toast. "We meet again."

"Bryan!"

"You know each other?" Eric sounded confused. "How?"

"We met earlier," I said. "Do *you* know each other?"

"We do now," said Bryan smoothly. "Give the girl a drink, Eric, Where are your manners?" He gestured to a bottle of Captain Morgan rum on the bay window ledge.

"Not for me, thanks," I said.

"Go on," said Bryan jovially. "Just one." By the color of his red nose I suspected he had definitely had more than one, and even Eric had the glassy-eyed look of someone who was three-sheets to the wind.

"Go on, Kat, please." Eric sounded unusually desperate.

"Just one," I said. "But small."

"Take a seat," said Bryan magnanimously.

I perched on the edge of the stained banquette opposite. As Eric poured me a glass I looked around his so-called office. I'd never been invited inside before. It was a typical six-berth layout with the two banquettes that Bryan and I were sitting on that could be converted into beds. Next to the door was a kitchen sink and primer stove. Opposite that was an island table that could fold away to allow for a Murphy bed to pull down from the rear wall.

Engine parts were spread over sheets of newspaper on every available surface and everything seemed smudged with axle grease.

At the far end I caught a glimpse of what would have been the main bedroom but looked as if Eric used it as his office.

"Bryan here was telling me all about his life in the Navy."

"Really?" I made a mental note for Mum's family tree.

"Joined up at eighteen. Traveled the world," said Bryan. "I was just telling Eric that it's time to put down roots in my old age."

"He's looking for work," said Eric.

"She knows." Bryan nodded at me. "We're meeting tomorrow up at Jane's, aren't we?"

"Yes." And then I remembered I hadn't actually mentioned Jane's Cottage. "Are you related to Laney—I'm afraid I don't know his first name—the dowager countess's land agent?"

Bryan seemed startled but then smiled. "He's a distant cousin."

"Maybe he can help you find a job in the area?"

"Yeah. Maybe he might." Bryan took a large draught of rum.

"So, you must have lived around here in the fifties?" I said.

"Yep," he said. "Right in the village. Not like Eric here whose folks got one of the estate cottages—or Joan."

"You know Joan Stark?"

"She was Banks back then," said Bryan. "I was sorry to hear about her Alzheimer's. Bloody shame that. She grew up at Jane's Cottage, you know. Damn good with a twelve-bore. Joan was a crack shot."

I made a mental note to tell Mum that, too.

"I've got good memories of Honeychurch back then," Bryan went on. "Those were the days."

"Do you remember Bushman's Fair and Traveling Boxing Emporium?" I said suddenly.

"Sure I do. I boxed a bit myself." Bryan cricked his neck and flexed his knuckles. I wondered why men always felt compelled to do that. "Did a fair bit of boxing in the Navy as well."

Eric stirred. "Yeah well, Kat's mother—"

"There was this one girl who fair broke my heart, she did," Bryan said. "Always ready for a romp in the hay. She was the one who got away." He paused for a moment, brows furrowed. "*Iris*—that was her name, Iris."

I practically choked as the rum shot up my nose and even Eric spluttered.

"Are you alright?" said Bryan.

"Fine!" I muttered as I tried to compose myself. "The rum..."

"She was a stunner," said Bryan. "Electra! The Twenty-seven-thousand Volts Girl!"

"She was... *what?*" I remembered the flyer. "Iris *was* Electra?"

Eric laughed. "Bloody hell!"

"Iris had long dark hair and deep violet eyes. She reminded me of Elizabeth Taylor. All the local lads were in love with Iris." Bryan grinned. "Let me see, how did it go, *'Expect shocks, sparks and an electric atmosphere... but don't get too close!'* That's how she was introduced and I got far too close. I'll never forget her."

I really did not know what to say. My mother had never said she'd performed in any sideshows.

"I always wondered what happened to her," said Bryan wistfully.

"Why don't you ask Kat?" said Eric, barely able to contain his mirth.

"Eric—wait—"

"Iris lives next door!"

Bryan's eyes bugged out. "Iris lives *here?*"

"Kat's her daughter."

Eric seemed to be enjoying himself. He looked at me and grinned. "Hey, everyone loves an admirer—I bet Iris will be chuffed."

"She's *here.*" A strange expression crossed Bryan's features but I couldn't say if it was hope or despair. "You mean she married one of the toffs?"

"Of course not," I said.

"But she *is* a widow," said Eric.

"Iris is *here.*" Bryan sounded like a lovesick teenager. "Blimey. I don't believe it."

It occurred to me that when I'd mentioned the name Bryan Laney, my mother had given no indication that she remembered him at all. If Mum had broken all the boys' hearts across the countryside, maybe Bryan had just been one of her many suitors. Electra! I couldn't wait to have *that* conversation with her.

"So you must have remembered the summer balls at the Hall?" I asked.

Bryan nodded, obviously still trying to take in the fact that my mother was close by.

"What about Pandora Haslam-Grimley," I said. "She was American. Do you remember her?"

Bryan frowned. "I remember her alright," he said darkly. "She was a friend of Lady Edith's. Much older than us lads but she liked a bit of rough."

"A what?" I exclaimed.

"Bit of rough." Bryan winked at Eric. "You know, a bit of the other with the local lads. Course, I only had eyes for Iris and that drove Miss High-and-Mighty mad. She couldn't stand Iris but then a lot of the girls here couldn't stand Iris, either. They were a bit afraid of her."

"Afraid of my mother?" I said with disbelief.

"Not only was she Electra, she was Madame Z—Madame Z's Psychic Touch." Bryan chuckled. "All the girls went to Iris to have their fortunes told."

"Did Pandora?" I asked.

Bryan shrugged. "No idea. When Pandora wasn't hanging about the stables she was messing around with the lads at the boxing emporium. I often wondered what happened to her, too."

"She's dead," Eric said bluntly.

"That wouldn't surprise me," said Bryan. "She would have been pushing ninety by now."

"Kat and I found her body today in a priest hole," said Eric.

Bryan's jaw dropped. All the color drained out of his face. I thought he was going to pass out.

"Are you alright?" I said. "Get him a glass of water, Eric."

"No! I'm okay. I'm fine." Bryan waved us away but he just stared at his feet. "Give me a minute."

Eric and I exchanged concerned looks.

"Bit of a shock, that's all." He still couldn't look up. "Don't like hearing that kind of thing."

"It *was* a horrible shock," I said.

"When I heard on the radio that a body had been found in a priest hole, I assumed it was—well, a priest from centuries ago." Bryan seemed incredulous. "What the hell happened? I mean—how could Pandora have ended up there?"

"They're investigating, obviously," I said. "They're asking anyone who would have been at the Hall at the time. I expect they'll want to talk to you as well."

"Yes, yes, of course. I'll call—who should I call?"

"Detective Inspector Shawn Cropper," I said.

"Cropper?" Bryan thought for a moment. "Peggy's grandson?"

"Yes."

Bryan got to his feet. "I'd better be off. I'll see you tomorrow morning." He paused at the caravan door. "Pandora was a nasty piece of work. She was cruel . . ." He stopped, as if lost in a distant memory. "But we can all be cruel when we're young, can't we?"

And with that, he left. After several false starts, we heard the engine of the camper van turn over and drive away.

"Well that was interesting," I said to Eric.

"You'd better warn Iris," said Eric. "He'll be after her fortune."

"Not if you don't tell him she's got one." I frowned. "What was he doing here?"

Eric shrugged. "He just said he was moving back to the neighborhood and looking for a bit of work. Looking up old friends, that kind of thing. He's been away at sea for years so he hadn't heard about my Vera—" Eric crossed himself and said a silent prayer. "Or about Joan's Alzheimer's and Sunny Hill Lodge. He seems set on paying her a visit but I told him not to bother. She's completely doolally."

Something felt off to me. "How did he know you'd be here so late tonight?"

Eric shrugged. "No idea. He just turned up and knocked on the door."

"And you didn't think to ask him?"

"Not really. He was looking for Joan."

"Well, tell Bryan to be careful," I said. "We don't want him to get accidentally shot for trespassing."

As I walked back to the Carriage House I felt thoroughly unsettled but I didn't know why. Bryan had been obviously shocked and upset about Pandora's demise. I didn't think he'd faked that. He also seemed genuinely surprised that Mum was living here.

As I let myself into the Carriage House I heard peals of laughter and shouts of "Snap!" I only knew of two grown-ups who played a children's card game with so much glee—my mother and Alfred.

Since Alfred had been camped at the Hall in the fifties too, maybe he would be more forthcoming.

Chapter Eight

I knew Alfred made my mother happy and I was pleased for her but sometimes I felt left out. The pair of them shared a lot of inside jokes. Alfred had this habit of shadow boxing around the kitchen that for some reason had Mum shrieking with laughter and darting off to the loo. I just didn't get it. Of course, he was nimble on his feet but after years of smoking, his efforts would always end in a coughing fit and once he actually passed out.

Mum accused me of being a killjoy and maybe she was right. When she broke the news that her stepbrother had been released on parole and was coming to work at the Hall—carefully hiding his prison record from everyone on the estate—I was certain I wouldn't like him but there was a charm about Alfred that I found endearing and besides, who can't like a man who claims he can talk to animals?

I braced myself, plastered a smile on my face and strolled into the kitchen. As usual, the room was filled with cigarette smoke but I did see that Mum had opened the window a crack in my honor. It mingled with the smell of fish pie, wafting from the oven. It was at times like this that I couldn't wait to live on my own again.

Both gave me grunts of acknowledgment but their fierce concentration for the card game didn't waver.

With his small, wiry frame, complete with arms heavily tattooed with birds of prey, it seemed hard to believe that Alfred had been a champion boxer. But his face bore all the scars of the ring—a squashed nose and a cauliflower ear.

"Snap!" Mum shrieked.

"You're here just in time, Kat," Alfred said grimly. "She's clearing me out tonight. I must have lost ten quid."

"Ah! Here comes the queen of the body snatchers!" said Mum triumphantly scooping up a mound of coins.

"It was the *Invasion of the Body Snatchers*," I said somewhat primly. "And it's got nothing to do with finding bodies."

Alfred leapt to his feet and did an impersonation of a zombie, thrusting his false teeth out at a disgusting angle.

"No zombies, either," I said but laughed all the same.

"She laughs!" Alfred exclaimed.

"I don't know why you don't think I have a sense of humor," I said.

"I'll pour you another drink," said Mum. "Pie's almost done."

"No, I'm fine," I said. "I'll handle the vegetables."

"I think they'd like that," said Alfred. "Nudge nudge, wink, wink, say no more."

Mum roared with laughter.

"Is everyone okay with peas?"

"Oooh." Mum clapped her hands. "I just love peas."

"You alright, luv?" Alfred said, suddenly all serious. "Not nice finding a body."

"Her name was Pandora Haslam-Grimley," I said.

"Never heard of her," said Alfred.

"Yes, you have," Mum insisted. "American. Smoked Lucky

Strikes. Awful person. Remember that time she struck one of the girls in the kitchens with a whip?"

"Pandora actually *hit* someone?" I was appalled.

Alfred's face darkened. "Yeah. That's right. Now I remember. Always hanging around the boxing emporium hoping to get lucky."

"Thrashed her, right across the back of the legs," Mum went on. "I was in the passage and about to walk into the kitchen and heard her cry out. Saw Pandora do it with my own eyes."

Alfred shook his head with disgust. "Do the cops have any leads?"

"They want to talk to everyone who was here at the time," said Mum.

"Maybe you can offer your services to the police, Alfred," I teased. "You're good at channeling the dead."

"Pandora had a thing about Alfred," Mum declared.

"Pandora had a thing about all the lads—not just me," Alfred protested. "And all the lads had a thing about Iris."

"So I hear," I said. "And Bryan Laney being one of them."

Mum shot Alfred a nervous look.

"Who?" Alfred demanded.

"No one." Mum shook her head furiously at me.

"I heard what you said. Bryan Laney." Alfred's expression changed. His good humor evaporated and in his eyes was a hardness I'd never seen before. "I remember *him*. Sniffing around underage girls—"

"I was mature for my age," Mum protested.

"You were fifteen!" Alfred was clearly unhappy. He popped his knuckles.

"He mentioned you performed in one of those sideshows," I said. "Electra! The Twenty-seven-thousand Volts Girl and that you told fortunes as Madame Z."

"Me? Never!" said Mum, giving Alfred a wink but he ignored it.

Alfred slammed his hand down on the table. "I told Laney that if he ever came anywhere near Iris again, he was a dead man."

"Oh, Alfred!" Mum forced a laugh. "Don't be daft."

"You don't know the half of it." Alfred's eyes grew flinty. "I punched his lights out in the ring and I enjoyed every minute of it."

"Well, we're all much older now," said Mum hastily. "None of that matters. Water under the bridge."

"A Bushman never forgets," Alfred growled. I decided now was not the time to mention that Bryan was back in the neighborhood.

"I'll get the pie." Mum got to her feet and joined me at the counter.

"For God's sake, don't tell Alfred that Bryan came here," she whispered urgently.

"If he finds out, it won't be from me," I said.

"And don't mention *that* book, either," Mum said.

"Lady—"

"Shh!"

"Okay. But if the police ask—"

"I'm not deaf, you know," Alfred shouted out. "What book?"

"Nothing!" Mum and I chorused.

"I'll lay up the table. You dish up the pie."

Ten minutes later we were all tucking into Mum's fish pie. Alfred hadn't said another word and the atmosphere was tense. I wracked my brain for something to say.

"This pie is delicious," I said.

"These peas are like bullets," Mum grumbled.

"You boil yours to death."

Mum turned to Alfred. "Remember Kat's old boyfriend, David?"

"The bloke with the fancy shoes?"

"Mum—"

"He went back to his wife," she said. "They renewed their vows under the Hawaiian sun."

"That journalist lassie?" Alfred exclaimed. "The one who looks like she'd kill a few puppies?"

"That's the one. Cruella," said Mum. "Kat's finished with him for good now."

"I never liked him," said Alfred.

"Nor did I," Mum agreed.

"Bit full of himself."

I got up from the table. "Okay, excuse me. Whilst you discuss my love life I'm going upstairs."

"It's only nine o' clock," Mum cried. "What are you going to do up there? You're not getting maudlin are you?"

"I'm fine!" I shouted from the doorway.

"You've upset her now, Iris."

"She's so serious all the time."

I didn't hear the rest as I climbed the stairs to my bedroom.

Mum was right. It *was* only nine in the evening. I was so bored. Is this what my life had come to? Perched on the bed I saw the old steamer trunk full of dressing-up clothes that my mother had made. When I was little, the costumes had been far too big for me to wear but I had never thought why.

I'd taken a look in the trunk before when Mum had broken her hand and couldn't wear any clothing with buttons or zips. We'd dug out a purple harem outfit that now took on a more sinister meaning. Digging a little deeper, I pulled out exactly seven brightly colored veils, a brocade bra with tassels and a wrap sewn with little bells. It was fairground style—gaudy, brash and very tacky and without doubt, the outfit used for the Dance of the Seven Veils.

I delved deeper and retrieved a short blue dress with zigzag-shaped epaulettes. Down at the bottom was an extraordinary wig with the white hair lacquered to within an inch of its life, standing upright. I found fake glittered eyelashes that had to be a half-inch long and a long cord with a huge three-pronged plug. This had to be Electra's, the 27,000 Volts Girl.

I started to laugh. Really, it was all so ridiculous. Mum accused me of being too serious. We'd soon see about that!

I tried on the harem outfit and gasped. I really had piled on some pounds. So I changed into Electra—wig, eyelashes, the lot—and trooped downstairs feeling very pleased with myself.

I burst into the kitchen. "Ta-dah!—Oh! Shawn, hello."

Three pairs of eyes swiveled in my direction. I was mortified. Shawn's jaw dropped. Alfred cackled with glee but Mum looked absolutely horrified.

"Oh, darling," she groaned.

I stood there feeling rather cold and silly.

"That's just *not* a good look for you."

"I was just going through that old trunk," I said lamely.

Shawn was grinning from ear to ear. "Well, well, well," he said. "I was just telling Iris that we've found out that the clothing Pandora wore the night she died was actually a fancy dress costume." He took in my appearance. "Isn't that fancy dress?"

"I hope so," I said. "It's not something I'd usually wear to the pub. Mum's very good with the needle. She made all my dressing-up clothes."

"How interesting," Shawn said. "We've learned that the

theme for that year's ball was Cleopatra. Pandora Haslam-Grimley had been dressed as Cleopatra."

"Ah, the wig," I said, recalling the beaded black wig.

"Did you make any costumes for the midsummer ball, Iris?"

"No!" said Mum quickly. "Why?"

Shawn's jaw hardened. "Look, Iris. I know you are holding something back from me or..." He turned to stare at Alfred who stared defiantly back. "Perhaps you are protecting someone else...?"

"Don't look at me," Alfred protested. "I don't know anything."

"Would you like to continue this conversation down at the station?"

"Am I under *arrest*?" Mum gasped.

"No," said Shawn. "But with the discovery of the book in the double-hide—"

"What book?" Alfred demanded.

Shawn turned pink. *"Lady Chatterley's Lover."*

"Lady Chatterley's Lover?" Alfred's eyes widened. "What's that *filth* got to do with my Iris?"

"I'm being framed," said Mum quickly. "The book isn't mine."

I felt as if I was in the middle of a farce.

"Iris is certainly—shall we say—a person of *interest*."

Alfred got to his feet. Despite his small size, he looked menacing. "I know her rights and unless you've got anything concrete to link her with the crime, you can't arrest her."

"Thank you for telling me my job," said Shawn tightly. He turned to me. "I only came by to let Kat know that she is free to return to the King's Parlor and remove the drawings."

"Thank you," I said. "What about the old tools?"

"His lordship is ninety-nine percent positive that they were the tools used for the Honeychurch mint."

For a moment, Shawn's eyes shone with boyish excitement but then he scowled. "But we haven't finished with you yet, Iris."

"I have absolutely nothing to hide." Mum flashed a smile. "Kat will see you to your car. Do go through the carriageway. We're using that as the main entrance now."

I ushered Shawn out but he paused and gallantly gestured for me to go ahead. I waved him on, very conscious of what I must look like from the rear in Mum's old Electra costume. He then waved *me* on. We both stepped forward and collided in the doorway.

"Sorry," he said.

I darted ahead.

"Kat, wait!"

I turned and was startled to find Shawn right behind me. Without my shoes, he towered above me. I felt surprisingly vulnerable. I also felt an unexpected rush of what I can only describe as electricity. Perhaps it was Mum's costume!

I waited expectantly for Shawn to say something. He looked into my eyes and my stomach did a peculiar somersault. For heaven's sake, Kat, get a grip. I was years older—or was I? I'd always dated much older men. Maybe the age difference between us wasn't as big as I thought. Five years? Seven?

"This is awkward." He took a deep breath. "I don't know what is going on but my grandmother told me that Iris made the Cleopatra costume for the midsummer ball."

"What?" I whispered as all romantic thoughts vanished. "I don't understand. Why would she make it for Pandora?"

"It wasn't for Pandora," Shawn said bluntly. "It was made especially for the dowager countess to wear to her birthday ball."

"Are you *sure?*" But of course, I knew he was. Mum had known about it but in typical fashion, had decided not to tell me.

"And there is something else," said Shawn. "Gran told me that she saw Iris and Pandora arguing out on the terrace on the night of the ball."

"Oh."

"The terrace was out of bounds apparently to everyone except the help they hired from the village."

"I really don't know what to say," I said miserably.

"Look, I just want to get to the bottom of it," said Shawn. "The problem is that we can't keep quiet on this one. In a matter of days this story is going to be all over the newspapers. You and I both know that your mother is hiding something."

"I'll talk to her," I said.

"Please do. Good night."

As I watched Shawn get into his car, I suddenly realized exactly what this could mean. It wasn't just about Pandora's murder being exposed, it was much, much more. Mum's alter ego as Krystalle Storm was bound to come out, too. Her carefully groomed persona, which was splashed all over her website, included owning a Devon manor house, an Italian villa and a Pekinese called Truly Scrumptious. None of which were true.

Mum also claimed that my father had been an international diplomat who had died in a plane crash and not a tax inspector for HM Revenue & Customs. This could trigger an investigation into her substantial earnings that she had given Alfred to manage and that were currently stashed in an offshore account in Jersey.

I didn't care about myself—after years in the public eye, I

was used to it—but such revelations could really damage my mother.

It was time to have a heart-to-heart chat. But first, I had to get out of this ridiculous costume.

Chapter Nine

"Yes, I did make Edith's costume for her birthday," Mum said hotly. "What is this? The Spanish Inquisition?"

"Where is Alfred?"

"Gone home," said Mum. "Police officers make him nervous."

"They should make you nervous, too!"

"I've done nothing wrong." Mum poured herself another gin and tonic. "If anyone is making me nervous, it's you. Sit down."

So I did.

"You looked quite fetching in that little blue Electra dress," Mum mused. "You should have seen Shawn's eyes pop out. Why did you take it off?"

"Because I'm cold and the wig was heavy—and don't change the subject. Come on, Mum, I'm just asking."

"Very well." Mum frowned. "You have to understand this happened donkey's years ago. Memories can be funny things. What I remember as one thing can be seen in a completely different light to someone else."

"Let's just start with your memories and go from there."

"I spent weeks making that beaded headdress. Everything

was sewn by hand, of course—and a beautiful toga that was threaded through with gold. I stole the material from the *Arabian Nights* sideshow and got into awful trouble with Aunt June."

"Go on."

"I sewed tiny sequins along the hem, sleeves and neckline," Mum continued. "Alfred knew a trapeze artiste from the circus that had set up in Plymouth. She gave them to me. It was a beautiful costume."

"What about the jewelry?"

"I borrowed the bracelets—"

"And the heart-shaped pendant?"

"I know nothing about that," said Mum hastily. "Her ladyship looked stunning. She said I was very gifted."

"You are."

"The next thing I know is that Pandora is wearing my Cleopatra costume. I was furious. I couldn't understand why she was wearing it and not her ladyship. I'd worked my fingers to the bone and it had all been for nothing."

I thought of Shawn's grandmother seeing my mother and Pandora arguing. "And you confronted her?"

"You bet I did," said Mum. "I waited until she walked out on the terrace. I followed her into the topiary garden. There was a topiary maze back then. She was obviously planning on meeting someone, having some kind of *tryst* because the moment she saw me she said, 'Oh, I was expecting someone else.'"

"What else did she say?"

"She pretended she didn't know what I was talking about and when I told her I'd made the costume for her ladyship, she said her ladyship didn't like it so she'd given it to her."

"I don't blame you for feeling upset."

"Of course her ladyship didn't do that! She wouldn't. She'd even had a fitting that morning. If Joan were still compos mentis, *she* would back me up. *She* was there. *She* heard her ladyship praise my work."

"You mean Joan at Sunny Hill Lodge?"

Mum nodded. "Of course, she didn't like me much, either, because she had this obsession with Bryan—"

"And he was just interested in you."

Mum gave a mischievous grin. "I can't help it if I'm naturally alluring."

"Yes, you certainly are."

"It was all so childish. There was Pandora wanting Alfred, then she wanted Bryan—who was dressed as a slave in a loin-cloth, I may add; Joan pining for Bryan but of course he wasn't interested in anyone except for me."

"That must have made you popular," I said dryly.

"I admit I did kiss Bryan once," said Mum. "It was horrible. Rather like being washed by a cat."

"Ugh!"

"And speaking of cats…" A shadow crossed Mum's features. "Women can be cats. They can say the most horrible things. Things I will never repeat."

I reached out and touched Mum's hand. It couldn't have been easy growing up on the road. "I know, Mum."

"But I found a way to get my revenge," said Mum briskly. "Madame Z's Psychic Touch! Women can be so gullible. You just tell them what they want to hear."

I thought for a moment. "What was Edith wearing?"

"Just an evening gown—gray-green satin and taffeta," said Mum.

"Didn't you ask Edith why Pandora was wearing her costume?"

"No. Because Pandora told me that her ladyship had given

it to her," Mum said. "I was only fifteen, remember, and a bit in awe of the toffs. So, no, I let it go."

I nodded in sympathy but in the back of my mind was the word "motive" that just wouldn't go away.

"Oh, I know what you're thinking," said Mum. "I did Pandora in. The last time I saw her was when they started to play that game of squashed sardines—"

"Rupert calls it Smee," I said mildly.

"Whatever it's called. Hide-and-seek in reverse, you know what I'm talking about."

"I thought you weren't allowed in the Hall."

"I told you, Alfred and I used to sneak up into the minstrels' gallery and spy on everyone."

"So Pandora must have disappeared during the game of squashed sardines," I said slowly. And then it hit me. "When she went off to hide or look for someone, perhaps?"

Mum nodded. "She could have triggered the catch, just like you did?"

"The location of the body just doesn't make sense," I said. "She'd broken her neck—"

"Oh! Don't!" Mum flapped her arms in horror. "Don't say that!"

"You must tell Shawn what you have told me," I said.

"Oh, Kat," Mum wailed. "What if, what if it was ... her *lady-ship* who did it? Her brother could have told her where to find the double-hide."

"Is *that* who you're protecting?"

Mum shuddered. "I don't think I want to talk about this anymore."

"Mum? *Tell* me."

"I always felt there was something more going on. I think

Pandora knew about her ladyship's love affair with the game-keeper but wanted him for herself."

"How do you know that?"

"Because we camped in the park and once I was walking in the woods and came across Pandora talking to him," said Mum. "He wasn't interested, of course, he adored her ladyship."

"But she could have threatened to tell Edith's brother out of spite," I suggested.

"We'll never know, will we? They're all dead now." Mum looked sad. "Some things are best left alone."

We fell quiet for a moment. "But why leave a copy of *Lady Chatterley's Lover* in the priest hole? Is that supposed to be a clue or just a way to frame you? It doesn't make sense."

Mum shrugged. "None of it does."

The doorbell rang—a continuous buzz, urgent and insistent, and then a second long, loud burst.

Mum turned ashen. "Is that the door? Oh God. They've come to arrest me."

"Don't be silly." Or had they? It was nearly ten-thirty. "I'll go."

The doorbell rang again followed by persistent knocking. "Wait!" I shouted. "I'm coming!"

I threw open the front door and to my surprise Ginny Riley was standing on the doorstep.

"I'm sorry—Oh!" Ginny's eyes widened when she saw what I was wearing. "You're in your pajamas! Did I get you out of bed?"

"No," I said. "Whatever's the matter?"

Dressed in sweats and devoid of makeup, Ginny's face was pale. She looked terrible. "Are you alright?"

Ginny looked over my shoulder. "Are you alone?"

"My mother is here but come in."

She shook her head. "Is there somewhere else? Somewhere private where we can talk?"

Grabbing a coat from the coat stand, I ushered her outside. "This way. We'll go into the old feed shed."

We crossed the cobbled courtyard and headed for one of the outbuildings. I led the way inside and turned on the electric light. It was full of disused metal grain bins, rolls of chicken wire and bits of an old henhouse.

"What's going on?" I said.

Ginny looked as if she was about to cry. "I'm really sorry, Kat. And you've always been so nice to me."

I put my arm around her shoulder and gave her a hug. "Tell me."

"You're going to hate me," she whispered.

"Of course I won't!"

"I didn't mean it to happen. I swear I didn't." She took a deep breath, and then, "You're going to be on the front page of the *Daily Post* tomorrow."

For a moment, I wasn't sure I had heard her properly. "I don't understand. You don't work for the *Daily Post.*"

"They heard my story about the priest hole on the local radio station and called me," Ginny went on. "They asked for more information so I filed a story and ..." Ginny's lip began to wobble. "I just saw it. They said they rewrote it a bit and ..."

"Don't worry," I said. "I'm sure it's not as bad as you say."

"But it is. They got the missing heiress in there and everything."

"But how?" I was confused. "We only found out ourselves this afternoon."

"I didn't know anything about that, I swear," said Ginny.

"Well, we all knew that sooner or later it would all come out," I said. "Who called you from the *Daily Post?*"

Ginny hesitated and then said, "I should never have spoken to her. I know how much she hates you."

And then I knew. "Trudy called you," I said quietly. Would I ever get away from my nemesis? She even had David all to herself now, too.

"I had to warn you," Ginny went on. "I'm sorry."

I felt disappointed but I knew only too well how these things could happen. It was the dowager countess that concerned me.

Ginny pulled out a tissue from her pocket and blew her nose. "I'm sorry you're mixed up in it but I suppose your name still sells newspapers."

"In a day or so it will be someone else in the news," I said.

"I wish that were true."

"What do you mean?"

"The newspaper wants to serialize the story—you know, make a feature of Honeychurch Hall and all the things that have gone on up there."

"But... what kind of things?"

Ginny shrugged. "I don't know. Something about a romance writer, other stuff that's been kept quiet over the years."

"That's ridiculous." But it wasn't, and I knew it. It was just as I feared. Everything was going to come out, after all.

"Trudy's assistant called me," Ginny went on. "She asked me about my job at the *Dipperton Deal*. She said that they wanted access to all the archives."

"What did you tell her?"

"I said I could get them—oh, Kat, I'm sorry." Ginny wailed again. "I was excited. I didn't know it was all going to come out."

I studied Ginny's face and felt a flash of anger. Ginny had known how I felt about Trudy Wynne and yet she'd still gone ahead with her story. "Really? You really didn't know what would happen?"

"What? You think I did this deliberately?"

I wasn't sure. I desperately wanted to believe her. "I wasn't born under a rock, Ginny."

"I know, but you sound like you're accusing me of something! I mean, what's it all to you? You weren't even alive in 1958."

"Who told you about 1958?" I said sharply.

Ginny reddened. "Whatever. Whenever. Be it 1950, 1960, 1970. Who cares?"

"I think you should leave now."

"Seriously?" Ginny gave a snort of disgust. "Just because David went back to his wife in the end there's no need to take it out on me!"

"Good night Ginny." I pushed past her and strode back to the Carriage House.

I found it hard to get to sleep. Thoughts of what would be revealed in the *Daily Post* filled me with dread. I wondered if I should warn Edith but decided against it. Ginny had very little to go on but when it came to the *Daily Post*, what they didn't have, they implied, which was often far worse.

I kept wondering if Edith had been involved in Pandora's death. I thought of Edith and the costume Mum had labored over. These things really mattered when you were young but was it enough to commit a murder?

And then there was Bryan Laney. It seemed odd that he'd suddenly reappeared and yet he seemed genuinely shocked upon learning of Pandora's death. I suppose he'd be calling on my mother soon as well. Oh dear, Alfred would really love that.

As I lay there I thought of Mum at age fifteen with all the

boys falling in love with her. *Electra! The 27,000 Volts Girl!* I was beginning to see her in a different light—I chuckled to myself at the unintentional pun.

I'd always taken my mother to be frail and a little bit feeble judging by the hours she used to spend up in her bedroom. I had never dreamed that she had been faking a migraine just so she could write her books. I was actually incredibly proud of her.

Tomorrow was going to be a busy day—a meeting with Bryan, a ride with Harry, valuing the Hollar drawings—and all overshadowed by the exposé from the *Daily Post*.

I pulled the duvet up under my chin and turned over to get some sleep.

Chapter Ten

Jane's Cottage had been built as a summer house in the 1800s on the foundation of Warren Lodge. It was constructed of red brick with stone dressings under a pyramidal slate roof. Two bay windows flanked a Venetian entrance with ionic pilasters under a pediment door with a fanlight over. Inside there were two bedrooms downstairs, a spiral staircase leading to an upstairs loft area in the eaves and on the ground floor, a living room with what would soon have a wood burner stove to heat the whole house. The kitchen was a galley affair and beyond that was a small bathroom that had been tacked on under a cat slide roof. The outside loo or "privy" was still there, just visible in the undergrowth.

Jane's Cottage was quirky and unusual and I really loved it.

Now that I had seen the Hollar drawings showing the original building, I was struck by how much the place had altered over the centuries. The solitary oak tree was now joined by dozens of other trees and dense undergrowth, blotting out the spectacular view.

As I walked up the rise to the entrance I was surprised to find Bryan's green-and-white camper van was already parked out front. He was early.

In fact, he was actually inside the house. It really bothered me that he hadn't waited. I found him in the kitchen, brandishing a retractable tape measure and a screwdriver. He turned and greeted a hello, looking rather dapper in cavalry twill trousers and sport coat with a paisley cravat underneath. Coupled with the odd green-and-white camper van, my doubts about him being up for the job increased.

"Did I leave the house unlocked?" I said.

"I know a way to get in." He grinned. "The window in one of the back bedrooms has a quirky catch. You should get that looked at." Upon seeing my surprise he added, "I used to come up here as a kid. It looks like the place has been empty for decades."

"You know that's trespassing," I said lightly but Bryan didn't seem to have heard.

"What was this place like when you first saw it? Find anything of interest?"

"Why?"

"No reason. Just curious."

"Just a lot of rat droppings," I said. "Pieces of old furniture riddled with woodworm. I did quite a lot of clearing out."

Bryan made a meal of strolling around the kitchen, staring up at the ceiling and muttering to himself.

"Are you going to Sunny Hill Lodge to visit Joan?" I said to make conversation.

"I'm thinking about it. My aunt suffered from Alzheimer's and didn't recognize my dad but remembered every single detail of what she got for Christmas in 1914."

"I've heard that can happen," I said.

Given that Joan had been at Sunny Hill Lodge for years, I thought that was pretty optimistic but it made me wonder.

"What about Pandora?" I said. "Can you remember anything about her?"

Bryan shook his head. "Got nothing to add. I've already called the police but had to leave a message. What kind of police station is closed on the weekends?"

"Little Dipperton." I smiled. "Open nine to five—although I have Shawn's mobile phone number if you'd like it."

Bryan duly wrote it down in a small notebook and then I told him what I wanted him to do.

"Tiling?" he said with a frown. "I'll be honest—tiling is not my strong point."

"What about the kitchen floor?" Currently it was covered in quarry tiles but most were cracked.

Bryan hummed and hawed but then shook his head. "You need a professional."

"Maybe you can help with replacing the shelves in here?"

I opened the door to a walk-in pantry and stopped in astonishment. Several of the shelves were covered in the same red shelf-liner paper that adorned *Lady Chatterley's Lover.* It was too much of a coincidence.

"Did Joan's mother work at the Hall?" I said suddenly.

"Eh?"

"Joan's mother," I said again.

"She was Lady Edith's maid," said Bryan. "Why?"

"Did Joan have any siblings?"

"A brother. He died though. Accident with a tractor. Why?"

"Just wondered." I gestured to the pantry. "I'd love to replace the missing shelves in here."

"You want a carpenter for that, luv," said Bryan.

"Okay. A carpenter. Fine. How about a few mirrors? Can you help me put them up?"

"Are they heavy? Only I've got a bad back."

"Okay. Too heavy. Fine. Follow me." I led Bryan into the bathroom and gestured to a mahogany medicine cabinet that was propped against the wall. "How about that? I'd like to put it above the washbasin. It's not very heavy."

Bryan hummed and hawed *again*. "Look, I'll be honest, I'm good with a hammer and a few nails but for this"—he shrugged—"you need raw plugs and a drill."

"I know I need raw plugs." I was starting to lose my patience. "You don't have a drill?"

"Never seen the need. Hammer is just as good."

"So you can't really do anything at all."

Bryan gave a sheepish smile. "I'll be honest," he said. "It's just a bit too advanced for me. I can do a spot of painting and pop up a few pictures, but"—he shrugged again—"you need a professional builder."

"I thought you were a professional builder."

"Not me, luv." Bryan shook his head. "You advertised for someone who can do a bit of D-I-Y."

I was about to argue but realized it was a waste of time. "You're right. I do. Thanks for coming up here this morning."

"Anything I can do to help."

I bit back the obvious retort.

As I waved Bryan out of the house I realized he hadn't once mentioned my mother. So much for Iris being the "one who got away."

I felt really bothered by the whole thing but couldn't put my finger on what it was. How long had Bryan been snooping around and what was he looking for? Jane's Cottage was empty. I had no furniture, just new curtains and blinds at the windows. I also wondered what he had actually been measuring when I'd arrived given that he had no intention of hanging anything.

Still, I'd made some progress with the walk-in pantry. I would never have connected the shelf-liner paper with *Lady Chatterley's Lover* if Bryan hadn't turned up. Joan's mother had worked for Edith. Perhaps the book had belonged to her?

Fifteen minutes later I walked through the archway and into the stable yard.

Compared to the rest of the property, the stable yard was immaculate. I absolutely loved coming here and soon forgot about Bryan Laney.

The stable yard was built around a stone courtyard with three sides of the quadrant housing four loose boxes. The fourth side was divided by a second archway—topped with a dovecote and clock—that led to the rear of the Hall.

Horses peered over green-painted split-stable doors, each bearing a name plaque. A saddle with a bridle looped over the cantle straddled the top of Thunder's loose-box door.

Winter pansies bloomed in wooden barrels; a mounting block stood beside an outside stone staircase that led up to Alfred's flat above. It used to belong to William Bushman, the former stable manager, but had been Alfred's home for the past six months.

William, now serving time at HM Prison Exeter, had often visited Joan Stark at Sunny Hill Lodge. It was a kindness that seemed at odds with what happened in the end. But before I could dwell on that any longer, Lavinia Honeychurch emerged from the tack room.

"Ah! There you are, Katherine!"

Tall, thin and with an aquiline nose, Mum unkindly referred to Lavinia as "horse face."

"Morning!" I said cheerfully but Lavinia didn't return my smile. She looked worried and beckoned for me to join her.

I followed her into the tack room.

"Do sit down, Katherine." She gestured to the old sofa that was oozing stuffing and covered in dog hair.

"I'm fine standing," I said. "Is everything okay?"

Lavinia perched on the edge of a huge pine chest that contained horse blankets and gave a heavy sigh.

I decided to sit after all. Her sigh sounded serious. I took in one of my favorite places—there was something warm and cozy about the tack room. Whether it was the smell of oiled leather or just the feeling of much-loved horses, I wasn't sure. One wall was lined with saddle racks and bridles each bearing the name of its owner on a brass plaque. There were also a dozen racks holding ancient saddles with tarnished brass plaques, the owners of which lay buried in the equine cemetery that overlooked the River Dart.

A pegboard was tacked to another wall, covered in rosettes along with photographs of Edith, Lavinia and William—the three of them pictured driving four-in-hand when they used to compete in carriage driving competitions. Edith at the reins with William alongside, and Lavinia directly behind as the "navigator." All that ended when William went away.

I caught a glimpse of myself in the mirror that was attached to the back of the tack room door and grimaced. Mum had a point. I really was turning into a frump. My jodhpurs were definitely too tight and with my hair clamped under one of Lavinia's slumber nets—"honestly, Katherine, it's the only way to hold one's hair orrf one's face"—she had a way of pronouncing off as "orrf"—I tended to agree with her.

"This is frightfully awkward," Lavinia began at last. "But I really *have* to talk to you."

"Is this about Harry?"

Lavinia seemed startled. "No. Why should it be about Harry?"

"Well, more about Harry's friends really."

Lavinia looked puzzled. "What about Harry's friends?"

This was exactly what I had hoped to avoid. "Has Max been here since Harry started his school year?" Of course I knew that he had not.

"No, thank God." Lavinia pulled a face. "Rupert dreaded having the local boys here but luckily, Harry hasn't invited any of them over."

Lavinia really was one of the silliest women I had ever met. "And that doesn't worry you?"

"Good heavens, no! We're *frightfully* relieved." Lavinia gave a dismissive wave of her hand. "This is far more important."

Was it more important than her son's happiness?

"Rupert told me that Edith is very cut up about this Pandora business," Lavinia went on.

"It's awful," I agreed.

"That's why she won't be riding out this morning. She's still in shock. They were great friends, you know."

"I had heard something like that. Did they meet at boarding school?"

"Good heavens, no!" Lavinia declared. "Pen friends and whatnot. Introduced by some mutual chum."

"I see."

"The silly thing is..." Lavinia rolled her eyes. "And I told her she was being ridiculous...the silly thing is that Edith blames herself for what happened to Pandora."

"Blames *herself*?" I said sharply. "Why?"

"For not guessing that something was horribly wrong. *Apparently*. Up until Pandora's visit they exchanged letters regularly as one did in those days. I had a pen friend in Switzerland actually. Even went to visit her once or twice."

"Did Edith say anything about Pandora being reported as missing?"

"That's just the thing," said Lavinia. "Pandora and Edith had a lot in common. As you know, her parents were killed in the Blitz and *apparently* Pandora was an orphan, an only child, too. Had a guardian but he couldn't handle her. She was quite wild, I believe—and of course, she was over twenty-one so free to do as she pleased."

I waited politely for Lavinia to come to the point.

"So *apparently* Pandora told Edith she was orrf to the Orient and that was that."

I nodded. "And?"

"Of course Shawn has done what he can to keep it quiet. Keep it out of the newspapers and whatnot but..." She rewarded me with an unnerving smile. "Rupert's frightfully worried that everything is going to come out."

He's not the only one. Then I realized that Lavinia had obviously not seen the *Daily Post*. Yet.

"You do know what I mean by *everything*," said Lavinia. "You do know what I mean, don't you?"

I nodded again. My mother's past was actually quite fascinating but the Honeychurch clan's was steeped in all sorts of murky scandals.

I thought of Ginny again and our unpleasant conversation from the night before and her decision to delve into the archives of the *Dipperton Deal*.

"We can't allow this to happen, you must know that." Lavinia regarded me in earnest. "You have to help."

"Me?" I exclaimed. "I'm not sure what I can do."

A faint flush began to bloom on Lavinia's cheeks. "This is horribly awkward," she said again. "But I—well Rupert, really..." She cleared her throat. "He wants you to talk to Alfred and your mother about it."

"About what, exactly?"

"The fair, boxing emporium and whatnot were here the summer it happened," said Lavinia. "Shawn will have to tell New Scotland Yard or Interpol or whomever they involve in these international cases. You do *know* what I mean, don't you?"

"I really don't, sorry." And I didn't.

"Oh for heaven's sake!" Lavinia snapped. "Rupert doesn't want them to talk to the police, that's all. We can handle Shawn and that other policewoman—"

"Shawn has already spoken to my mother and Alfred."

"Oh God, no!" Lavinia groaned. "I don't belieeeeeve it."

"I'm still not sure what you want me to do."

"Well *really*. This is so maddening!" Lavinia gave an exasperated sigh. "We're actually trying to help Iris and Alfred. All they have to do is say they weren't here that summer."

"Why?"

"Because we don't want to implicate them, that's why!" Lavinia stood up, clearly flustered. "Rupert wants the gypsies to take the blame."

I stiffened. "They are not gypsies, Lavinia."

"You know what I mean! Fairground people. Travelers. I don't know what they're called. It was decades ago. Most are probably dead by now and even if they aren't, where would one start to look?"

I was stunned. "You'd rather shed suspicion on my mother's family, to save yours?"

"You're a Honeychurch now," said Lavinia. "And the Honeychurches close ranks. Always. It's the way it's done."

"I'll pass the message on to my mother," I said. "But I don't think she'll be very happy."

"This *is* for your mother!" Lavinia's voice had gone up a few decibels. "Edith is *frightfully* fond of Iris and she thought it was a very good plan."

"Aren't you curious about what really happened to Pandora?"

"No. Not really. I just want it all to go away and it would have if you hadn't fallen into the double-hide in the first place."

I let that comment go.

"Don't you see? If there are no leads, the coroner will just pronounce Pandora's death as an accident."

"What about her broken neck?" I said.

"I don't know!" Lavinia shouted. "Perhaps she tripped over her toga!"

"Alright. I will speak to my mother."

"Good," said Lavinia. "I'm sure she'll be relieved."

My stomach gave a jolt. Why would my mother be relieved?

"And no talking to the press," Lavinia went on. "No interviews. At least we agree on that score."

"Ginny Riley has already been here," I said.

"Oh, I'm not worried about the *Dipperton Deal*," Lavinia said with a sneer. "Shawn's on great terms with the editor. We can handle him."

"Ginny doesn't work for the *Dipperton Deal* anymore," I said but before I could go on, the tack room door flew open and Edith's Jack Russell terrier, Mr. Chips, bounded in.

"Hello, boy," I said. He circled my feet, sniffing the floor and barking. I reached down to fondle his ears, welcoming the distraction.

"It's Harry," Lavinia whispered urgently. "It's very important that he know nothing about finding Pandora until Rupert has worked out the official story. You know what his imagination is like!"

Harry strolled in dressed in his Biggles regalia of flying helmet, goggles and white scarf.

"Isn't it exciting, Mummy?"

"What is, darling?" said Lavinia.

"The skeleton!" he clapped his hands with delight. "Alfred told me that Kat found a skeleton in the secret chamber!"

Lavinia looked horrified. "It's not a real skeleton, silly. Alfred was just teasing. A skeleton! Whatever next!"

Harry's face fell. "Oh. I was going to ask Father if I could bring it to show-and-tell next week."

Lavinia blanched and silently appealed to me for help.

"Ready for our reconnaissance mission, sir?" I said, addressing Harry's alter ego.

"What a jolly good idea," said Lavinia. "Leave Mr. Chips here though, Edith wants him to stay with her today."

"I thought we should check the boundaries this morning, sir," I said. "There have been rumors of enemy activity overnight."

"Good idea, Stanford," Harry said crisply. "Prepare the engines and chocks away!"

Chapter Eleven

Moments later Harry and I clattered out of the yard on Thunder and Duchess. Harry adored his little black pony and since I always rode the dapple-gray mare, I liked to pretend she was my very own. I felt very lucky.

It was a cold morning and the horses were anxious to get warm. Everything sparkled with a layer of frost.

"I like Alfred," Harry said cheerfully.

"Good. I'm glad to hear it."

"He's going to teach me to box this afternoon."

My heart sank. "Does your mother know?"

"We're keeping it between us as a surprise," said Harry.

Some surprise!

"Alfred told me he's knocked out hundreds of men in the ring," Harry went on. "That's what I want to do. Show the boys at school who is boss."

Already I could see trouble ahead. "I really think you should at least tell your father."

"No. I told you. It's going to be a surprise!" Harry turned his face to mine and gave me a big smile. His Biggles goggles glinted in the morning sunshine.

We broke into a trot and headed up the hill to Hopton's

Crest—one of my favorite rides. It ran along the top of a ridge and had the most amazing views.

On one side nestled the small village of Little Dipperton and on the other, tucked between trees and centuries-old dry stone walls lay the magnificent Honeychurch Hall estate. My mother's Carriage House stood adjacent to Eric Pugsley's hideous scrapyard.

I glanced over to the gatehouses, the peculiar equine cemetery, ornamental grounds, Victorian grotto and the vast walled garden that was lined with near-derelict glasshouses.

And then I saw it.

Partially hidden on the other side of the wall and half in the undergrowth, was Bryan's green-and-white camper van. He had to have driven down a bridleway to get there—no easy job given the narrow access and rutted ground. What was he up to?

"Can we go to The Spinneys?" said Harry, breaking into my thoughts.

Oak Spinney, Pond Spinney and Home Spinney were three little connecting woods that bordered Home Farm. "Granny says that some trees came down in the last storm and there are some jumps."

"That's a great idea," I said. "And then we can circle back through Jane's Wood."

We turned off the ridge and took a winding animal track down through the forest that came out near the ruins of Bridge Cottage.

Harry and I crossed the road and started to climb the rise at a brisk trot. It was at the second bend that I almost knocked a woman and her tricycle over. She was draped in a bright yellow sou'wester cape and rain hat. The horses were terrified.

Duchess shied. Thunder ploughed into the back of Duchess

who squealed and lashed out narrowly missing Harry. Thunder then nipped Duchess's hind leg and the two horses sprang apart. It was a blessing neither of us came off but by the time we'd calmed them down, the woman had vanished.

"Are you alright?" I called out.

"What a funny bicycle," said Harry. "It's got three wheels."

"Are you okay?"

"Just a bit of turbulence, Stanford," said Harry, resorting to his alter ego. "But I held her steady."

"You certainly did."

"Stanford . . ." Harry said as we set off once more.

"Sir?"

"We have a problem."

"I'm sure it's nothing we can't handle."

"We're going to have to move one of our men," Harry went on. "And quickly. I'm afraid his identity has been compromised."

"What happened, sir?"

"We'll need a safe house," Harry said. "Perhaps Jane's Cottage might fit the bill?"

"Is this to do with Ella Fitzgerald?" I hadn't seen Harry's Merrythought Jerry mouse now for weeks. Harry had even shunned Jazzbo Jenkins, claiming that the vintage velveteen toys were too "babyish."

"No. This is far more serious," said Harry grimly.

"More serious than the mice?"

"Oh, Kat," Harry wailed, swiftly dropping the Biggles accent. "Granny wants to sell Douglas bear. She says he's very valuable and he'd fetch so much money we can repair the ceiling in the King's Parlor."

"Douglas, as in the Steiff bear, Douglas?"

Harry nodded miserably. "Granny said he'd be sacrificing himself for the cause and that he wouldn't mind. She said she'd make sure he would go to a good home."

I was dismayed for many reasons. Edith was right. Douglas, the *Titanic* mourning bear, was extremely rare. As one of just six hundred bears made to commemorate the sinking of the *Titanic* in 1912, they were given to the families of relatives who had perished when the ship went down. Edith's great-uncle, the tenth Earl of Grenville, had been one such victim.

Harry had inherited the black bear and christened him Douglas in honor of the real boy who had owned a Steiff bear called Polar, immortalized in *Polar the Titanic Bear* written by Daisy Corning Stone Spedden. The tragedy was all the more acute because both boy and bear survived the actual sinking of the ship but three years afterward, Douglas was killed in a car accident. Polar was never found.

I knew that the bear was important not just to Edith, but to Harry, too. I also knew that the sale of such a rare item would definitely help to pay toward the staggering restoration costs of the plasterwork ceiling. But what neither Edith nor Harry could know, was that in 1990, the Steiff bear had been reported as stolen in an insurance scam masterminded by Edith's late husband, the fourteenth Earl of Grenville. The Steiff bear was on the watch list because I had seen it.

"I'll talk to your grandmother," I said. "We'll find something else to sell. Don't worry."

"We could sell Mrs. Cropper," said Harry. "Granny says she's very valuable."

I laughed but Harry seemed serious. "What would Mr. Cropper do without her?" I said. "They've been inseparable for decades."

"Oh, he's not worth anything," Harry went on cheerfully. "Granny said he's useless. But you will talk to Granny, won't you?"

"I promise."

"Why can't we make our own money?" Harry said. "Then we wouldn't have to sell anything."

"Wouldn't that be lovely!"

I braced myself for the skeleton conversation but fortunately Harry didn't mention it.

"Father told me that Honeychurch isn't the only house to have a priest hole. Lots of them did. Sometimes they were built inside chimney shafts or under fireplaces. Did you know that a priest built them—Nicholas something—he was made into a saint, but anyway, he was captured and tortured in the Tower of London. Do you know how they tortured him?"

"No. And I really don't want to." I gestured to a wooden signpost bleached white with age that pointed to THE SPINNEYS.

"I think we go down here, Harry. Come on, let's canter."

We turned into a green lane—something I'd never heard of until I moved to Devon. According to Edith, there were over three hundred green lanes in South Devon. These grassy tracks were the remains of old communication patterns that formed a network of lanes, many of which are now cut through by present-day roads. I thought back to the retreating Royalists as they fled Cromwell's approaching army, possibly down this very track.

Harry was right about the jumps at The Spinneys. There were a lot of trees that had come down during last month's storm. We spent almost an hour jumping over trunks that crossed the pathway until Thunder got bored and actually bucked Harry off.

"I think we've had enough now," I said as Harry scrambled back on, none the worse for wear. "Let's head home."

There were many ways back to the stables but today I decided we would go via the rear of Jane's Cottage. I was curious as to whether Bryan might still be snooping about.

I had never ridden up the back track before. On this side, there were no trees, just a panoramic view that stretched to the horizon. A patchwork of fields fell away to my left and on my right were rows and rows of straight-sided mounds with rounded ends and raised profiles.

"What are those things, Harry?"

"Bunny pillows."

"*Bunny* pillows?" I laughed. "You're just being silly."

"No, I'm not. Granny told me that when the warrener—he's like the gamekeeper only he used to look after the rabbits—well, when he lived here thousands and thousands of years ago, he dug trenches for the bunnies to live in."

"Ah! So they're man-made warrens?"

Harry nodded. "They were bridged over with stones and covered with earth."

It was at times like this that I felt such a city girl. "Really, whatever for?"

"Mr. Barnes—he was my history teacher at my old school—Mr. Barnes said that during medieval times rabbits used to be reared for their meat and fur. It was quite a decalasie."

"Delicacy, you mean?"

"Mr. Barnes said that rabbit meat used to cost five times more than chicken." Harry paused for a moment. "Mrs. Stanford has a coat made of rabbit, doesn't she?"

I hardly thought my mother would be pleased to have her mink mistaken for rabbit but I didn't correct him.

"And it was such a decalasie that there were always poachers about. Do you know you can be hanged for poaching?"

"Not these days," I said.

"Yes. You can," said Harry solemnly. "That's why we have poaching signs everywhere."

"And I suppose the warrener lived in Warren Lodge?"

"Yes, but Cromwell burned it down. The warrener *had* to live close to the bunnies to make sure they weren't stolen. In his house he used to keep nets and traps and lanterns—oh, and he washed the carcasses that he'd skinned with a knife. Only the well has gone now, too."

I had never noticed a well at Jane's Cottage. "I wonder what happened to it?"

"I don't know," said Harry. "But I do know about murder holes."

"Murder holes?" I exclaimed. "That sounds gruesome."

"The proper name is a me … me … tri something, anyway, sometimes, if the warrener found someone trying to break down the door downstairs, he'd throw burning oil through the hole and they'd explode!"

"Wow. That sounds painful."

"Did you know that in the thirteenth century, a rabbit was worth more than a workman's daily wage?" Harry went on.

"I did not know that, Harry," I said. "You are a mine of information."

"And do you know how they caught the bunnies?"

"No, but I suspect you do."

"They'd send ferrets into the burrows or wait until they were outside feeding and catch the bunnies in nets."

"That sounds cruel."

"Did you know that a ferret's teeth are so sharp that they

can bite off your hand and sometimes"—Harry's eyes widened—"they even kill babies!"

"I think it's more like a finger, Harry," I said. "And I am pretty sure that ferrets don't go out to kill babies."

"I wish I could have a ferret," he said wistfully.

"Well, I am impressed by how much you know about your home," I said.

"Father told me everything because one day all of the Honeychurch Hall estate and most of the village is going to belong to me and he said it was very important to know the history of everything that happened here."

"I like that—oh!" Suddenly Duchess shied and almost unseated me. There was a rustle in the undergrowth. I spotted Bryan lurking in the bushes.

"Hello there," I called out.

I was right. Bryan *was* still snooping around. I saw a flicker of annoyance cross his features before he broke into a wreath of smiles.

"Excuse me, sir, I'm afraid you're trespassing," Harry said politely. "Didn't you see the warning signs? You could have been shot!"

"I'm a lucky man," said Bryan smoothly. "You must be Master Harry. I hardly recognized you under your Biggles disguise—and a fine disguise it is, I must say."

"Thank you."

"That means . . . let me see, one day you will be the fifteenth Earl of Grenville."

"No—the sixteenth, actually. Father is the fifteenth." Harry sat up straighter in his saddle. "And who are you?"

"Bryan Laney at your service, m'lord," said Bryan, touching his forelock. "My ancestors used to work on the estate."

"Yes. Nearly everybody did." Harry turned to me. "Isn't Granny's land agent called Laney?"

I will say one thing for Harry—he didn't just have a vivid imagination. He was a very smart boy.

"That's right," said Bryan. "He's a distant cousin."

"I suppose that doesn't quite count as trespassing," said Harry, adding, "So what *are* you doing here if you're not trespassing or poaching?"

"I'm going to be doing a bit of work for Kat here at Jane's Cottage." Bryan gave me another smile. "I thought I'd come back and take another look at those shelves you wanted me to put up. I reckon I can do it. I mean, how difficult can it be?"

I had changed my mind about hiring Bryan but didn't want to say so in front of Harry. "We'll talk later," I said. "I have your number."

"But where did you leave your car?" Harry demanded.

"I parked it on the top road. I like the walk."

Harry thought for a moment. "I'll tell Granny we met you."

"There's no need to bother her ladyship," said Bryan quickly.

"It's not a bother." Harry beamed. "Granny has always felt sorry for Laney. She told me he has no family left but now he does!"

I swear I saw Bryan blanch and wanted to laugh. Why Harry decided to grill Bryan was beyond me but he seemed to be asking all the questions I'd wanted to ask Bryan myself.

Bryan touched his forelock again. "It was a real pleasure to meet you, Master Harry. Enjoy your ride and Kat—we'll talk tonight."

And with that Bryan turned back into the woods and disappeared from sight.

Harry leaned toward me. "That was a spy, Stanford," he whispered.

"I think you might be right, sir."

Sometimes children could sense things adults could not. "Why do you think he was a spy?"

Harry thought for a moment. "I *know* Laney doesn't have any relatives because that's why he always comes for Christmas... and Easter lunch."

"That's a good point," I said.

"But we don't want him to know we're on to him, Stanford," said Harry, reverting to his alter ego once more. "We should wait until he makes a mistake."

Back at the stables, I helped Alfred untack Duchess and Thunder. Harry had completely forgotten our conversation with "Klaus the German spy"—his head was full of boxing—but I hadn't.

I wanted to see Edith and decided to pay her a quick visit. I had quite a few questions to ask her myself—to stop the sale of the *Titanic* mourning bear for one—and about that fateful night in 1958.

Chapter Twelve

I was surprised to find my mother sitting in Mrs. Cropper's kitchen. "What are you doing here?"

"Having coffee with Mrs. Cropper. Why?"

This was a first. Mum had never warmed to the cook and not once had she ever "had a coffee."

"She's just taken the dowager countess a pot of chamomile tea," said Mum. "Thought it would calm her nerves. Her lady-ship is very cut up about Pandora."

This was also a first. Edith had always seemed to have nerves of steel and kept her emotions in check.

"What are you doing here?" Mum demanded.

"I've come to see Edith," I said. "But I suppose I won't be able to now."

I pulled out a chair at the vast kitchen trestle table that had to be a good fifteen feet long. "Never mind. I'll sit and talk to you and Mrs. Cropper."

"Why?"

"I might learn something."

Mum grunted. I was clearly not welcome. She pulled her mink coat closer. "It's freezing in here."

I took in the old kitchen with its high-gabled roof and clerestory windows. Despite a lively fire burning in the grate under an elaborate arrangement of roasting-spits—long since abandoned—the room felt cold. There was an old-fashioned range flanked by warming cabinets, but even that didn't seem to put out much heat.

"Are you going to ask Mrs. Cropper about Bryan Laney?" I said.

Mum looked startled. "Why?"

"I saw him up at Jane's Cottage. There is something odd about him that I just can't put my finger on."

Mum's face paled. "He's not coming here, is he?"

"As far as I'm concerned, he's not coming anywhere," I said and went on to tell her how my initial hopes that he put up a few shelves and hang some mirrors had vanished. "I don't think he's ever held a hammer in his life."

"But—if Alfred finds out he's even here ..."

"If it makes you feel any better, Bryan didn't ask after you once."

"Oh!" Mum seemed miffed. "Perhaps he was too shy to ask?"

"Perhaps."

"So much for me being the one who got away." Mum gave a sigh. "Well. I suppose it's for the best."

"Have you asked Mrs. Cropper about him?"

"I was just about to when"—Mum pointed to the row of servants' bells on the wall—"her ladyship rang. Mrs. Cropper will be back in a minute but I don't think she'll be so forthcoming if she finds you here."

I had a sudden thought. "Did you ask her about the shelf-liner paper?"

"I already did but she said that when the other girl was

here—you know the one who had that accident with those cows—she cleared the whole lot out."

"Did you describe the paper?"

"Of course not," said Mum. "I didn't want to be too obvious. And besides, she's very busy. The woman who comes up from the village to help with the housework called in sick again today. They just can't seem to get a new housekeeper—or at least one who stays."

"Well, I saw the shelf-liner paper in Jane's Cottage," I went on. "In the walk-in pantry."

Mum brightened. "You see! I knew it was nothing to do with me."

The wall phone rang. It was an old-fashioned ring—earnest and persistent. Mum was within arm's reach so she snatched it up. "Honeychurch Hall," she said in a grand voice, giving me a wink.

I couldn't hear the voice on the other end. "No, this is not Peggy. Can I take a message?"

She cocked her head and listened. Mum's eyes widened. "Well, my daughter Katherine has." And listened a little more. "You want me to tell Mrs. Cropper that a friend called. She has lots of friends. Who is this?" Mum frowned. "Who am I? Iris— yes, Iris. Hello?" The click was audible. Mum looked at me in surprise. "How odd."

"Who was that?"

"No idea—ah, here she is."

Mrs. Cropper hurried in. She was wearing her usual pink-striped pinafore over a plain white linen short-sleeved dress. I'd never seen her wear anything else. This morning, her gray hair seemed unusually disheveled with strands falling from beneath her white mobcap. "She's up and about, thankfully—oh, Katherine. Good morning."

"Kat was just leaving," said Mum pointedly. "She just came here to ask after her ladyship."

"The dowager countess is much better, I think," said Mrs. Cropper. "It's so hard to tell. She's taken Mr. Chips down to the equine cemetery. Did I hear the phone ring?"

"It was most odd," said Mum. "Some woman asking if Bryan Laney was here."

I caught a flicker of alarm cross Mrs. Cropper's features. "Did she leave a name? A number?"

"She hung up."

"I'm sure if it's important she'll call back," said Mrs. Cropper briskly.

I regarded the two women with suspicion. Something was going on.

I got up. "Right, I'll take a walk down to the cemetery, in that case."

"I really think her ladyship should be left alone," said Mrs. Cropper.

"That's right," Mum chimed in. "Don't go asking all your questions, Katherine."

"I need to talk to her about the Hollar drawings." In fact, I really did. "If Edith wants to sell them, I must take them to Luxton's today. As it is, I had to pull a few strings to get them into Thursday's sale."

"Well—don't mention anything else," said Mum.

"Oh—Mrs. Cropper." I paused at the door. "I just wondered if you had any red shelf-liner paper left—"

"I already asked—"

"It's called Royaledge," I cut in. "I saw it in the walk-in pantry at Jane's Cottage and since I'm going for a retro look in my kitchen, I wondered if you still had some laying about?"

"All the larders down here were lined with that but as I told your mother, it was all thrown out."

"I just wondered," I said. "Okay—I'll leave you both to it."

Edith's equine cemetery was set on a gentle slope and enclosed by a thick, ancient yew hedge. The fourth side lay open affording a spectacular view of the River Dart. It was a beautiful, peaceful spot and I loved it.

Even though I'd been here countless times before, I still glimpsed at each headstone as I headed down the hill to the wooden memorial seat. I could see Edith sitting there, gazing out over the water with Mr. Chips lying at her feet.

I knew the epitaphs off by heart.

MR. MANNERS

MAY 1958–DECEMBER 1970

A REAL GENTLEMAN

AND

APRIL SHOWERS

FEBRUARY 1914–JANUARY 1935

ALWAYS GRACIOUS

I'd grown to love this sanctuary more than I imagined anyone could. Each one-line inscription revealed the personality of a much-beloved horse. There was Sky Bird, Nuthatch and Braveheart: "Adored Mud," "Unstoppable!" and "Never Beaten: A True King." Old horses from the Carriage House were laid to rest here, too, Fiddlesticks, China Cup and Misty—their names still living on in the tarnished plaques in their abandoned stalls and in the tack room.

There was a freshly dug grave with a brand-new headstone dedicated to Pixie Dust, who, at twenty-nine, was the youngest of the three "old ladies." Her epitaph was touching.

PIXIE DUST

DECEMBER 1987–APRIL 2016

SPRINKLE YOUR MAGIC IN HEAVEN

I felt a lump in my throat as I remembered the morning I found Pixie Dust motionless in the straw. Ian Masters, the vet, told us that she'd just fallen asleep in the night and didn't wake up. I found some consolation in knowing that her passing had been so peaceful.

"Mind if I join you?" I asked Edith.

She looked up and nodded. Her face was pale and drawn. For once, Mr. Chips seemed subdued—as if he was sensing his mistress's distress—and only acknowledged my presence with a desultory wag of his stumpy tail.

I sat down on the wooden bench, glancing at the gold-plated plaque inscribed with the words RUPERT—MY BROTHER, MY BEST FRIEND. I wondered if Rupert had ever told his sister about the location of the double-hide but didn't think this was the right time to ask. It was obvious that Pandora's death had upset Edith far more than I realized.

"How is Harry?" said Edith at last. "Has he settled into his new school?"

"I think he's still trying to make friends."

"He should have stayed at Blundell's," she said bluntly. "He was with his own kind there and not the riffraff from the village. It doesn't do to mollycoddle boys. The world is a hard place. No one is doing these children any favors by fussing over them and making it easy."

"I think Harry is more sensitive than most," I protested.

"All the more reason for him to toughen up."

"Harry mentioned you are thinking about selling the *Titanic* mourning bear," I said, changing the subject. "Don't you think the Hollar drawings should generate enough revenue? A lot of Hollar's work was lost in the Great Fire of London and it's highly sought after by collectors."

"I have no idea," said Edith. "Rupert has arranged for a restoration expert to take a look at the ceiling next week."

"What about Rupert's train set?" I remembered he'd mentioned having one up in the attics. I suspected it could be highly valuable.

"Frankly, it's all a drop in the ocean, Katherine," said Edith. "We're slowly going bankrupt."

"I know you are against opening it to the public—"

"Absolutely not—"

"Please hear me out," I said. "The Historic Houses Association offers tours of private homes. You'd be open whenever you wanted to be. The tours are for a limited number of people and it's ticketed."

"What could anyone possibly find interesting about the Hall?"

"The Museum Room, for one," I said. "And the grounds— the grotto, stumpery, sunken garden—there is so much here to see."

"But even to get it to a point of being acceptable to visitors would cost a fortune."

Edith definitely was right about that. We lapsed into an uncomfortable silence.

"Rupert was so sure that he'd find the silver coins in the double-hide," she said at last. "So *sure*! Finding the tools..." She shook her head. "All so frightful."

I knew I had to say it. "I'm so sorry about your friend."

"Friend? I'm not sure if I would call Pandora a friend," said Edith with a trace of bitterness. "We were pen friends. I had met her in London just the once. We had a lot in common. My parents had died in the Blitz and hers had been killed in a car crash on the Continent."

"So you were both orphans."

"She had a guardian but of course, Pandora did exactly as she pleased." Edith paused. "She was unforgivably rude to the servants. Even struck poor Joan who couldn't have been more than eighteen at the time. My mother always told me that servants are trained to do skilled work that we could not possibly do and should be treated with the utmost courtesy. They are in no way inferior. They are part of the family."

"And Pandora didn't understand?"

"Well. She was American. Of course she didn't understand." I could see it still upset Edith. "You must always be polite to people whose position forbids them to be rude to you, Katherine. Otherwise they will despise you."

"And they despised Pandora."

"We had a frightful row the night of the ball. It all sounds so childish now, but it was my birthday and she stole my costume."

"The one my mother had made for you?"

"I've never seen anyone so angry. Iris was devastated." Edith fell quiet again, and then turned to me saying, "Pandora sent me a thank you note, you know."

"A *thank* you note?" I gasped. "But how ... ?"

"Someone forged her name," said Edith. "That's why I didn't think twice about her vanishing. But to know she has been here! Here! *For all these years!* It's just ... it's just too frightful to bear."

"You couldn't possibly have known."

"Of course I couldn't have known," Edith said hotly. "But don't you see? Someone from *here* forged that note. I am quite certain that it would *never* have been one of the servants."

The silence between us lengthened. A peculiar feeling started to form in the pit of my stomach as I realized exactly what Edith was implying. "You think my mother had something to do with this?"

Edith didn't answer.

"But . . . how would she have known about the double-hide?" I went on. "How could she physically have put Pandora in there?"

"Perhaps Iris didn't act alone," said Edith quietly.

"You mean . . . ?" I couldn't even finish my sentence. Edith's meaning was clear. "Surely it could have been anyone who went to the ball," I protested. "And besides, Mum told me that they were not permitted to roam around the main house."

"I know," said Edith.

"But . . . when did you receive the thank you note?"

"One week later," said Edith. "I distinctly remember the day because it was the same morning that Braveheart was born."

I recalled the epitaph on the hill above us: BRAVEHEART: NEVER BEATEN: A TRUE KING.

"He was born prematurely but we couldn't get him out," said Edith. "It was touch and go whether he would survive." She took a deep breath. "So I can assure you that I didn't give Pandora or her thank you letter another thought. The following week, there was all that frightful business with my brother and Walter."

I knew that Edith was alluding to the duel that ended in both their deaths but I was surprised that she was being so candid, especially to me. It was hard to know what to say.

"I should have suspected something was wrong," Edith went on. "I knew Pandora had planned a trip to the Orient. I should have written to her but I didn't. She used to send me postcards on her travels—to brag, naturally—but I didn't receive a single one. As far as I was concerned, our friendship was finished."

"Have you told the police about the thank you letter?"

"Good gracious, no," Edith exclaimed. "It would prompt all sorts of questions. No, far better to let things be. Pandora stumbled into the double-hide by accident—just like you did."

"But her . . . injuries?"

"She died from her injuries," Edith said firmly. "*We* may know the exact placement of the body but we can keep that between ourselves."

Roxy was right when she'd mentioned Honeychurch hushups. "What about your brother? As the head of the house, wouldn't he have known about the double-hide?"

Edith regarded me coldly. "What exactly are you trying to say, Katherine?"

"Nothing." I faltered. "I just meant—or wondered if your brother knew Pandora." I wanted to add that according to Mum's family tree, the thirteenth Earl of Grenville would have been quite a catch and perfect marriage material for the American heiress.

"Rupert and Pandora barely exchanged more than two words the entire time she was here," said Edith. "No, I'm afraid . . . I'm sorry, my dear. Your mother has always been very loyal to me."

My dismay must have been obvious because, in a rare show of affection, Edith reached out and patted my shoulder. "So you see, that's why it's best if we keep it quiet about her being here with the fair and boxing emporium that summer."

She clicked her fingers and Mr. Chips leapt to attention, patiently waiting for further instructions. Edith got to her feet. I knew I was being dismissed.

The pair turned and began the trudge back up the hill.

"Wait!" I raced after her. "Why do you think my mother posted the thank you letter?"

"It was postmarked St. Ives in Cornwall—one of their stopping places," said Edith. "It had to be Iris."

"Do you still have it?"

"I'm afraid not. Please tell your mother what I said. She and Alfred were never here that summer. It's for the best."

I watched the slight figure weave in and out of the gravestones until they were out of sight. Did Edith know something? Was it possible that Mum and Alfred had been involved somehow and if so, why?

There were too many unanswered questions. I didn't want to cause my mother any trouble but I just had to find out the truth.

Chapter Thirteen

"Wait a minute!" Mum shouted in answer to my knock at her office door. I heard the grumble of the rolltop desk lid come down. "Don't come in yet!"

Balancing a tray of cheese and pickle sandwiches and two packets of crisps in one hand, I threw open the door with the other and strolled in. "I thought you might like a spot of lunch."

"Oh, how lovely." Mum beamed. "I was getting a bit peckish. You can just leave it there, dear." She pointed to the coffee table next to the wingback armchair. "Off you go."

"I thought we could eat lunch together."

Mum looked irritated. "I'm rather busy."

"Just for five minutes." I opened her bag of crisps, sprinkled them onto a plate and passed her a sandwich. "Don't you want to know what Edith had to say to me?"

Mum rolled her eyes. "You've got that expression on your face again."

"Which expression?"

"The accusatory expression," said Mum. "The one that means we'll probably argue."

"We won't if you are truthful."

"I was talking to Peggy—"

"*Peggy* now, is it?"

"I was telling her how oppressive you could be."

"What else did *Peggy* have to say for herself?"

"Never you mind," said Mum. "It's private."

"Well—I wish I could say my conversation with Edith was private, but unfortunately it involves you."

Mum put her sandwich down. "What do you mean?"

"Did you know that Edith received a thank you letter from Pandora after the ball?"

Mum frowned. "But how can that be possible?" She thought for a moment. "You mean, she left the Hall, someone killed her and then took the body back to hide it?"

"I wish that were true, but Edith believes the thank you letter was forged."

"Just like the book," Mum said thoughtfully.

"Mum, I won't be cross, just tell me the truth," I said. "Did you write that thank you letter?"

Mum's jaw dropped. "What are you talking about? Me? Write the thank you letter? Why would I do that?"

"Maybe you were covering something up—or you and Alfred were covering something up. I don't know, just tell me!"

Mum's eyes flashed with anger. "I don't know anything about a thank you letter."

"Just like you didn't know anything about *Lady Chatterley's Lover*!"

"That was different! Anyway, I didn't even know about the double-hide."

"The problem is that I never know what to believe and what not to believe."

"You mean . . . you can't possibly mean . . ." Mum spluttered with indignation. "You think *I* had something to do with Pandora's death? Are you *mad*?"

"Alfred, then?"

She got to her feet. "I think you should leave now before one of us says something they will regret."

"Lavinia said, well, it was Rupert really—actually, no, Edith—"

"What?"

"They would prefer it if you and Alfred said you weren't here that particular summer it happened."

"I see." Mum fumed.

"They just want to protect you."

"So everyone here thinks I'm a murderer! How lovely."

"That's not what I said."

Mum strode over to the door and dramatically flung it open. "Good-bye!"

But I stood my ground. "I'm just the messenger! Just tell me—please tell me what's going on."

"Oh for heaven's sake." She strode back to the desk and threw open the rolltop lid. Inside was a rusty cash tin speckled with lumps of earth.

"What on earth is that?"

Mum didn't answer. She opened it, took out an old exercise book and then closed the box with a snap. Silently—she handed it to me.

"What is this?"

I stared at the battered cover. Written in the subject box was the title, THE AMERICAN HEIRESS—NOTES. The date said June 17, 1958—that would have been six days before Edith's birthday bash.

"Well—aren't you going to read it?" said Mum.

I cracked open a page and tried to make sense of my mother's scribbles. *"Dunna fret thysen about lovin' me. Sit 'ere I'th 'ut. Dunna ax me nowt now.* Is this in code?"

"No, it's not in code!" Mum exclaimed and snatched it out of my hands. "It's written in dialect—gamekeeper dialect, that's all. I told you, I just wanted to borrow *Lady Chatterley's Lover* to see how it was done."

"But you've called this *The American Heiress*," I pointed out.

"Oh. Well, I wrote it so long ago, who knows what it's supposed to be about."

"But why is it in that cash box?"

"I told you there was no privacy in Aunt June's caravan," said Mum. "And in fact, there seems to be no privacy here, either."

"I'm sorry. You're right, it's none of my business."

"If you must know, I buried the cash box out in the woods over fifty years ago and just remembered where. The trees have grown quite a bit since then."

"Oh so *that's* what you remembered burying," I said.

"Yes, it's my little time capsule."

"What else is in there?"

"Never you mind—can you hear that knocking?" Mum cocked her head.

"Don't dodge the question!" But I heard the knocking, too.

"I'll go."

Mum hurried out and then shouted, "You've got a visitor!"

To my dismay, Rupert was standing in the hallway. His expression was thunderous. In his hands was a copy of the *Daily Post*. I knew I should have warned him.

"Just in the middle of something. Sorry," Mum muttered and slipped past me, darting back upstairs.

"You've seen it," I said flatly.

"Why would you do such a thing?" he raged. "Why would you give an interview? How could you, Katherine!"

I was horrified. "I did not give an interview. The press are wolves. They take everything out of context. You know that."

"Really?" He thrust the newspaper into my hands. "*Really? Well, explain that!*"

It was everything a tacky sensational tabloid newspaper could possibly be. A recycled photo of me had been superimposed in front of Honeychurch Hall along with a pixilated holiday snap of Pandora Haslam-Grimley laughing aboard a yacht. The caption said, "Cannes: 1957." She looked young and beautiful, with a cloud of dark hair. There were accounts of wild orgies, costume parties and the implication that this was a house where anything and everything was possible, all told in lurid detail by a "family friend."

I stared blindly at the thick, black headline and shook my head.

"Read it!" Rupert hissed.

HONEYCHURCH HOUSE OF HORRORS
NO MORE SECRETS
AMERICAN SOCIETY HEIRESS DISCOVERED
BETWEEN WALLS
EX TV CELEBRITY HOST, KAT STANFORD, NOW SHARES
HER NEW HOME WITH ONE OF THE OLDEST FAMILIES
IN ENGLAND—BUT WILL SHE KEEP ITS SECRETS?
*The Grenvilles date back to Henry V and have had more
than their fair share of scams, scandals, crimes of passion and
cold-blooded murder.*
*What really happened to the stable manager who mysteriously
left to walk the Himalayas? What is the real story behind
the body in the grotto or the minister in the mire?*

*Join Ginny Riley in the first of an exclusive behind-
the-scenes look at the shocking truth of what lies beneath
the upper-class façade.
Follow us on Twitter for updates and like us on Facebook.*

A further paragraph in bold print promised a financial reward for anyone living in Little Dipperton who could "share
memories" and help bring the killer of the latest tragedy to
justice.

I couldn't speak. All I felt was white-hot anger. How could
Ginny do this?

"Eric told me Ginny was here yesterday," said Rupert.

"She was." I thought of how desperate she had been when
she'd called around later that night. "But this isn't her doing.
She told me her article had been rewritten. She was upset."

"*She's* upset?" Rupert was trembling with fury. "Have you
any idea what this will do to my mother?"

"Yes. Of course I do," I exclaimed. "Yes. Ginny came here.
No, I did not tell her anything. She obviously got her information from somewhere else!"

"And what about Harry?" Rupert demanded. "Didn't you
stop to think how this would affect him?"

I didn't know what to say.

Rupert shook his head. "You and your mother," he said with
disgust. "I wish you'd never come here. You've been trouble
from the very beginning." At some point, I no longer heard Rupert's insults until he started shaking a finger at me. "I want
you to fix this, do you understand? I don't care what you have
to do but fix it *now!*"

"I was going to talk to Ginny anyway," I said coldly. "You
seem to forget that this isn't just all about *you* and your wretched
reputation."

Rupert's eyes narrowed. "You are no longer welcome at the Hall—nor is your mother. The sooner you move back to London, the better."

And with that, he turned on his heel and stormed out of the Carriage House. I heard the front door slam.

I didn't hear Mum come down the stairs. I didn't even jump when she put her hand on my shoulder and pulled me into her arms.

"I heard every word," she said.

"Oh, Mum."

"I wish I could make it better. When you were little I could wave my magic wand."

"I just feel so conflicted. I'm angry at being accused of something I didn't do. I'm *furious* with Trudy for being so vindictive."

"Let me see the newspaper."

We sank onto the stairs and Mum started reading, muttering under her breath and getting angrier and angrier.

"It wasn't Ginny's fault," I said. "She came here to warn me that her article had been rewritten."

"Some women just don't know when to let go. Even now Trudy can't stop herself from putting in the knife."

"But there is truth to it all, isn't there?" I said quietly. "The cover-ups, the secrets."

"Don't we all have those, Katherine?"

"I don't." And I didn't—or did I?

"The question is," said Mum. "Who has been talking to Ginny? Who has been feeding her information?" She regarded me keenly. "Eric?"

"No. He's still very upset about having to take the fall for that railway fiasco. She told me that Eric wouldn't even talk to her."

"Then *who?*"

"Someone in Little Dipperton?" I suggested. "The newspaper is offering a reward for information. You said yourself that there were people from the village helping at the Hall on the night Pandora disappeared. What about Bryan Laney?"

"It *is* odd that he is back," Mum agreed. "And he hasn't been to see me, either."

I got to my feet. "Well, I'm going to talk to Ginny."

"Shall I come with you?" said Mum. "I'm pretty good at wringing necks and throwing bodies into cellars."

"I think you're in enough trouble as it is."

"I think that goes for the both of us," she said darkly.

Promising I'd be careful, I headed to my car. The one thing that I hadn't voiced to my mother was my concern about Ginny's safety. The article recklessly implied that she could know the person responsible for the "latest tragedy" and that could put her in danger.

Chapter Fourteen

Ginny rented The Granary, a one up, one down stone building that was part of a converted farm complex that now housed holiday homes for tourists anxious to visit the South Hams and neighboring Greenway, Agatha Christie's summer home.

The farm used to belong to the Honeychurch Hall estate and was one of several that had been sold off years ago to meet the excruciating death duties enforced following the fourteenth earl, Edith's husband's, death back in the 1990s.

I liked the conversions. They had been very well done despite the twee-sounding names like The Piggery, The Cowshed and The Henhouse.

The farm was on the other side of Little Dipperton. On a clear day, I could see it from Jane's Cottage. Before Ginny had gone to work for the *Western Times,* she and I had joked about sending each other signals—a red tablecloth in the window would mean that it was time to come over for a glass of wine—but not anymore.

During the drive over, I'd calmed down. There was little point in getting angry about what had already been printed.

What's done is done. The problem was, what to do about the future.

And then all thoughts of that flew out of my mind as Bryan's camper van shot out of a concealed driveway and pulled right across in front of me. I slammed on the brakes, fishtailing violently. I thought Bryan would stop—but he didn't so much as slow down.

All I saw was a grim look on his face as he sped past.

It was then that I saw the sign: Sunny Hill Lodge: Residential Home for the Elderly. Bryan must have visited Joan Stark after all and most likely not gotten very far.

I thought of his camper van being hidden on the estate. I had intended to tell Rupert but not now. Let him deal with his trespassers. I'd interfered enough.

I turned into the deserted farmyard. In the winter months it looked so dreary. The color scheme was a uniform brown with doors and windows, all matching perfectly. Each front entrance was flanked with wooden barrels filled with soil for summer flowers. I didn't know the new owners of the farm who lived elsewhere, but I had heard that the village had fought— and failed—to stop the development.

I parked my Golf behind Ginny's black Peugeot and felt a sudden pang of anxiety. I hated confrontation of any kind but I had to sort this out.

There was no response to my knock on her front door. "Ginny? Are you at home?" I shouted. "It's Kat!"

I took a few steps back to look upstairs and saw the curtains were still closed.

A bitingly cold rush of wind sent a plastic bag skittering across the smart courtyard. I suspected in the holiday season the farmyard would be bustling with holidaymakers and children—but this afternoon, the place gave me the creeps.

I tried the door, but it was locked. I walked around to the back of The Granary and called out again. I was positive she had to be avoiding me.

"Ginny?" I cried. "We've got to talk. I'm not angry with you. I promise. Please?"

I touched the back door and it swung open. I heard the blare of BBC Radio Devon and felt a rush of annoyance. She really was avoiding me.

"I know you're here," I called out. "Come on, Ginny, I just want to talk."

The Granary was set up as a holiday cottage with the bare essentials. A small kitchenette with fridge, two-plate stove and kitchen sink, an open-plan living area with a spiral staircase leading upstairs where there was a bedroom and tiny bathroom. Ginny had added personal touches—photographs, one of the two of us drinking at the Hare & Hounds last Christmas—and books and fashion magazines. A copy of the *Daily Post* lay tossed on the floor.

I walked to the bottom of the spiral staircase and called out again, but there was still no answer. In fact, it sounded very quiet. Tentatively, I climbed up and found her bedroom was empty. The clothes she wore the night before were pooled on a small chair. She was not in the bathroom, either.

I spotted her handbag hooked over the kitchen chair. A half-eaten piece of toast and full mug of tea were on the kitchen table. But it was only when I saw Ginny's iPhone peeping out from under the sofa that my heart missed a beat. Something was horribly wrong.

I hurried outside to her car. It was unlocked and the keys were in the ignition. Trying to keep calm, I scanned the deserted courtyard. "Ginny! Where are you?" I yelled.

Of course I could be overreacting. Maybe she was so afraid

to face me that she tore outside and was hiding somewhere behind the farm.

"Come on! Don't be so childish. We're friends, remember?"

I took one more look around the yard and ventured into the surrounding woodland but there was no sign of Ginny.

I called Shawn's mobile but the number had been forwarded to Roxy—Shawn had taken the twins to a soccer game. I had hardly finished telling her what happened when she cut me off in midsentence—"I'm on my way"—and disconnected the line.

During the fifteen minutes it took for Roxy to arrive, I was beginning to have second thoughts. Maybe I *was* overreacting—but it was seeing Ginny's iPhone that worried me. Generation Y and their iPhones were inseparable. Then I thought of Bryan. He'd been in the area.

Roxy barreled into the yard in her own car—a white Ford Fiesta—and scrambled out. She was dressed in jeans and a sweatshirt and hadn't even put on her uniform.

"What happened?" she said as she flew past me and straight to the front door.

"It's locked, but the back door is open." I hurried after her as she jogged around the side of the house. "I found her handbag and iPhone . . ."

"She's never without that!" Roxy's face was white. Her panic was contagious. It was so out of character that I began to wonder. Were the two women, in fact, friends?

We stepped into the kitchen but Roxy stopped abruptly. "No, don't go any farther," she said. "Don't touch anything."

"You don't think—?"

"Did you touch anything?"

"Just the door handles but—"

"We'd better get forensics in here. I've got to think. Got to get ahold of Shawn." I could tell she was sick with fear and it made me scared, too. She turned away, running her hand through her thick red hair.

She pulled out her mobile and left Shawn a message.

"Did you check the other buildings?" Roxy demanded. "The woods behind?"

"The buildings are all locked up. I did look in the woods but they're huge. You don't think she'd be hiding from me, do you?"

Roxy shook her head. "If you think that, you don't know her."

If I'd needed confirmation about their relationship, this was it. It would certainly explain how Ginny had gotten ahold of the details of Pandora's death and Roxy had made no secret of her disdain for the upper classes—"a rule for them and a rule for us."

I was disappointed. Roxy was a good policewoman. I just hoped I was wrong.

Roxy looked at me with suspicion. "What are you doing here anyway?"

"I came to talk to her about her article," I said pointedly. "The one in the *Daily Post.*"

"She's such a fool!" Roxy exclaimed. "I told her to be careful."

"So it *was* you who gave her the details about Pandora?"

"Some but not..." Roxy swallowed hard. "Not what she wrote about in the papers—*nothing* like that! You have to believe me!"

"She's your friend, isn't she?"

"We've known each other since we were born," said Roxy. "I just wanted to help, that's all. I just gave her Pandora's name. That was it. No details. Oh, God. Shawn's going to kill me—oh!" She looked horrified at her choice of word. Her distress was so acute I felt sorry for her.

I tried to stay calm. "Look, there could be a perfectly reasonable explanation. Her car is still here. She may well have gone for a long walk."

"I saw her wellies by the back door," said Roxy miserably. "The woods are muddy at this time of year."

"Roxy—I have to ask you this," I said. "Does Ginny have any idea who might be responsible for Pandora's death?"

"Of course she doesn't!" Roxy shouted. "It's a bluff, that's all."

"I can't believe she's in any real danger," I said. "I mean, this is Little Dipperton, isn't it?"

"You have no idea what these people are capable of," she insisted. "They'll do anything to protect their own. They close ranks. It's as if the law doesn't apply to them. They're not like the rest of us. You know that's true."

"All I know is that Ginny has vanished," I said carefully. "And we're going to find her."

Roxy bit her lip. She was practically in tears. "Ginny should have left well enough alone. I told her she was out of her depth."

A tap at the window startled both of us. Shawn waved and gestured to the front door.

I let him inside.

"Any news?" said Roxy.

He shook his head. "A word, Roxy?" He took her elbow and gently steered her outside, into the courtyard and—unfortunately—out of earshot.

I couldn't hear their conversation but when the pair came back inside, Roxy seemed to have composed herself.

"I suggest you go home," said Shawn. "We'll take it from here."

"But I might be able to help," I said. "Ginny was also a friend of mine."

"Roxy said you came here to talk to her about the article—and yes, we've all read it. The village is talking about nothing else."

I was about to protest but Shawn raised his hand. "Don't bother. Not important right now."

"She came to see me late last night," I said. "She was very upset. Different. I'd noticed a change in her since she left the *Dipperton Deal*—"

"Smart clothes," Roxy chimed in. "New teeth—she told me those veneers cost her three thousand quid."

"Why would she come to talk to you?" Shawn demanded.

"She knew that the article—her original article—had been heavily rewritten," I said and went on to explain my relationship with the *Daily Post*'s Trudy Wynne and her personal vendetta against me.

"Because you slept with her husband," Roxy stated flatly.

"They were separated—"

"Carry on." Shawn looked daggers at Roxy. "And I believe David and his wife are back together again anyway now so I assume the piece was just plain spite."

I felt my face redden but didn't comment.

"Look, I know it wasn't Ginny's fault," I said. "I know how newspapers work; how they twist things out of context—"

"But isn't her exclusive an ongoing series?" Roxy seemed to have returned to her old self. "I'm sure you would have wanted to stop that."

"Oh for heaven's sake!" I exclaimed. "Aren't we wasting time talking about this when we should be out looking for her? Have you called her parents?"

Both of them gave me a look that implied I was stupid.

"They live in France," said Roxy.

"I know that," I said. "But maybe she went there?"

"Without her iPhone and her handbag?" Roxy shook her head. "I don't want to frighten them. Not yet."

Shawn donned disposable latex gloves and started pacing around the room, poking into corners and drawers, studying walls and moving books around as if he were expecting the answer to jump right out.

"What if someone came here and abducted her?" I suggested. "Kidnapped her. Right here."

"There doesn't seem to be any sign of either a forced entry or violence, Shawn," said Roxy.

"Only the dropped mobile phone," I pointed out. "I saw Bryan Laney drive by in his camper van. He's been hanging about a lot."

Shawn picked up Ginny's iPhone. He scrolled through the call log nodding silently until he said, "Ah, so you called Ginny this afternoon?"

"Yes. I rang her on my way over," I said.

"And there are four unlisted numbers that last just a few seconds. Hmm."

"How easy is it to get Ginny's number?" I asked.

"She lists it with her byline and e-mail address," said Roxy.

Shawn carried on looking. "Nothing in her e-mail. But we'll have our chaps take a look at it on Monday."

"Did you look inside Ginny's car, Roxy?" said Shawn.

"Not yet. I was waiting for you."

"I just found the keys in the ignition," I said. "Nothing else."

We trailed outside and Shawn opened all four doors, removed his Mini Maglite and started inspecting all the corners, under the seats—even in the glove box. I watched him carefully as he zeroed in on the seat belt on the rear seat. It wasn't sitting right. He lifted the lever and urged the rear seat back. It hadn't been locked in place.

"Someone had this down," he said. "Roxy, open the boot."

Roxy's face paled. She nodded. I found my heart was hammering in my chest as the hatchback slowly opened.

Roxy gave a cry of dismay.

"Is it Ginny?" I gasped. "Please tell me it's not."

"No. But that's hers!" Roxy pointed to a solitary Ugg slipper. "She got a pair for her birthday from her mum and dad."

Shawn removed a plastic baggy from inside his voluminous trench coat, speared the Ugg slipper with his flashlight and handed it to Roxy. I watched him carefully examine the interior of the trunk.

"What are those strange marks?" I said, pointing to deep scores in the paintwork on both sides of the door frame.

"I have no idea." Shawn stepped back and shone his flashlight along the bumper. "And here, too." He turned to Roxy. "Did you call forensics?"

"I wanted to wait for you."

I stood watching feeling utterly useless as Shawn made the call. "Yes," I heard him say. "Right now."

"So you think Ginny was driven somewhere in her own car," Roxy said to Shawn.

"It looks like it."

I couldn't put into words my biggest fear. That something terrible had happened to Ginny and her body had been dumped. I thought of Bryan again. Was it possible that he'd parked his camper van nearby, taken Ginny somewhere and returned? I shared my thoughts with Shawn, especially my misgivings about him claiming to be an expert at D-I-Y.

"He told me he was going to call you," I said.

"He did call and left a message," said Shawn. "We'll be calling him back."

"Oh." I had to admit that surprised me.

"Did you get a license plate for the camper van?" Shawn asked.

"No, but it's very distinctive. It's old—seventies, perhaps? Green-and-white VW," I said. "I think he might be sleeping in it. It was parked in the field behind the walled garden."

"Trespassing, eh?" said Shawn thoughtfully. "I wonder what his game is?"

Dick's black Fiat 500 entered the farmyard.

"Perhaps you'd better go home," said Shawn. "If Bryan is our man, he may be wanting to see who else remembers that night in 1958."

"What . . . you mean . . ." I felt cold all over. "Do you mean my mother could be in danger?"

"Unless she did it," said Roxy.

"Mum was with your grandmother this morning, Shawn," I said. Roxy was becoming really annoying.

"We don't know what time Ginny was snatched at this point, Roxy," Shawn replied. "Let's deal with the facts." Shawn handed me a scrap of paper. "My private mobile phone number. Go home. Be careful."

Chapter Fifteen

"That's the most ridiculous thing I've ever heard," Mum fumed and slammed her gin and tonic down on the kitchen table. "So now I'm able to clone myself, zip over to Ginny's, abduct her...pop in for a quick cup of coffee with Peggy... and all before lunch?"

"I'm under suspicion, too."

"It's obvious that Bryan Laney has something to do with it," said Mum. "They should be questioning him."

"They will. Oh, Mum, I'm worried sick about Ginny. Roxy told me that it was a bluff—that she didn't really know who was responsible for Pandora's death."

"Ginny will turn up. This is Little Dipperton. Maybe someone put her in an abandoned shed until she agrees not to write any more stories about Honeychurch Hall. We should get Alfred to do some channeling."

"This isn't a joke."

"He's been very successful in the past," Mum protested.

"With finding Mr. Chips," I pointed out.

"You have no idea what Alfred can do."

"I don't think I want to."

"All he needs is something Ginny has worn. An old sweater, perhaps."

I laughed. "I know that Alfred can communicate with animals but are you assuming he can change into a bloodhound?"

"He's done it before."

"I'll let you tell Shawn," I said.

"And there is something else," said Mum. "Eric has already taken the Hollar paintings to Luxton's but I don't want you to worry. Everything is under control."

"I'd forgotten all about that," I said. "Well, since we're both banned from the Hall, I'm not getting involved anymore."

"Good."

I regarded Mum with suspicion. "Why? What's going on?"

"You don't remember, do you?"

"What?"

"Remember the insurance scam?" said Mum. "And that list of items that had been reported stolen and some were hidden in the underground tunnel?"

"Yes, I remember. Why?"

"The Hollar drawings were on that list, too."

"No, they weren't," I said. "You're talking about the oil paintings by John Collier, not the drawings by Wenceslaus Hollar."

Mum looked smug. "It's just as well you've got me, dear."

"What do you mean?"

"Well. Peggy mentioned that her ladyship had changed her mind about selling the Steiff bear and that Eric had gone off to Luxton's with the Hollar drawings."

"And?"

"I had one of my weird premonitions so I went and took a look at that list."

"You went through my private things *again*?"

"You told me that David had given you a copy, remember? Wait! Where are you going?" Mum shouted as I tore up the stairs. "Guilt!" she yelled. "I bet he already knew ahead of time that he was going to renew his vows with Cruella."

In the drawer in my night table I still kept a box with all my letters from David that I'd been meaning to throw out. There, in an envelope marked June 21, 1990 was a photocopy of the police report detailing the fact that an intruder had entered the French windows in the dining room in the middle of the night; that there had been no alarm; no broken windows and no witnesses. A list, handwritten by David, itemized the pieces that were claimed as stolen.

Mum was right. Alongside the Collier painting, was the word *Hollars*. The ink was smudged and I suppose the spelling looked so similar I hadn't thought to take a closer look. The minute the paintings entered the cataloguing database, the Art & Antiques Unit would get an alert.

I raced back to the kitchen, flapping the list. "What are we going to do?"

Mum beamed. "You've got absolutely nothing to worry about."

"Are you mad?" I shrieked. "There is everything to worry about!"

Mum carried on smiling.

"When did Eric take them? I need to talk to Eric."

"Calm down!" said Mum. "Alfred is taking care of everything. And I mean ... *everything*."

"What has Alfred got to do with this?"

Mum's smile kept growing broader. She tapped the side of her nose. "The less you know, the better."

I thought for a moment. "He's going to steal them back, isn't he?"

"I'm afraid I can't tell you the details," said Mum. "I'm sworn to secrecy."

"He is, isn't he?" The thought was horrifying. "When?"

Mum's eyes were alive with excitement. "All I can say is that you are in excellent hands."

"Please don't tell me he's going to break into the warehouse?"

"It's Saturday night. No one will be there. I thought it was a jolly good idea."

I could feel myself becoming hysterical. "They have security guards. There are surveillance cameras everywhere. Who does Alfred think he is? Tom Cruise?"

"Don't worry," said Mum again. "He's used to all that. He's an expert."

"Not so much of an expert. He's been caught enough times."

Mum frowned a bit. "He's not as agile as he once was, I admit, but he's very fit for a man of his age."

"Call him," I said. "Call him right now and tell him to come back."

"I can't call him. He doesn't have a mobile."

I made a beeline for the door.

"Where are you going?"

"I have to stop him," I roared.

"You're too late. Alfred is probably doing it right now."

I thought for a moment. "Wait—Alfred doesn't have a car."

"He borrowed my MINI."

"Oh great, so if he's caught, it'll be in your car." I thought again. "Does he actually know what the Hollar paintings look like?"

Mum's smile faltered. "Perhaps you'd better go after him, after all."

"God help me," I muttered.

"And put on something black!"

Chapter Sixteen

All thoughts of Ginny and Pandora's demise flew clean out of my head as I drove the twenty-five miles to Newton Abbot as fast as I dared.

For a Saturday night, the roads were busy and it took me a full forty-five minutes to reach Heathfield Business Park where Luxton's had their storage facility.

The land had once belonged to a stately home called Heathfield Place. The eighteenth-century house had been pulled down thirty years ago to make way for the town's bypass—yet another casualty to progress. All that was left were the two stone pillars that used to flank the main entrance but were now covered in graffiti.

I pulled up next to a large board that mapped the location of each company in the business park. Luxton's was on the far side of the park in unit 23. A sign warned of twenty-four-hour surveillance and a security guard patrol ... with a dog.

I'd been to Luxton's once before and had gotten horribly lost. It was a warren of roads lined with square, flat-roofed, windowless boxes that all looked the same. It was dreary enough during the day, but at night, the empty car parks took on a rather sinister air.

I set off again and tried to concoct a feasible story in case I was stopped. Wouldn't that look peachy on the front page of the *Daily Post*! Heathfield Business Park was hardly somewhere anyone stumbled upon.

And then I saw Mum's MINI and I swear my heart skipped a beat.

It was parked in the *middle* of the road and what's more, it was empty.

I drew up alongside and got out. The door was unlocked but the keys were still inside. I just didn't know what to do. Perhaps Alfred had his reasons to continue on foot. After all, he *was* the expert—apparently.

With a feeling of dread, I got back into my car and began crawling the roads looking left and right for Alfred. I took the spur down to unit 23 but there was no sign of him anywhere.

I was growing increasingly nervous. Had the security guard picked him up for questioning—or maybe, the worst had happened and he had been arrested! It was the only reason I could think of for abandoning Mum's car.

I was about to turn around and head home when out of the corner of my eye I caught sight of a dark figure in the shadows. He was holding two large rectangular packages.

It had to be Alfred.

I flashed my headlights.

For a moment, nothing happened.

I opened my window. "Alfred!" I called out urgently. "Quickly. Get in."

Alfred part-ran, part-staggered under the weight of his heavy load. He was dressed all in black and was actually wearing a balaclava.

I leapt out, threw open the hatchback—and gasped. There were four boxes, not two.

"Drive, just drive!" Alfred shouted.

I slammed down the hatchback and jumped in, executed a perfect three-point turn and we sped away.

"Why are there four boxes?" I demanded.

"I took a couple of others." Alfred was wheezing from exertion. He ripped off his balaclava. "It's got to look like a break-in."

"It *was* a break-in!" I shrieked. "Why would you do that? Oh God, we'll all be arrested."

"Calm down, luv," said Alfred. "This isn't my first rodeo and put your foot down. I reckon we've got five minutes before this place is crawling with coppers."

We sped toward the main entrance but I suddenly remembered and slammed on the brakes. "Mum's MINI!" I cried. "We have to go back and get it."

"Can't. Guard won't be knocked out for long."

"Knocked *out?*"

"And there's a snag," said Alfred.

"A *snag?*"

"Old Iris... she really should keep her petrol tank filled up."

"You ran out of *petrol?*" I gasped.

"But don't you worry about that. I've got you covered, luv."

"No, no! We can't leave it."

"Pull yourself together!" Alfred said sharply. "We're not going back."

I practically took the corner out of the business park on two wheels. Moments later, three police cars with flashing lights sped past us with their sirens howling. As they receded into the distance Alfred started to cackle with glee then promptly dissolved into one of his coughing fits.

"I don't know how you can find this funny!" I was severely shaken up. "They'll see Mum's car! They'll find it. We're doomed."

"Stop panicking," said Alfred. "We got out. We're fine. And

good job on driving the getaway car. Didn't think you had it in you. Wait until I tell Iris."

"If she hasn't already been arrested."

"We should take a back road," said Alfred. "Just in case."

I took the long way home, winding up and down narrow country lanes where some even had grass growing down the middle. Now that there were a lot of miles between Newton Abbot and us my heart rate had returned to normal.

"I'm glad you know where you are going." Alfred sounded impressed.

"I ride around here," I said. "I know all these roads—oh!"

Up ahead I saw the rear of a white Vauxhall Astra parked on the side of the road. "It's the police!"

"No, it's not," said Alfred with a confidence I definitely did not feel. "Just a couple getting a bit of nooky. Take it slow. Don't attract attention."

In fact, the car was empty but as we drove by, I noticed the dent in the rear passenger door. It threw me for a moment. Surely, it wasn't Pippa's car? But no, that made no sense. She'd never leave Max at home alone.

Alfred gave a sigh of relief. I stole a glimpse at my mother's stepbrother and for the first time, saw that his face held traces of fear.

"Alfred, you're supposed to be on parole," I said. "You took a huge risk doing this for Edith and the family."

"Yeah, well, her ladyship took a chance on me. I wanted to help."

"But what are we going to do?" I said.

"Trust me," said Alfred. "Just trust me. The main thing is that we didn't get caught."

The lane ended in a T-junction. I turned right, went straight across a tiny crossroads, turned left and then we were back in Cavalier Lane.

"See!" I said. "One more hairpin bend and we're home."

A pair of headlights swept around the corner.

"Are we?" Alfred croaked. "I'm not so sure."

I pulled over to allow the car to pass and my heart sank.

It was a police panda and in the driver's seat sat Shawn. Even worse, he stopped and opened his window.

"Act normal!" hissed Alfred.

A glance at the clock on my dashboard declared it was anything but normal. It was gone midnight. "How can they have gotten here so fast?"

Alfred didn't answer.

I had to shield my eyes from the glare of a flashlight that Shawn shone full in my face.

"Good heavens!" he cried. "Katherine?"

"Evening, Shawn," I said gaily.

Alfred leaned over me. "Evening, Officer."

Shawn turned his flashlight onto his watch. I saw the cuff of striped pajamas beneath his trench coat sleeve. "I would say it's good morning, wouldn't you?"

"I suppose it is." I gave a silly grin. "How time flies."

"Where have you two been?" Shawn went on.

"I'm glad we've bumped into you, Officer," said Alfred smoothly. "Iris's car was stolen this evening and we've been looking all over the countryside for it."

"That's right!" I exclaimed. "Stolen. She's really upset."

"*Stolen?*" Shawn frowned. "What time was this?"

Alfred leaned over me again. "This evening, Officer," he said. "Silly woman always leaves the keys in the ignition. I told her one day this would happen."

Shawn had to know about the break-in at the warehouse. He *had* to—and the paintings were in the back of my car!

"Tonight, eh." Shawn stroked his chin thoughtfully. "And you reported this theft, I presume?"

"Not yet."

"Then I will do so for you. License plate?"

"I don't know," I said. "We'll call you tomorrow with the information."

But then I had a horrible thought and my mother's MINI was forgotten. It was a question I just had to ask.

"You're out late," I said. "Is this about Ginny? Have you found her?"

"Unfortunately no," Shawn said grimly. "I just hope this isn't a sign of things to come."

I didn't think I could handle any more shocks today. "Why? Whatever's happened?"

"Bryan Laney has been murdered."

Chapter Seventeen

"Murdered!" I squeaked.

"*Who* did you say was murdered?" Alfred demanded.

"Bryan Laney," said Shawn.

Alfred went perfectly still.

"You knew him?" Shawn asked.

"No," said Alfred quickly.

I thought back to the comment Alfred had made in the kitchen and started to wonder. Other than the break-in at the warehouse, I was Alfred's only alibi unless...

"When did this happen?"

"We're waiting for confirmation but he was last seen alive at nine forty-five," said Shawn. "So between then and when his lordship discovered the body."

"Rupert found him?" This was a surprise.

"His lordship was taking the tradesman's entrance and found his body in the culvert."

This was odd. To my knowledge, Rupert rarely used that entrance.

"What happened to him?" I asked.

"That's all I can tell you at this time," said Shawn. "Obviously we will be talking to everyone and ascertaining their movements this evening. We'll be taking *particular* note of any unusual behavior—such as your little jaunt to find a stolen car."

"Do you think this could be connected to Ginny's disappearance?" I said.

"We're not ruling anything out at this time."

Bryan had been my prime suspect for both Pandora and Ginny. His death truly shocked me.

"Now, it's late," said Shawn. "I suggest you go home. We'll want to speak to everyone at the Hall later this morning."

We set off once more, both of us unable to speak. I realized my hands were shaking. "Aren't you going to say anything?"

"About what?" Alfred said.

"Bryan Laney has been murdered."

"Nothing to do with me."

"And what about Mum's car," I exclaimed. "Who is going to tell her?"

"Pull yourself together and let a man think," snapped Alfred. "This is serious and I don't need a hysterical female flapping about and making it worse. Do you *understand*?"

I was so taken aback by this unexpected flash of anger than I realized what I was really dealing with. Alfred was a hardened criminal who had served time.

As I turned into the courtyard, my heart sank even further.

"Oh blimey," said Alfred. "This is all we need."

Mum was sitting on the mounting block wrapped in her mink coat. She scrambled down and hurried over before I'd even turned off the ignition.

"Where have you been?" she demanded. "Something awful has happened. Where's Alfred? Oh—what are *you* doing here? Where's my car?"

"We'll explain in a minute, Mum," I said. "You've heard about Bryan?"

"Of course I have!" Mum exclaimed. "I've been worried sick. There's obviously a killer on the loose."

I regarded her with suspicion. "But you thought it was okay to wait outside in the dark?"

"I kept thinking you would be back at any minute," Mum protested. "I'm frozen to the bone."

"I suggest we all go inside and have a brandy," said Alfred. "It's been a long night."

"I thought you'd have the sense to check the petrol tank," Mum shouted ten minutes later.

"I didn't expect you to be driving around on empty," Alfred shouted back.

We were sitting at the kitchen table with three balloons of brandy.

"This is disastrous!" Mum exclaimed.

"But not as disastrous as Bryan Laney lying dead in a field," I pointed out.

Mum lifted her glass and as she did so, I caught a glimpse of bruise marks on her wrists. The minute she saw I noticed, she hastily pulled her sleeves down to cover them.

"Mum?"

"It's obvious that Rupert did it," said Mum, giving a barely perceptible nod to Alfred who was nursing his brandy. "He found the body."

"But why would he kill Bryan?" I demanded.

"Trespassing," Mum declared. "Shawn said—"

"Shawn came . . . *here*?" I cried.

"Oh yes. When he turned up in his pajamas, I felt so sure Alfred had been caught." I caught a distinct slur in her voice.

"Have you been drinking all evening?"

"Just one or two," said Mum defensively. "For shock. Gin doesn't cut it."

"The copper came here, did he?" said Alfred at last.

"Yes. And I was so sure. So *sure*"—Mum slammed the brandy balloon onto the table—"that Alfred had been caught and what with you being on parole."

"Well, we weren't caught, Iris."

"There is no *we*, Alfred," I said primly.

"But I was so *sure* you were—"

"Pull yourself together, Iris." Alfred's voice was hard again. "We've got to get our stories straight. What did you tell him?"

Mum nodded. "Yes. Sorry." She took another sip. "Shawn seemed surprised when I answered the door because he thought I was out. And then he thought you were out. Which you were." Mum nodded again. "So I told him that you'd both gone to Plymouth. To the cinema."

"The *cinema*," Alfred and I chorused.

"You stupid, stupid woman!" Alfred yelled. "Why would you say such a thing? *Why?*"

"I panicked," Mum wailed. "I said Plymouth because it's in the opposite direction from Newton Abbot."

"But why would we go in separate cars?" I said.

Mum clapped her hand over her mouth in horror.

"That's not the point." Alfred was struggling to keep his temper. "Why do I always have to clear up after your mess, Iris?"

"What do you mean, *always* having to clear up *my* mess?"

"Do you want a list?"

"Children! Children!" I exclaimed. "Let's focus now. Let's look at the facts. Mum, your MINI ran out of petrol at the business park. Alfred told Shawn that your car had been stolen—oh, wait..."

"Exactly!" Alfred snarled. "That copper knew we were lying about the car being stolen because he never mentioned the cinema."

"You're right," Mum groaned. "He would have said, 'Did you enjoy the film?'"

"Hang on!" Alfred frowned. "Shawn didn't ask us *where* the car was stolen."

"We could say it was stolen *at* the cinema?" I suggested. "The keys were left in the ignition and someone drove it away."

"It's the perfect alibi!" Mum enthused.

We all fell silent. Twice, Mum opened her mouth to say something then snapped it shut.

"So...what did we go to see at the cinema?" I said gingerly.

"I'll get the local paper." Mum got up—somewhat unsteadily I noted—and grabbed the *Dipperton Deal* from the oak dresser. She gave it to me.

I couldn't help but scan the headlines. "Interesting that the lead story is about finding the double-hide."

"I know," said Mum. "Not a squeak about Pandora's murder at all."

"What's playing, then?" said Alfred. "I hope it's something I've seen before. We had a Friday night film club at the Scrubs but they always showed kiddy movies."

I turned to the back of the newspaper and laughed. "Oh dear."

"What's on?" said Mum.

"What time would we have seen the film?"

Alfred frowned, then said, "It would have to have been a late-night showing unless we went out for a curry afterward—"

"Which we wouldn't have done because we would have discovered that Mum's car had been stolen."

Alfred nodded. "She's right."

"I'm sorry to say that it limits us to one film. *Fifty Shades of Grey.*"

"I can't believe they're still showing that," said Mum. "What happened to the sequel?"

"I'm just telling you what's playing. I don't know the details."

"Fifty what?" said Alfred. "The last film I saw was called Freeze or *Frozen.*"

Mum reddened. "It's a spoof on *Houdini* only with whips."

Despite the seriousness of the situation I couldn't help chuckling.

"Oh, that'll be easy enough to remember." Alfred ran his fingers through his thatch of hair. "If that's our alibi. Then that's our alibi. I'm off. I'm tired. I'm not as young as I was."

"But what about all that stuff in my car?" I said.

"I'll sort it out tomorrow." Alfred shuffled out of the kitchen. We heard the door to the carriageway slam.

"I'm off to bed, too," I said.

"No," said Mum quickly. "Not yet. I need to talk to you about something."

"You mean Houdini?"

"Oh. Right. Well—Alfred can be a bit *prudish,*" she said.

"After all those years in prison?" I took one look at the expression on her face and my heart sank. "Oh God. Please tell me you didn't have anything to do with Bryan—"

"Of course not," Mum exclaimed, "but he *was* here earlier."

"O-kay," I said slowly.

"I heard a noise outside and thought you were back."

"Go on."

"Well ... it was Bryan. I caught him coming out of that old feed shed, snooping about."

I waited for her to continue.

"He thought everyone was out—no cars, you see. Of course he turned on the charm. He said he'd recognize me anywhere because I hadn't changed a bit."

How original.

"And?"

"He started talking about Pandora and if I remembered anything about the night of the midsummer ball," said Mum.

"And?"

"I said, not really. Just the fact Pandora had been wearing the Cleopatra costume that I'd made for her ladyship," Mum went on. "Then he said something about telling fortunes and I said why, did he want me to tell him his and he said, 'So you don't remember?'"

"Remember what?"

"He wouldn't say." Mum bit her lip. "He was acting very funny," she said. "All jumpy. Nervous. He asked when I'd last seen Joan Stark—"

"Joan." I remembered seeing Bryan's camper van leaving Sunny Hill Lodge and told Mum so.

"Well, I haven't for donkey's years so I told him," said Mum. "He asked if I'd seen the *Daily Post* and I said yes."

I thought for a moment. "Mum, I think Bryan either saw something or knew something about that night—something that actually got him killed."

Mum's eyes widened. "Well, I nearly killed him myself—before someone else did, I mean. I haven't finished my story, yet!"

"Okay."

"And *then* Bryan seemed to relax and he asked for a tour of the Carriage House."

"He wanted to see the Carriage House in the *dark*?"

"I know. I thought it was a bit odd," said Mum. "We went into the carriageway and he started poking around the stalls and tack room—really nosing about and asking questions. We reminisced a bit about—well, the past."

"Okay."

"He kept calling me Electra, which to start with was funny but after ten minutes, became very annoying," said Mum. "And then he pointed to the hayloft and winked. He wanted a bit of nooky for old time's sake. Can you believe it?"

"I thought you just kissed Bryan, mother. You never told me about—nooky."

"Didn't I?"

"No wonder Alfred didn't approve of Bryan," I exclaimed. "You were underage!"

"It was different back then," said Mum. "I was very mature for sixteen."

"Fifteen."

"And we didn't go all the—"

"Argh! I get the picture, spare me the details."

"Well—that was then. This is now but Bryan wouldn't take no for an answer."

I was appalled. "Is that where you got those bruises from? On your wrists?"

"Oh don't look so surprised," said Mum coyly. "I told you that men still find me—"

"*Alluring,* I know," I said. "But I thought you told me that when you kissed him it was like being washed by a cat."

Mum's face fell. "Well. It is—was," she said. "He hasn't changed."

"You mean—he tried to *kiss* you?"

"Tried? He did!" Mum said indignantly. "He got me cornered in the tack room. Apparently I'd promised him—whatever it was I promised him—back in 1958 and he'd come back to claim it."

"What a creep!"

"He never forgot me. Or so he said." Mum's expression was hard. "I'm not stupid. He was a womanizer then and he's a womanizer now—*was* a womanizer." Mum was growing angry. "He was Mr. Charming—all hearts and flowers—and jewelry as a matter of fact. Bryan loved the chase but once he got his girl, he lost interest. He went through all the girls in the village but of course, I was always the one who got away ... because we went away!"

"I don't feel so sorry that he's dead now," I said.

"He broke a lot of hearts—even poor Peggy although she daren't admit it."

"Mrs. Cropper," I said. "You don't think Seth Cropper—"

"I wouldn't know," Mum said darkly. "But she told me that Seth has a bit of a temper."

"Seth Cropper has got about as much backbone as an amoeba. I can't see him beating Bryan to a pulp." I thought for a moment. "Why didn't you tell me all this before?"

"I'm telling you now."

"How did it all end this evening?"

"For him? Not very well."

"Mother! It's not funny!"

"I hit him."

I groaned.

"Gave him a right hook," Mum went on. "He went down and caught his forehead on an old saddle peg."

"But he was *alive*."

"Of course he was alive!" Mum said hotly. "I grabbed a pitchfork and threatened to hit him with that unless he left me alone. He got up, apologized for his behavior and walked out as fit as a fiddle."

"I really want to believe you," I said.

"It's the truth. I swear to God. Cross my heart and hope to die."

"So you'll tell Shawn what you've just told me?"

Mum shook her head vehemently. "Of course I can't tell Shawn! If Alfred found out he'll take the blame. I know he will."

"Why would he do that?"

"Katherine," Mum said sadly. "There is so much you don't know about me."

It was with a heavy heart that I climbed the stairs to my bedroom. Mum was right. It was only since my father died that I was beginning to really get to know my mother for the first time. I'd known nothing about her colorful past and I'd never thought to ask her. To me, she was just my lovely Mum who was always waiting for me to come home from school. I hadn't even thought to question her frequent migraines that turned out to be excuses for her to keep writing her romance novels in her bedroom. But I'd accepted her reasons for not telling me the truth and had forgiven her. It just seemed that the proverbial skeletons kept on coming out of the closet.

At first, I'd been angry and disappointed that she had kept so much from me about the traveling fair and boxing emporium and her life on the road. Perhaps ten years ago, I would have been embarrassed at my background. Back then I was a different person and was the first to admit to being a bit superficial and materialistic—but not anymore.

I stood at my bedroom window gazing out at Cromwell Meadows. I could see the glare from the halogen lights through the trees that presumably marked the location of the culvert and where Rupert had discovered Bryan's body.

I was deeply troubled. I didn't want to accept the obvious. My mother was absolutely involved. Mum had admitted to finding *Lady Chatterley's Lover* in the hayloft. This same book then turned up in the first hide and even had Mum's name in the flyleaf for good measure. Then, there was Mum's fight with Pandora over the Cleopatra costume that had been witnessed by Peggy Cropper. And most damning of all, someone had forged a thank you letter purporting to be from Pandora and posted it from St. Ives, a known stop made by the fair and traveling boxing emporium. I had to wonder if Alfred was involved, too.

I kept replaying the scene from the warehouse. What had possessed Alfred to steal other works of art? And even worse— they were still in my car! Hopefully, David would still be on his honeymoon in Hawaii but it wouldn't take long for him hear about it. In situations like this he was always the first man they called.

And then there was Ginny.

Chapter Eighteen

"We've been summoned to the Hall at ten," said Mum as I joined her for breakfast.

She looked very much the worse for wear with large dark rings beneath her eyes although I wasn't sure if that was a hangover or a sleepless night from a guilty conscience.

She took one look at me and said, "You look awful."

"You don't look so bright, either."

"I've got a headache," Mum grumbled. "Now I remember why I never drink brandy."

I poured myself a cup of tea and Mum clutched her head when I thrust the bread into the toaster. "Do you have to *thrust* it down like that?"

"Have you seen Alfred this morning?" I asked. "He's still got those paintings in my car!"

"Stop fussing," said Mum. "Alfred knows what he is doing."

Even so, it made me very nervous.

At five minutes to ten Cropper answered the front door dressed in his butler regalia. He did not say good morning or utter a greeting of any kind. In fact, he just opened the door and drifted off at his usual glacial speed. I tried to imagine him as a young lad with raging testosterone, bouncing off the walls and wooing Peggy Cropper. I was quite relieved that I couldn't.

How quickly life changed. Just two days ago, the biggest problem seemed to be how to repair a rare plasterwork ceiling. Now, we were discussing two murders and one missing person.

Cropper ushered us into the library. It was freezing cold with the only heat coming from a fire that roared in the grate. Unfortunately, Rupert, dressed smartly in cords and tweed jacket, was standing with his back to it absorbing most of the warmth. Cromwell, his deaf, old English setter, lay dozing, stretched along the hearth. Edith and Lavinia were sitting on the leather Chesterfield sofa with ramrod straight backs. Lavinia was dressed in jodhpurs and jacket with her hair clamped under a thick hairnet. Edith wore a navy calf-length suit with a cameo brooch at her throat. Her gray hair lay in neat pin curls and she held a pair of dark navy gloves in one hand and a small purse in the other. She looked dressed for an occasion.

None of them looked up as we walked in and when I said, "hello," no one acknowledged us whatsoever.

Presumably, news that a serious crime had been committed was no substitute for my so-called interview with the *Daily Post*.

"Where would you like us to sit, your lordship?" Mum meekly asked Rupert.

Rupert gestured to the window where Eric and Alfred stood to attention in their socks, with caps in hand.

"I'm sorry, your lordship," said Mum. "But you mean you want us to stand?"

Rupert just glared. Mum pulled her mink closer. We trooped over to line up with the men.

During the uncomfortable silence that followed, I took in
the room—a man's domain that I always admired. The walls
were papered with marbled pages from old books and smelled
of cigars. One entire wall sported a mahogany floor-to-ceiling
bookcase filled with leather-bound collections. Heavy dark
crimson brocade curtains framed the two casement windows
that overlooked the parkland toward the ornamental lake.

A captain's chair stood behind a walnut partners' desk. I noticed that Rupert had deliberately propped the *Daily Post*—
showing the headlines—up against a letter rack.

"How immature," Mum muttered, echoing my thoughts.

Oil paintings of animals—stags, dead pheasants and shot
rabbits—cluttered every empty wall space.

On top of a long mahogany dresser were display cases filled
with carefully posed stuffed animals—a Victorian hobby that
I never really understood—badges, foxes, ferrets, an owl and
various birds of prey. One glass case held the famous blood-
stained hawk that one of the Honeychurch ancestors had
brought back from the Crimea. A pair of rabbits, playfully
dancing on a bed of imitation grass, reminded me of Harry and
his pillow mounds at Jane's Cottage.

"Where is Harry this morning?" I asked.

"Roxy has taken him out for a walk with Mr. Chips," Shawn
answered as he breezed into the room followed by Detective
Constable Clive Banks—who Mum insisted on calling Captain Pugwash thanks to his heavy black beard. He was carrying
a plastic shopping bag.

"Uh-oh," whispered Mum. "They've found something."

Mrs. Cropper wasn't far behind. Judging by the amount of
flour that covered her pink striped pinafore over her plain white
linen dress, she had probably been in the middle of baking. She
stopped next to Mum. The two of them exchanged a look that

smacked of some kind of agreement. When I searched Mum's face for a clue, she just smiled.

We fell into *another* uncomfortable silence whilst Shawn and Clive went into a huddle in the corner.

"Is this going to take long, Shawn?" Lavinia demanded. "I'm frightfully busy this morning now that Edith's going to church."

"Church?" Rupert exclaimed. "You never go to church, Mother."

"Well today I am going to church," Edith declared.

Mum whispered into my ear. "That's a sign of guilt if ever there was one."

The comment wasn't lost on Shawn, either. I caught an exchange of looks between himself and Clive.

"The sooner we get this over with, the sooner you can all go about your business," said Shawn somewhat pompously. "And you can go to church, m'lady."

"Surely we're not suspects, Shawn." Lavinia gave a nervous laugh. "Golly. You don't think this has anything to do with that frightful reporter being abducted, do you?"

"We're not ruling anything out at the present time." Shawn took a deep breath. "The truth is, I want to give each of you a chance to tell me what happened before the boys from Plymouth sweep in."

Lavinia gave a cry of dismay. "Why can't we keep it between ourselves?"

"Don't be ridiculous, Lav," said Rupert. "The *Daily Post* let the cat out of the bag by covering the Pandora fiasco."

"It wasn't a *fiasco*!" Edith's face was a sea of emotions—something I'd never witnessed before and judging by Rupert's surprise, he hadn't, either. "How can you be so callous, Rupert? Say what you like about Pandora but the thought of the poor girl being here all the time, right under this very roof is too frightful to bear. I am deeply shocked. I want to know who did such a terrible thing."

Rupert had the grace to look embarrassed. "Whoever was responsible is most likely dead themselves by now, Mother. That's all I meant by that."

"Not according to the article in the *Daily Post*," Edith exclaimed. "That young girl implied she had firm evidence to prove otherwise."

"Have there been any more developments yet, Shawn?" Rupert demanded.

"We have a few leads, m'lord," said Shawn. "But obviously, Bryan Laney's *murder* must take priority."

"The press will be back." Rupert glowered at me. "But I'm quite sure that Katherine here will have learned her lesson and not agree to any more interviews."

"I can assure you that nothing will come from me," I said sharply. Although I had to admit I was growing tired of the Honeychurch clan feeling that they were above the law.

"Right then, let's get started." Shawn took a deep breath. "Bryan Laney was killed last night. He was attacked out in Eric's field—"

"The culvert," Eric piped up. "Not my field. I wasn't there."

"You'll get your turn in a minute, Eric," said Shawn. "Now, where was I?"

"Was there a weapon?" Mum demanded.

"Ah—yes, I'm coming to that," said Shawn. "As I was saying, we're waiting for the results of the postmortem but we're confident that he was struck over the head with a tire iron that had been purloined from Eric's scrapyard."

There was a universal gasp of horror. Including one from me. "How horrible!"

"Thank God," Mum whispered to me. "That lets me off the hook."

"Tire iron?" said Eric. "How do you know it belonged to me?"

"The weapon was discovered in a nearby hedge," said Shawn. "But as I was saying. "Bryan Laney grew up here…""

"Bryan was a distant cousin of my land agent's," Edith said suddenly. "I believe he enlisted in the Navy the minute he was eligible to apply. That's all I know."

"Where *is* Laney?" Rupert demanded.

"He's on safari," said Edith. "He won't be back for two more weeks."

"We've not been able to reach him yet, sir," Clive said to Shawn. "They're somewhere out in the bush."

"I bet Bryan had a girl in every port," Mum whispered to me.

"If you have something to add, Iris," Shawn said. "I'm sure we're all ears."

"I said I bet he had a girl in every port," Mum declared. "Don't you agree, Peggy?"

"I wouldn't know," said Mrs. Cropper hastily and found something very interesting to brush off her apron.

"Yes, you do," Mum persisted. "Remember?"

"I don't know what you're talking about," said Mrs. Cropper, shooting a look at her husband who was dozing in the corner.

"Can we get on?" said Shawn. "I don't want to be here all day."

"We're waiting for you." Lavinia sounded exasperated.

Shawn brought out a battered notebook from his trench coat pocket, removed the pencil from the elastic holder and stood there, pencil poised.

Clive crackled the plastic shopping bag expectantly.

"Not yet, Clive." Shawn turned to Edith. "Your ladyship, I'm sorry but I have to ask," he began. "Can you account for your movements last night?"

"Do you know how old I am?" Edith snapped. "Where do you think I was? Tripping the light fantastic?"

Shawn duly noted it down. He turned to Lavinia. "Where were *you* last night, m'lady?"

"In bed."

"And this can be verified?" He looked pointedly at Rupert who suddenly seized the fire tongs and started poking the log in the grate. It flared up so violently that he had to jump back. Sparks fluttered onto the rug, startling poor Cromwell and sending Rupert into a frenzy of ember stamping.

Lavinia gave him a filthy look. "Rupert was out but I was with Harry. He had had a horrid dream about his bear being drowned in a bucket."

"And what time was that, m'lady?" Shawn continued to scribble.

"Let me see. Harry came into my room around ten-ish. We went downstairs to make some cocoa. I read him a story and that was that."

"And what story would that be, m'lady?"

Lavinia let out a little gasp. "You're not going to ask Harry, are you?"

"Not if we can't help it," said Shawn.

Lavinia bristled with indignation. "Are you accusing me of lying?"

"Should I remind you that in these past few months you seem to have been involved in one case of manslaughter and another of fraud?"

Lavinia's eyes practically bugged out. "But ... but that was just frightfully bad luck!" She turned to her husband. "Rupert? Are you just going to stand there whilst I am insulted?"

Rupert continued to stamp out the stray embers, clearly ignoring his wife.

"It was the story about the bear on the *Titanic*," said Lavinia with a sniff. "I don't recall the title."

"I think it's *Polar the Titanic Bear*," I said. "Written by Daisy Corning Stone Spedden."

Edith sighed with exasperation. "I've already told Harry I'm not selling the Steiff. What is he worrying about?"

"He's worrying about his frightful new school," said Lavinia. "We should never have sent him to the local primary. Frightful children. Awfully common."

Mum nudged me and said in a low voice, "I told you not to get involved."

"And where did you go after putting Harry to bed?" Shawn said, ignoring their exchange.

Lavinia rolled her eyes. "To bed myself and no, I can't prove it. Frankly, I've never even met Bryan Laney. I don't see why I should be here at all. He was well before my time."

"As I've told you before, Shawn," Rupert chimed in at last. "We don't leave Harry alone in the house. So if Lavinia says she was here, then she was here."

Shawn seemed to write copious notes. "And you, m'lord?"

"I already told you. I had a drink at the Hare & Hounds. On my way home, I took the back road—"

"And why would you do that, m'lord?"

"Because I had been drinking," said Rupert coldly. "I came in through the tradesman's entrance and down the service road. That's when I saw Bryan Laney."

"Saw Bryan Laney where?" said Shawn.

"I've already told you this," said Rupert again. "He was

lying in the culvert. I thought someone had been fly tipping, dumping their household rubbish and whatnot."

"And then what happened?" said Shawn.

"I realized he was dead. I called you."

"You *recognized* him?" Shawn said sharply. "But earlier on, you told me that you'd never seen him before."

Rupert turned pink. "Well, I had. But that's irrelevant."

"I don't think so, m'lord." Shawn cocked his head. "When did you last see Bryan Laney?"

"Months ago," said Rupert. "Last August. He was trespassing. I gave him a flea in his ear and he went off. I have no idea where he went to or why he suddenly came back."

"I see." Shawn studied Rupert's features. Rupert stared defiantly back.

"A man has a right to protect his estate—"

"It's not your estate, Rupert," Edith chimed in. "It's still mine."

"Did Bryan tell you *why* he was trespassing?" Shawn demanded.

"Said he was looking for work," said Rupert. "I didn't think any more of it."

"I see." Shawn nodded. "So . . . you say you saw Bryan *in* the culvert but as everyone here knows," Shawn made a grand sweeping motion, "the service road passes *over* the culvert."

"Perhaps his lordship has X-ray vision?" Mum put in.

"I stopped—" Rupert turned pink. "I . . . I . . . I had to relieve myself."

Mum started to snigger.

"You couldn't wait until you got home?" Shawn asked politely.

Mum's sniggers turned into snorts.

"Good God, man," said Rupert. "Do I really have to go into details?"

"Rupert has a prostate problem," Lavinia declared. "That's why we have separate bedrooms. Every time he has to use the lavatory, he turns on the light. It's ab-so-lutely infuriating."

"How unfortunate," Edith muttered.

Rupert was mortified and just glared at Lavinia, sending my mother into silent convulsions. I could feel her shaking with mirth. To my horror, I fought the urge to giggle, too. It was rather like being in church and knowing you shouldn't laugh, which made it all the more funny.

There was a rustle of plastic and Clive stepped forward with the plastic shopping bag. "I think now is a good time, sir."

"Not yet, Clive." Shawn waved him away and started pacing around the room before coming to a stop in front of Rupert. "The problem is, m'lord—according to a witness, you were at the Hare & Hounds for only one hour. Where were you between the hours of seven-thirty and the time you made that phone call?"

"Eric will confirm my story," said Rupert.

"Me?" Eric looked horrified. "I—I—that is . . . yes."

"You don't seem so sure," said Shawn.

"I'm sure," he mumbled, not sounding sure at all.

"What's Rupert up to now?" Mum whispered. "I almost feel sorry for Eric. He's always having to cover for him."

"Gran?" Shawn turned to his grandmother.

"Mr. Cropper and I were at home in bed," said Mrs. Cropper. "We heard an argument outside."

"An argument?" Shawn said sharply. "And what time was this?"

"As I told you last night—it woke us up—we go to bed early," she added helpfully. "But I think it was around eleven."

"And did you recognize these voices?"

"I'd say it was a man and a woman, wouldn't you, Mr. Cropper?"

I looked over to where Mr. Cropper was propped up in the corner with his eyes closed.

"Take my word for it," said Mrs. Cropper. "It was a man and a woman."

"A *man* and a *woman*," Shawn said slowly as he scanned the room.

Of course I thought of my mother.

Lavinia rolled her eyes and muttered something that sounded like "pompous."

"But as I said, dear..." Mrs. Cropper seemed apologetic. "It could have been a fox. They scream something dreadful."

I'd often heard the unnerving scream of a fox's mating call, too.

Clive stepped forward again and jiggled the plastic shopping bag. "Now, Shawn?"

"Not *yet*, Clive," said Shawn with a hint of annoyance. Clive looked crestfallen and stepped back to his post.

Shawn started pacing around the room *again*. He stopped in front of Eric. "What about you?"

"I saw Bryan late last night."

Everyone gasped.

"You didn't mention *that* when we had a drink, *Eric*," Rupert said pointedly.

Eric hesitated. He fixed his gaze on my mother and said, "The thing is, Shawn, Bryan turned up at my caravan with a black eye. He told me that Iris—I'm sorry, Iris—attacked him."

Mum stood there, utterly shell-shocked. "And to think I was feeling sorry for you!" she exclaimed.

Eric nodded. "That was the last time I saw Bryan alive."

Chapter Nineteen

"It's a lie!" Mum exclaimed. "Bryan attacked *me*!"

"Attacked you?" everyone chorused in unison.

"The bastard!" Alfred bristled with fury and raised his fists. "Why … if I could only get my hands …"

"I think that ship has sailed, Alfred," said Edith dryly.

"But why did he come to your caravan again, Eric?" I demanded.

"No idea," he replied but I noted that Eric refused to look me in the eye. "He was upset. Very upset."

"Whoa, steady on everyone, please! Quieten down now," Shawn said above the ensuing pandemonium. "So it's true, Iris, you admit to attacking the deceased?"

"I admit I gave him a black eye," said Mum.

"I thought you hit him on the chin?" I said.

"Eye, chin—what does it matter?" Mum exclaimed. "But I didn't bludgeon him to death with a tire iron. Anyway he deserved it."

There was another universal gasp of horror.

"He made a pass at me," Mum shouted. "Cornered me in the old tack room but I soon made him change his mind. Peggy knows what he's like—or was like, I should say."

"I don't know what you're talking about," Mrs. Cropper said again, and *again* glanced nervously over to Cropper who *again,* seemed not to have heard. "Iris has always been one to tell stories."

"Excuse me?" Mum gawked. "Talk about the pot calling the kettle black!"

"You probably encouraged him, anyway," said Mrs. Cropper childishly. "Seth always said you were a tease, didn't you, Seth?"

Cropper grunted, cleared his throat and muttered something inaudible.

"Don't you dare insult my Iris," Alfred yelled from the sidelines.

"A leopard never changes its spots," Mum went on. "And that goes for you, too, Peggy Cropper."

Lavinia glowered at Rupert. "I couldn't agree more."

I felt as if I were in the stands at Wimbledon as insult followed insult. Even Edith caught my eye and winked. She seemed to be thoroughly amused. I would have been, too, had it not been my mother in the hot seat.

"But I can assure you," Mum went on, "thanks to Alfred who taught me how to defend myself, Bryan ran off like the coward he *always* was."

"And presumably, neither Kat nor Alfred can verify this story because..." Shawn paused dramatically. "Apparently, they were at the cinema."

"Yes, we were," Alfred and I chorused.

All eyes swiveled to us.

"And what were you watching at the cinema?" said Shawn.

"Fifty Shades of Grey," Alfred declared. "And very enjoyable it was, too."

"Fifty Shades of Grey!" squeaked Lavinia.

"Good heavens," said Edith. "What happened to the sequel? *Fifty Shades Darker?*"

"It's not coming out until 2017, m'lady," said Mum. "According to the *Daily Post* there were problems finding a director."

"I do wish you had told me," said Lavinia, shooting Rupert another mutinous look. "I would have liked to have come."

"And then what happened?" said Shawn wearily.

"My MINI was stolen," Mum declared. "Right outside the cinema."

"With all due respect, if you've stopped talking about Bryan, I have a meeting to go to this morning," said Rupert.

"On a Sunday?" Lavinia demanded.

"Of course, m'lord. But please, wait for just one minute. Clive?" Shawn snapped his fingers and Clive leapt forward brandishing the plastic shopping bag. His fifteen minutes of fame had finally arrived.

"Oh, I do declare," said Lavinia, rolling her eyes. "It's time for Shawn's show-and-tell."

There was a tense silence as Clive passed the plastic shopping bag to Shawn. He opened it and withdrew a small Ziploc bag containing a piece of jewelry.

Mum gasped. "What on earth—oh. Never mind."

The library fell silent as Shawn began to glide around the room with his Ziploc bag. "We found this necklace caught in the shrubbery next to the culvert."

Edith, Rupert and Lavinia barely gave the Ziploc bag a passing glance but when Shawn stopped in front of his grandmother, she let out a cry of horror and tore out of the library muttering, "Kitchen!" "Potatoes on stove!" and "Burn!"

"Gran?" said Shawn anxiously.

Cropper hurried after her at quite an astonishing speed for once but before we had time to rally, Shawn was standing before Mum and me, Ziploc bag in hand.

Inside was a gold-plated heart-shaped pendant with a fake diamond in the center. It was tarnished with age.

My heart skipped a beat. "Wasn't *Pandora* wearing something very similar?"

"Well spotted, Katherine," said Shawn. "She was indeed."

"How the hell did that end up in the shrubbery?" Alfred exclaimed.

"At last!" Shawn was triumphant. "We're getting somewhere." He nodded eagerly at Rupert, Edith and Lavinia, who had suddenly grown interested and were all craning forward for a better look.

"Perhaps we can get Katherine to value it?" suggested Lavinia with a sneer.

Alfred laughed. "I think you'll be disappointed. We used to give those necklaces away as prizes—what was the stall, Iris?"

"Hook-the-rubber-duck," Mum declared.

"What on earth are you talking about?" Rupert demanded.

"When the fair and traveling boxing emporium used to come here in the summer, m'lord," said Mum. "We ran quite a few sideshows. Hook-the-rubber-duck was one. And very popular it was, too."

"There are probably dozens of these trinkets all over the place," Alfred scoffed.

"You mean—this is worthless?" Shawn's disappointment was plain.

"Of course it's worthless, my man," said Rupert. "And obviously, since a similar necklace was worn by Mummy's friend, she probably won it at the ... what was it—?"

Lavinia rolled her eyes again. "Hook-the-rubber-duck..."

"Absolutely not," Edith chimed in. "Pandora would never have worn cheap jewelry—especially not to my birthday ball. She liked to show off. You must be mistaken."

"I'm afraid not, m'lady," said Shawn. "Pandora Haslam-Grimley was wearing one just like this around her neck."

"I thought her neck was broken?" Mum said bluntly.

"So basically, we're no further forward with this charade," said Rupert.

"I still think its evidence, sir," Clive protested and opened the plastic shopping bag for Shawn to drop the Ziploc bag back inside.

The library door opened and Roxy scurried in wearing a huge smile.

"Don't bring Harry in here!" shrieked Lavinia.

"He's helping Mrs. Cropper in the kitchen," said Roxy. "But I've got news that just can't wait." She grabbed Shawn's elbow and wheeled him into the corner. Then she passed him a note.

We all watched with bated breath as he read it and broke into a huge grin.

"Good news," he said. "Ginny has been found."

I'd never felt so relieved. "Thank God! Whatever happened?"

"Ginny who?" said Edith.

"That reporter," spat Rupert. "The one who Katherine talked to."

"Was she missing?" said Lavinia blankly.

I realized that Shawn was watching everyone's reactions keenly.

"Where was she?" I asked.

"A man walking his dog on Dartmoor found her wandering around in her pajamas."

"On Dartmoor?" everyone chorused.

"She could have died of hypothermia!" I said.

"Or fallen into a bog," said Roxy. "It's treacherous out there. Everyone knows that."

"Where is she now?" I asked.

"Totnes Hospital," said Roxy. "She's in no fit state to talk to anyone at the moment but when she can, we're confident we'll know what happened."

I was truly puzzled. Had Bryan abducted Ginny, driven her to Dartmoor in her car, dropped her off and returned the car? Why would he go to all the bother and not just use his camper van?

"I don't think we can help you any more, this morning," said Rupert briskly. "This newspaper girl has nothing to do with us. We all have alibis for the Laney chap's death—"

"Of course, m'lord," said Shawn. "You're all free to go—except for the Stanfords and Mr. Bushman, here."

"I hope you won't keep Iris long," said Edith, "because I'd like her to accompany me to church this morning."

"Me? To *church*?" Mum cried. "Why, yes, of course, your ladyship."

"And Rupert is going to drive us there."

"I'm afraid I've got a meeting," said Rupert.

"So you said." Lavinia sounded suspicious. "Where?"

"Why are you questioning me?" said Rupert. "If you must know, I'm going to talk to someone about the plasterwork ceiling."

"Where?" Lavinia said again.

"At his house in Exeter."

"Good. Then you can drop us off and pick us up afterward," said Edith smoothly. "We'll wait for you, Iris, in the car at the front of the house."

We moved en masse out of the library and into the icy-cold galleried reception area with Clive trailing behind still clutching the plastic carrier bag. Mum pulled her mink coat closer.

"Gather round, gather round," said Shawn. "Well, good news, Iris. We found your car."

"Oh, that's wonderful," gushed Mum. "Isn't that wonderful, Alfred?"

"Amazing," he said. "Bloody amazing—pardon my French."

"Yes, it looks like some kids had taken it for a joyride—just as you suspected," said Shawn. "Extraordinary isn't it?'

"May I ask where you found my car?" said Mum, feigning innocence.

"Heathfield Business Park in Newton Abbot—"

"A business park? In Newton *Abbot*? Fancy. Well I never." Mum looked to Alfred. "Did you hear that, Alfred? Newton Abbot."

"Was there any damage?" said Alfred. "Knowing what kids can be like."

"Happily, no," said Shawn. "It looks like they just ran out of petrol and abandoned the car. Right in the middle of the road."

"I'm so relieved!" Mum said happily.

"Of course you'll have to pick it up at the pound," said Shawn.

"Thank you so much." Mum beamed. "Excellent police work!"

"There is one thing, however…" Shawn turned his gaze to me. "Something that Katherine might find interesting."

My heart sank.

"Luxton's, the auctioneers, have a warehouse in Heathfield Business Park," he went on. "It was broken into last night."

"Oh no!" Mum exclaimed. "What a shame. But I can't see why that should concern us."

"Why *would* it concern us, Officer?" Alfred echoed with a complete poker face.

"Since your car was in the vicinity of the robbery, Iris, we'll need to dust for fingerprints—just as a precaution you understand," said Shawn.

"Kids!" Mum said with disgust. "What do they want with old drawings?"

Shawn frowned. "I didn't mention any drawings, Mrs. Stanford."

"Well!" Mum said gaily. "Kat told me about an auction and drawings or paintings or something...I just assumed..."

"Yes, that's right, I did." I had that all-too-familiar sinking feeling in my stomach. "In fact, Edith put two drawings into the sale."

"So I heard," said Shawn. "Eric dropped them off at Luxton's. I believe that they were the Hollars that were hanging in the King's Parlor."

"Oh dear!" Mum exclaimed. "Well, let's hope they weren't among the items stolen."

"We should have a list tomorrow," said Shawn. "We're confident we'll find the culprit."

"Kids can get sloppy," said Alfred.

"Oh no," said Shawn. "On the contrary. It was a professional job."

"Ah," said Alfred with a satisfied grunt.

"However, Heathfield Business Park is installed with the latest surveillance technology," Shawn went on. "Cameras are everywhere. I'm quite certain we'll catch whoever was responsible. We've already alerted the Art and Antiques Unit in London."

Mum gave a little gasp. I daren't look at her. The Art & Antiques Unit meant that there was no way that David would not find out.

"Well, thank you for tracking down my car," said Mum. "I have to go to church now."

"Are you planning on going to confession?" Shawn said.

Mum looked startled. "*Me?* No. Why?"

"Edith is Catholic, I believe."

"Oh," said Mum. "I'm a bit of a pagan if you really want to know."

"And I've got horses to see to," Alfred put in. I had to admire his sangfroid. His face gave absolutely nothing away whereas I was certain that mine did.

"Of course," said Shawn. "We'll be wanting to talk to you—*both* of you—again."

"Any time," Mum said cheerfully and followed Alfred out of the room.

"I'd better be going, too," I said.

"Let's go into the kitchen, shall we?" said Shawn. "I have a couple of things to ask you."

As we passed through the green baize door that divided the old servants' quarters from the rest of the house, raised voices could be clearly heard.

"Surely that's not Rupert?" I exclaimed.

Shawn stopped. We both strained our ears and heard every single word.

"I knew it!" shouted a man's voice. He was furious. "All these years, I *knew* it!"

Mrs. Cropper's answer was drowned out by another burst of indignation.

"Wait. That doesn't sound like Rupert," I said suddenly. "Is that ... surely ... that can't be Mr. *Cropper?*"

"Let's go somewhere else." Shawn grabbed my arm and steered me back the way we had come.

"Was he shouting at Mrs. Cropper?" I was still stunned.

"He's a bit deaf," said Shawn defensively. "He doesn't know how far his voice carries. That's all."

I felt reluctant to say the obvious. Shawn had to have seen how nervous Mrs. Cropper was this morning—especially when Mum talked about Bryan. She definitely reacted to the sight of the necklace, too. Perhaps Mrs. Cropper had been one of Bryan's many conquests and Mr. Cropper still bore a grudge. Yet, was it enough of a grudge to kill Bryan with a tire iron?

"How long have your grandparents been together?" I said to Shawn as we paused at the front entrance. The rain was coming down in sheets.

"I have no idea," he said. "Do you mind continuing this conversation in my car?"

He gallantly removed his trench coat and held it over my head whilst walking alongside me. In the twenty feet it took us to reach his panda, Shawn was utterly drenched.

He opened the front passenger side, helped me in—even protecting my head as I slid into the seat. Then, he hurried around to the driver's side.

Within minutes, the car windows steamed up. It felt unnervingly intimate and rather romantic in an odd sort of way with the rain hammering down on the roof. I could smell bananas—the peculiar scent that always accompanied Shawn wherever he went.

I bundled up his trench coat and handed it back to him. He tossed it into the backseat.

"Look, I'll come straight to the point," said Shawn. "Everything points to your mother's involvement. The book with her name in it, the Cleopatra costume, the necklace—"

"Alfred said those necklaces were everywhere—"

"The motive, the opportunity—"

"Are you talking about Pandora?" I said.

"I'm talking about all three—Pandora, Bryan *and* Ginny." Instead of accusation in his eyes, I saw compassion. "We all know your mother has a lot to hide. We like Iris. I know that Edith is very fond of her—but . . . this is murder we're talking about, Kat."

I felt sick.

"You're not helping Iris by covering for her!"

"I'm not covering for anyone," I said.

"We *know* she was involved in Pandora's disappearance."

"I don't see how! It's just circumstantial evidence," I said hotly. "Just because Pandora wore the costume that was intended for Edith doesn't make my mother a killer. And anyway, what about the thank you letter that Pandora wrote to Edith?" I said. "Have you had any luck with that?"

"The dowager countess says she didn't keep it. We'll probably involve a forensic handwriting expert to take a look at the writing on the flyleaf of the book and—"

"But even if the book *had* belonged to my mother, I don't see how that proves she was there."

"It proves that she knew the double-hide was there."

"Perhaps Edith's brother Rupert told her?" I said. "Or told someone else who told her—"

"Or maybe she's covering for Alfred?" Shawn's eyes bored into mine. I had to look away.

I didn't even need to bring up Bryan. My mother had admitted she attacked him.

"And surely, if she is such a bad person, she would have done something far worse to Ginny rather than dumping her off on Dartmoor," I said. "I mean—why not hit her with a tire iron and be done with it?"

"I know it's hard to believe." To my surprise, Shawn reached over and squeezed my shoulder. "And then there is the car theft. I'm just not sure where that bit fits in."

I shrugged. "Your guess is as good as mine."

Shawn leaned back in his seat and gave a heavy sigh. We sat there in silence with the rain still hammering on the roof and the car getting so steamed up that I couldn't even see outside the windows.

"Kat," said Shawn gently. "Is there anything you want to tell me?"

"About last night's break-in, you mean?"

"O-kay. Yes. We can start with that." Shawn paused for a moment. "Dealing with Newton Abbot is not like dealing with . . . me. If you know what I mean."

I nodded. I knew exactly what Shawn meant. He may be willing to hush things up.

"They'll obviously be conducting the inquiry because the crime falls into their jurisdiction," Shawn went on. "If the drawings that Eric said he dropped off are on the list of items that were taken last night, then we'll obviously have to get involved."

For a wild moment, I hesitated. What if I told Shawn the truth—that the Hollar drawings had been reported as stolen over twenty-five years ago; that they were still on the watch list; that Alfred had broken in to steal them . . . but then I stopped. I knew I couldn't. Alfred was on parole. Shawn may have been easily swayed when it came to keeping the Honeychurch affairs under wraps, but Alfred had definitely committed a crime—no matter how noble it had seemed at the time.

"As I said, Alfred and I went to the cinema."

"I see," Shawn said curtly. "We'll know soon enough. First thing tomorrow we'll have access to the CCTV surveillance tapes."

"Good," I whispered. "I think I'd better go."

"It's still raining."

"I'm fine." I opened the door.

"I'll drive you to the Carriage House."

"No, really," I said. "I'm going to the stables, actually. It's not far."

"Remember what I—" but I didn't hear the rest of it. I'd already closed the door.

I set off at a fast walk. The only thing I was certain about was the theft of the Hollar drawings. It would take the police hours, if not days to screen the footage—wouldn't it? By then, Alfred would have put them back—I stopped in my tracks. No, of course he couldn't put them back! What was I thinking? It was better, far better for them to disappear altogether. But—damn—would Edith try to claim on insurance? She didn't know about the scam.

My head began to spin. I suddenly thought how apt that the woman who had started all this had been called Pandora. Discovering her body in a tomb-like box had certainly unleashed a lot of misfortune.

Hopefully, Alfred knew what he must do.

Chapter Twenty

"Ah, Katherine!" Lavinia poked her head out of Thunder's stable. "Any idea where Alfred is?"

"He's not *here*?" I said, feigning surprise.

"No. Why else would I be asking?" Lavinia said coldly. "We've been waiting around for the last half an hour. Alfred didn't even tack up the horses! It's frightfully inconvenient."

A sense of foreboding swept over me. This was most unlike Alfred. Of course, Alfred didn't have a mobile phone. He didn't need one. His new life was living above the stables in his little flat.

"Maybe he's taken Jupiter down to the paddock?" I said hopefully. But even as I scanned the yard, I knew he hadn't. All the loose box doors were shut.

"Alfred's not answering!" came a shout from above. I looked up to see Harry, dressed in his Biggles flying helmet, goggles and white scarf, standing at the top of the stone steps that led up to Alfred's flat.

"Oh, this is so *maddening*!" said Lavinia. "Alfred is usually so reliable. I hope this isn't going to become a habit."

It dawned on me that perhaps Alfred had been thinking what I'd been thinking and had already gone to get rid of the drawings. But no, of course he couldn't. Mum's car was at the pound and he didn't have the keys to mine.

"Perhaps Alfred had to go down to the bottom paddocks for Edith?" I suggested.

"No. Edith went to church," said Lavinia. "Though what possessed her I have no idea. She's never been before—apart from Christmas and Easter, of course."

"Did you go inside Alfred's flat?"

"Good heavens, no," said Lavinia.

"I'll go and look. Maybe he's fallen—"

"Fallen?" Lavinia looked horrified. "Why ever would you think that?" She shook her head incredulously and stomped off to the tack room muttering, "Have to do everything myself."

I took the stone staircase and met Harry coming halfway down. "It looks like Flying Officer Bushman went out on a secret mission this morning and didn't tell his commanding officer!"

"Oh dear!" I said with forced heartiness. "He'll have to be severely reprimanded when he returns to base."

"Now, Stanford..." Harry gestured for me to come closer and lowered his voice. "I'm sending you on a mission of vital importance."

"Yes, sir."

"It's about that spy we saw yesterday," he whispered. "I think I know where he is hiding out."

"That's very disturbing, sir," I whispered back. "Where?"

"Behind the walled garden," said Harry. "Spotted his bunker. He did a poor job of trying to disguise it. The man knows nothing about camouflage in hostile territory."

"May I ask which of our agents saw the—er—bunker and when he saw it, sir?"

"Yesterday afternoon," said Harry. "Agent Chips—"

"Ah, Agent Chips." I stifled a smile. Agent Chips being the Jack Russell terrier.

"We were patrolling the boundaries and he raised the alarm," Harry went on.

"Did you see the enemy, sir?"

"I got close but I had to retreat. When a man's been in the field for as long as I have, you get an instinct, Stanford."

I felt a tiny knot of fear. Had Harry seen anything?

"What happened, sir?"

"Someone was watching from the woods," Harry went on in his alter ego. "I thought I'd go back this afternoon for another look."

The last thing I wanted was for Harry to go anywhere near Bryan's camper van—if it was still there—by himself, especially if the police had found it and cordoned it off. "I'll go, sir."

"Good man." Harry nodded. "Take the gate next to the hothouse, but be careful. It could be a trap."

"Harry! Don't just stand there!" Lavinia emerged from the tack room with a saddle in her arms. "Come and help me!"

"I'm happy to help," I called out.

"No, thank you, Katherine," said Lavinia frostily. "We do not need your help."

I gave Harry a salute and he jumped down the last few steps and dashed over to where Lavinia was holding Thunder's bridle.

Once Lavinia and Harry had ridden out of the yard, I tried Alfred's door. It was unlocked.

The flat had been built under the eaves but was fairly spacious. It was furnished simply with a two-seater sofa, coffee table and bookcase. A TV sat on top of a sideboard against the end wall. There was a small kitchen table with four chairs, a kitchenette, a bathroom leading off and one bedroom.

I took a quick look around. It was neat and tidy. Alfred had very few possessions and as far as I could tell, everything was still there. He hadn't packed up and fled.

How well did I really know my mother's stepbrother? Mum said a leopard never changed its spots and that didn't just apply to affairs of the heart!

The more I thought about it, the more I was convinced that Alfred must have gone to move the drawings.

Taking the shortcut through the pine forest, I was back at the Carriage House in fifteen minutes. To my relief, my Golf wasn't there. I was right. Alfred *had* gone off to move the drawings. What's more, he must have hot-wired my car because I still had my car keys in my tote bag.

I glanced at the singing bird clock. Mum wouldn't be back from church for at least another hour. *Church!* Another strange development—and Edith insisting my mother go with her was just plain odd.

It was the perfect time to go and see if Bryan had indeed left his camper van behind the walled garden.

The Victorian walled garden looked dreary on this wet February afternoon and even more neglected than usual. Within the ivy-clad walls were wide borders that were bounded by a perimeter path that had two main central paths. One ran north to south, the other east to west, dividing the garden into four equal sections. A line of glasshouses stretched along one side. Behind them, hugging the boundary wall, were abandoned hothouse furnaces, potting sheds, tool rooms and a henhouse. It was easy to imagine how beautiful this would have been in its heyday.

I found the wicket gate and passed through into the field behind.

Bryan's camper van was still there. It was screened from the Hall, Honeychurch Cottages, Eric's scrapyard and Mum's Carriage House. As yet, there was no sign of the police.

I peered into the windows. I'd always thought that VW camper vans had a lot of charm and as a child had loved the idea of sleeping under the raised striped canopy roof. Perhaps I had inherited my mother's genes for life on the road, after all.

It started to rain again. I tried the door and to my surprise, it was unlocked. I stepped up inside and was hit by the smell of stale cigarettes mingled with alcohol. A duvet and pillow were scrunched up and shoved under one of the seats. I was right. It looked like Bryan had been sleeping here.

Although I was wearing gloves, I didn't want to get into trouble with Shawn for touching anything but when I spotted two plastic long-stemmed champagne glasses in the small sink, I couldn't help myself.

Bryan had been entertaining.

I opened the door under the sink and there, in the rubbish bin was an empty bottle of champagne.

My mother drank champagne.

I couldn't stand not knowing the brand. It sounded silly but I knew her tastes. I carefully took out the bottle. It was Freixenet—a cheap sparkling Spanish wine. Mum said she only drank real champagne but with everything that had happened over the past twenty-four hours, I was ready to believe anything. I'd never seen her drink brandy but she'd been knocking that stuff back last night as if it had been going out of fashion.

Suddenly, a phone rang and it wasn't mine. I searched to

see where it was coming from but the ringing stopped only to start up again a few seconds later.

It seemed to be coming from the driver's area.

I made my way to the front of the camper van and in the console between the seats was a mobile phone. I nudged it. The screen lit up. There was no password needed. I saw twelve missed calls, three voice mails and 10 percent of battery remaining.

Someone had been trying to get ahold of Bryan. Someone who couldn't possibly know that he was now dead.

In the passenger foot-well was a cardboard box containing a set of headphones and some magazines. I could just make out two of the titles—*Treasure Hunting* and *Searcher*. There was also an ordnance survey map and an exercise book.

It began to dawn on me why Bryan had come back to Honeychurch Hall and when my foot caught the coil of a long metal shaft, I knew.

It was a metal detector. Bryan's return had had nothing to do with wanting to find work.

I thought back to Rupert's comment earlier that morning. Bryan had been trespassing last August. That was around the time that the underground tunnel was discovered in Cromwell Meadows.

I remembered how quickly Bryan had turned up out of the blue on Friday. He must have heard about the double-hide on the radio and come straight away to nose around. I bet he was looking for the missing Honeychurch silver coins.

I picked up the ordnance survey map and spread it over the bench seat.

It was a detailed map of the Honeychurch Hall estate.

Bryan had painstakingly labeled everything—the Hall, the Carriage House, stable yard, Jane's Cottage, Eric's scrapyard and caravan, the Honeychurch Hall cottages next to the Victorian walled garden, Edith's equine cemetery, the Victorian grotto, the sunken garden, stumpery—even a boating lake and boathouse that I did not know existed.

Illegible hieroglyphics in tiny spider scrawl were scattered across the map. A blue line had been drawn in to mark the underground tunnel from the Hall to the exit on Cavalier Lane. A grid covered Harry's pillow mounds behind Jane's Cottage. It looked as if Bryan had been systematically working his way across the field.

Of course he had wanted to talk to Joan Stark. She'd lived at Jane's Cottage with her family and he probably thought she might have had a lucid moment and remembered something important.

The camper van door opened with a crash. Startled, I leapt to my feet and promptly hit my head on the roof, tripped over the coil again, lost my balance and fell onto Shawn who then lost his. We both tumbled out onto the muddy grass in an embarrassing heap with my face practically buried into the crotch of his trousers.

"I'm so sorry," I mumbled and struggled to push myself away without touching his legs only to collapse on him face-first *again*.

"Your elbow!" Shawn yelped.

"Oh God!" I was utterly mortified and hurled myself sideways, straight into a puddle of muddy water.

"Here, take my hand," said Shawn in a voice that definitely sounded a couple of decibels higher than it had this morning.

"I am so sorry," I stammered. "You startled me."

"So I see," he squeaked.

"I was going to phone you about the camper van but it started to rain—"

"I hope you haven't touched anything."

I held up my gloved hands that were now soaked with muddy water. The rain started to come down again.

"Let's get inside." Shawn gallantly helped me back into the camper van and pulled the door shut behind us.

"You've got mud on your nose," he said shyly.

"So do you." And he had.

We both self-consciously touched our noses.

It was the second time that day that I had found myself in an enclosed space with Detective Inspector Shawn Cropper. This time I was acutely aware of a strange tension between us. Shawn's face was flushed. His curly hair was wet with the rain and I knew that mine had expanded into a wild bush, just as it always did in wet weather.

"You look like Electra, the Twenty-seven-thousand Volts Girl," he said lightly. "I can certainly feel the electricity in here, can't you?"

I blushed and felt oddly pleased. Was he actually flirting with me?

"What's that?" he asked on spotting the ordnance survey map and our moment was broken. "I told you not to touch anything."

I was going to lie and say that the map had already been there but decided against it.

"So this was what Bryan was up to," said Shawn. "I had my suspicions."

"And the tools that were found in the double-hide must have confirmed that the Honeychurches really *had* minted the coins here," I said.

Shaw donned his disposable latex gloves and started going through the cardboard box. At the bottom was a Ziploc bag.

"Ah-ha!" he exclaimed. "I can never resist a Ziploc bag."

"What is it?"

"It looks like a receipt book," Shawn said with growing excitement. "Bryan was onto something. Has anyone told you about the role the Earl of Grenville played in the English Civil War?"

"I've heard bits," I said. "Rupert felt that the coins had been buried somewhere on the estate when the Royalists had to retreat."

"So goes the legend," said Shawn. "The Honeychurches were closely allied with the Vyvans—a very prominent and influential family in Cornwall. Like many Royalist supporters in the area, they were permitted to collect plate—that would be silver in today's terms—to melt it down and create money to support the Royalist army." Shawn pointed to the bag. "I am certain that this is a receipt book that would have itemized what the Honeychurches had taken from neighboring farmers all anxious to support their king."

"I wonder how Bryan got hold of it?"

"I suppose we'll never know," said Shawn. "You see, there were pockets of Royalist supporters called Cavaliers, and pockets of Roundheads from Cromwell's New Army—"

"Yes, I know about the Roundheads and the Cavaliers—"

"In fact, Lavinia's lot—the Carews—fought for Cromwell. Families were often split right down the middle—rather like the American Civil War, in fact, so you see..."

Shawn droned on about the Sealed Knot and all the different regiments and I duly listened. Much as I liked him, he had this awful habit of pontificating and now in this enclosed space, instead of enjoying the electricity between us, I was beginning to feel claustrophobic.

"I had no idea you were such an expert, Shawn," I finally managed to say.

"I'm a member of the English Civil War Reenactment Society," he said with a hint of pride. "This summer, we're hosting a reenactment group here at the Hall. Naturally Rupert will play his ancestor, the Earl of Grenville."

"That sounds exciting."

"It is," said Shawn eagerly.

"And who do you play?"

"Prince Maurice."

I thought of the Dobson painting hanging in the King's Parlor and suddenly, Alfred and the revelries of the night before at Heathfield Business Park came flooding back.

Shawn must have seen something in my face. "Sorry. I tend to get carried away. Trains and the English Civil War are my hobbies."

"No, it was interesting," I protested.

We fell quiet again as the rain continued to hammer down on the roof of the camper van and the windows started to steam up, again.

Shawn started to poke around as I watched. I couldn't deny there was some spark between us but I didn't want a relationship so soon, nor did I want to take on a man who already had two children and a wife who, by everything I'd heard, had been just wonderful. I'd always be second—just like I had been second in David's life.

As if sensing my eyes on him, Shawn turned and smiled but then he spotted the plastic champagne glasses in the sink, opened the little cupboard underneath and withdrew the rubbish bin. "Hello, hello, hello! What have we got here?"

And the policeman clichéd phrases, I thought to myself, could I live with those?

"Freixenet in the love machine," said Shawn.

"Excuse me?"

"Gran told me that Bryan was quite a Casanova in his day. He used to do a lot of…" Shawn blushed. "Entertaining in this old camper van."

Shawn delved into the rubbish bin and withdrew a crumpled greeting card. "Hmm … hello, hello, hello! What's all this then?"

No. The clichéd phrases would definitely be a problem.

Pictured on the front was a floral teapot with a cup and saucer inside a large red heart. The caption said, *"You suit me to a tea!"* "It's a Valentine's card."

"It looks pretty old, too," I said.

Shawn opened it and together we read the greeting inside, *"I'm all steamed up over you my Valentine,"* and under that, in spidery handwriting, *"Together forever—?"*

I thought of all the cards that David had sent me and that I still had. "Do you think Bryan Laney sent this? It looks like his handwriting."

"Someone has been holding onto that card for a very long time." Shawn removed a Ziploc bag and slid the card inside. "We'll get this handwriting analyzed."

Bryan's mobile rang from the central console again.

"Front passenger seat!" I said quickly. "I meant to tell you—"

But Shawn had already pounced on it. "Hello?"

I could hear a woman's voice twittering on the other end.

"No, this is not Bryan," said Shawn, all business. "He is unable to come to the phone. Who am I speaking to?"

More twittering.

"This is Detective Inspector Shawn Cropper," said Shawn.

More twittering that I could tell was becoming hysterical.

"I'm not at liberty to say, madame. Can you identify yourself? Oh!" Shawn's eyes widened with surprise. "I'm afraid I can't give out that information on the telephone," he said firmly. "Let me take your address." He fumbled in his top pocket. I helped him find a pen and opened his notebook for him.

"Hello? *Hello?*" Shawn looked at me and shook his head. "She hung up." He put Bryan's mobile into a fresh Ziploc bag. "We should be able to trace her address from Laney's phone."

"Who was it?"

Shawn paused for a moment before saying, "It would appear that Bryan had a wife."

Chapter Twenty-one

"She was calling from a Plymouth area code," said Shawn as we left the camper van. "Judging by her reaction, Bryan seemed to make a habit of disappearing and losing his phone."

I thought of the missed calls and ignored voice mails.

"Do you think his wife called to cover her tracks?" I suggested. "Plymouth isn't so far away."

"You mean, did she discover Bryan with another woman—but who?"

I shrugged. "That's why you are a detective and I'm not."

The rain had finally stopped. We cut through the walled garden in silence. Shawn seemed preoccupied and was walking quickly.

"Any news on Ginny?" I said.

"What?" he said distractedly.

"Ginny? Is she still in hospital?"

He nodded. "We'll be talking to her this afternoon."

"Will you let me know when I can go and visit her?"

He nodded. "I'm just going to pop in and see Gran." I noticed his panda car was parked outside the Croppers' cottage.

I headed back to the Carriage House wondering about Shawn's grandmother. The cottage was just a short walk from the camper van. Mrs. Cropper had said she'd heard a man and a woman arguing but perhaps she was lying? If she were involved, I wondered what Shawn was going to do about it.

Back at the Carriage House, my car still wasn't back. Hopefully Mum was home from church and might know what Alfred's plans were.

I found Mum upstairs in her office sitting at her desk and poring through the cash box.

"How was church?" I said.

"Good God!" she shrieked and shot out of her chair. "Why didn't you knock?"

"Were you struck down by lightning?"

Mum shoved something into her cardigan pocket and snapped the cash box lid shut. "What did you say?"

I regarded her with suspicion. "You're up to something."

"No, I'm not," she protested.

"What have you got in your pocket?"

"Nothing!"

I made a quick lunge for her hand. My mother spun away and dashed out of the office with me in hot pursuit. She darted into the bathroom and slammed the door.

I tapped quietly. "Hello? What are you doing? Flushing whatever it is down the loo?"

"I'm just having a pee. Why do you have to follow me everywhere?" Mum called out.

"Okay—well, that's a shame because I had something really interesting to tell you but I suppose I can't now."

There was a silence. And then:

"How interesting?"

"About Bryan Laney—or should I say, *Mrs.* Laney."

There was another silence and then the door opened a crack. Quick as a flash, I barged in and grabbed her wrist.

"Ouch, ouch! That's my bad hand!" Mum squealed as I plunged my own into her cardigan pocket.

"Ah-ha! What is this?" I withdrew a heart-shaped pendant with a fake diamond. It was identical to the one that Shawn had shown us in the library—and on Pandora's body.

"Really, Katherine," Mum said crossly. "You can be so dramatic!"

"Oh, so you have a necklace, too?"

Mum gave a heavy sigh and sank onto the edge of the bathtub. "I don't want you to jump to the wrong conclusions but . . ." She paused. "Alfred was right when he said these necklaces were all over the place. Bryan was very good at hook-the-duck—"

"I'm sure he was," I said dryly.

Mum smirked. "He used to win these necklaces all the time and give them to us girls. He was such a flirt, always swearing undying love to whomever caught his eye."

Mrs. Cropper had told Shawn the same thing. "Obviously I'm relieved that you have kept your necklace—"

"No idea why I did," Mum mused. "I think it was more of a memento from my Electra days rather than sentimental value . . ."

"Did he send you a Valentine's card?"

Mum thought for a moment. "Of course not. We were never at the Hall in February. We were only there in the summer."

"What about Mrs. Cropper?" I said slyly. "Does she still have her necklace?"

"How did you find out about her and Bryan?" Mum exclaimed. "If Peggy thinks I told you she'll be furious."

"It was a lucky guess," I said. "Did Bryan send *her* a Valentine's card?"

"I've no idea," Mum grumbled. "She's not really a friend, you know."

"I thought you'd gotten all chummy."

"For a moment, I thought we were chummy, too," said Mum. "She suddenly changed. I suppose she still doesn't like me. Her Seth used to have a thing for me—"

"It sounds like everyone had a bit of a thing for you."

"I know. They did," she said. "The boys went wild because they knew we never stayed around. It was the same for Alfred and Billy—the local girls just thought that life on the road was incredibly sexy. It was so silly."

"I don't think so," I said. "It sounds exciting—and sexy."

Mum seemed pleased. "I always thought you disapproved of me."

"Of course not!" I exclaimed. "I just felt disappointed that you didn't feel you could tell me. That's all. But now I know. And now I want to know *everything*."

"Well—Peggy tried to make Seth jealous by flirting with Bryan but she got more than she bargained for—and that made Joan furious! If anyone was jealous, it was Joan." Mum nodded. "*Apparently*, Bryan got Joan in the family way."

"Oh dear."

"And then he ran off to sea. Abandoned her. Peggy said he couldn't keep his torpedo in his trousers…"

"That's disgusting, Mother."

"Her words, not mine."

"What happened to the baby?"

"Peggy thinks there was no baby; that Joan tried to trick Bryan into marrying her."

"But Joan obviously did get married, eventually."

"To Peggy's brother," said Mum. "It's all so incestuous! But she never got over Bryan. Peggy feels that's what turned her brain."

"Alzheimer's is a horrible disease, Mum." I thought for a moment. "Did Mrs. Cropper keep her necklace?"

"She said she did."

"Did you see it?"

"No."

"So the necklace that Shawn found near the culvert just might belong to Mrs. Cropper?"

"I think I'm rather weary of talking about all this necklace nonsense now, dear," said Mum. "Can we change the subject?"

"Do you know whether Mrs. Cropper drinks Freixenet?" I persisted.

"That cheap champagne?" Mum said. "Why?"

"I just wondered." I still wasn't convinced that my mother was telling the truth. "So why did you tear off into the bathroom?"

"Force of habit," said Mum with a grin. "You scared me—but enough of that. I can't believe that Bryan had a wife! What nerve! Do you know what he said to me?"

"Before you hit him?" I said. "I think you should keep that to yourself. Bryan having a wife gives you a motive."

"You'll never guess why her ladyship wanted me to go to confession."

"I don't think I can but I suspect you're about to tell me."

"She asked me to put my hand on the Bible and swear that I didn't write that thank you note from Pandora."

I felt my jaw drop. "And did you?"

"Of course I didn't write it!" Mum exclaimed. "Her ladyship wanted to give me the opportunity to come clean. Pandora's death really upset her."

I thought for a moment. "Edith was protecting you."

"Yes. She had the thank you letter, after all," said Mum. "So she's going to give it to Shawn."

"Oh dear," I whispered. "Does this mean—Alfred had something to do with it? The letter was postmarked from St. Ives."

"St. Ives? We used to camp at St. Ives." Mum turned ashen. "No, I don't believe . . . Alfred wouldn't—why would he? Or would he? We'll ask him."

"You could, if he was here." I told Mum that not only had Alfred not shown up for work this morning, but that he had stolen my car with the drawings.

"Stolen?" Mum said with scorn. "Don't be so dramatic."

"Well, he certainly didn't use my car keys," I said. "They are in my purse. He must have hot-wired it."

"Alfred has always been good at that."

"Mum—"

"I don't want to talk about Alfred," she declared. "I want to know about Bryan's wife."

I filled Mum in on the little I knew about the existence of Mrs. Laney. "Shawn said they'd send someone out from Plymouth to break the news to her."

"Maybe she did it," said Mum. "Plymouth's not far. Maybe she found out about his past shenanigans."

"That's what I wondered, too," I said. "Or maybe there is another woman in the village who he's been messing around with."

"Like who?"

"Maybe one of your friends from the Women's Institute."

"Maybe," Mum mused.

"I was joking," I said.

"I wasn't," said Mum. "The body might give out but the heart goes on."

"You sound like Céline Dion."

"Speaking of the *Titanic*, it's feels like the arctic up here in this bathroom. Let's go downstairs for tea."

We trooped to the kitchen.

"And you really think Bryan just came back to the Hall to look for the silver coins?" Mum said as we sat at the table.

"Judging by the metal detector in the camper van and the books and magazines on coins and treasure," I said. "Yes. I think that's why he came back."

"Only to get hit on the head with a tire iron," Mum said with a sigh. "What rotten luck."

There was a loud knock at the door.

Mum leapt up from the table. "That'll be Alfred! Oh thank the Lord."

"Alfred doesn't knock," I reminded her but she'd already left the kitchen.

Seconds later Mr. Chips raced inside.

I heard Edith's voice call him to heel and then, "I'd like to talk to Alfred, please."

Chapter Twenty-two

"I'm sorry, your ladyship," said Mum nervously. **"But what** did you say?"

"Alfred? Where is he?" Edith demanded. "He's not at his flat."

"He's not at his flat?" Mum said. "Are you sure?"

"Of course I'm sure! That's why I am here." Edith's eyes narrowed. "It's frightfully important I speak with him. Since he has no car and no mobile phone, surely you must know where he is?"

"I do," said Mum suddenly. "He's upstairs. Sick as a dog. Isn't he, Katherine?"

Oh no! "It sounds like it."

"What's wrong with him?" Edith demanded.

"He's got a headache," Mum said hastily.

Edith frowned. "A headache?"

"Yes, but it's a bad one. A migraine, actually."

Edith fixed Mum with a look that implied she didn't believe her. "And you just remembered he was upstairs?"

"Not exactly, m'lady." Mum lowered her voice. "Alfred didn't want you to know. He told me he'd hate you to think he was a weakling. Men and their egos!"

"Perhaps it was the effects of watching *Fifty Shades of Grey*?" said Edith. "It's enough to give anyone a headache."

"With all due respect, m'lady, a migraine is not a headache. Have you ever had one?"

Mum seemed to warm to her theme. "Awful, it is. You get nausea, disturbed vision. You can't move—and the pain is excruciating. I suffered for years and years—didn't I, Katherine?"

I merely smiled. Of course Mum had never had a migraine in her life but she knew enough about them to fake one.

"So how long does this migraine go on for?" said Edith.

"Could be days," said Mum.

"Days?" I exclaimed.

"Just to be on the safe side," Mum said. "And if you're worried about the horses, Katherine will help, won't you?"

"I don't think her ladyship wants my help, Mother." Upon seeing Edith's confusion I added, "Rupert told me he'd prefer I stayed away."

"Rupert is an idiot," Edith exclaimed. "Hopefully Alfred will feel better soon. But in the meantime, we would appreciate your help. Thank you."

"You mentioned you had something important to ask Alfred?" said Mum. "Was it...was it something to do with anything we talked about in church this morning?"

Edith gave a dismissive wave. "Of course not. I needed a second opinion on Tinkerbell."

"Well, Katherine always has an opinion so perhaps she can help?"

"That won't be necessary tonight," said Edith. "But we'll expect you at the stables tomorrow."

"I'll be there!"

"I'll see you out, your ladyship." Mum tried to signal all sorts of messages as she ushered Edith into the carriageway.

"I see you are using this as the entrance now," Edith said, gesturing to the vast interior with its magnificent arch-braced roof.

"Yes. We've done a lot of work to tidy the place up," said Mum enthusiastically. "I know we talked about having horses back in here again one day."

Edith nodded but then looked around, frowning. "But where are your cars?"

Mum looked startled. "Cars? Where *are* our cars, Katherine?"

"Yours is still at the pound—"

"Ah, yes," Edith mused. "Wasn't it stolen from the car park at the cinema?"

"Yes. Dreadful, it was," said Mum.

"Not only do people gets headaches after seeing *Fifty Shades of Grey* but their cars are stolen, too—but Katherine's Golf?"

"Stolen," said Mum quickly.

"Good grief! From here?" Edith sounded appalled.

"Mum, I think you forgot that *Eric* borrowed my car last night," I lied.

"Eric," Mum said. "Yes, yes, of course he did! With all this upset over Bryan's murder and that Pandora person's death, I just can't think straight."

"Yes. Very upsetting." Edith snapped her fingers to call Mr. Chips to heel. "Please tell Alfred that I hope he feels better soon." And with that, she strode out of the carriageway.

The minute we were back in the kitchen Mum said, "You don't need to say anything!"

"What were you thinking? A *migraine*?"

"I panicked."

"What if Alfred just comes back and Edith asks him how he's feeling?"

"I *know*." Mum's eyes couldn't get any wider. "What are we going to do?"

"I have no idea what you are going to do, but I'm going up to the gatehouse to sort out a few things. I'll leave you to nurse your poor stepbrother with his migraine."

"You have no heart," Mum grumbled.

To be honest, I had to get away and gather my thoughts.

"You'll freeze up there," said Mum. "Do you want to borrow my mink coat?"

"As a matter of fact, on this occasion, I do."

I spent the next two hours sorting through my stock. Even with a paraffin heater going at full blast, it was cold and damp but I was warm as toast in Mum's coat.

It felt good to get organized and I found the mindless sorting out helped me sort out my thoughts, too.

Alfred was missing but hopefully he had merely moved the drawings to a safe location. He was on parole. He wouldn't want to jeopardize that. It wouldn't have mattered so much if he had just taken the Hollar drawings. But instead, for some unknown reason, he'd stolen a couple of paintings, as well.

Which led me to the forged thank you letter from Pandora being posted from St. Ives. Even though I knew my mother was not a Catholic or particularly religious, she did believe in the power of the Bible. Edith was satisfied that Mum had not written the thank you letter but *someone* had. Was Alfred covering for my mother?

The plethora of heart-shaped pendants seemed to indicate that Bryan had given them to all the young girls in Little Dipperton—including Pandora. But wouldn't Alfred have had access to the necklaces, too?

Mum hadn't wanted Alfred to know about Bryan being back in Little Dipperton. Yet the attack had seemed particularly violent and if anything, I would have imagined that Alfred would have given Bryan a good beating with his fists to teach him a lesson—not end his life with a tire iron—*especially since* Alfred was still on parole.

I also couldn't imagine the tremulous Seth Cropper brandishing a tire iron, either. Which left Mrs. Cropper.

Of course there was Rupert. He'd warned Bryan off last year and he'd been the one to find his body in the culvert. But again, what would have been the motive—unless it had something to do with the missing Honeychurch treasure.

And then there was the attack on Ginny. I'd seen Bryan in the area yesterday. He could easily have read the *Daily Post* and could well have had secrets of his own to hide. But now that Ginny had been found, did that mean she was still in danger?

A sudden loud crash stopped me in my tracks. It seemed to be coming from outside. It suddenly occurred to me that whoever had killed Bryan and attacked Ginny was still out there. Quickly, I flipped off the overhead light and grabbed a seventeenth-century fire-iron from my stock as a weapon. I was still waiting on having the blinds installed and felt very exposed.

I dropped to my knees and crawled to the front door where I'd left my tote bag. Pulling out my iPhone I first called Mum but she didn't answer. Then I called Shawn's private mobile number but I just got his voice mail—so much for that. *Then,* I called Little Dipperton's police station but—being a Sunday—it was closed. The recorded greeting prompted me to dial 999 but I didn't feel my life was in danger.

In the end, I rang Eric.

It took him less than five minutes to reach the gatehouse by which time I was feeling more than a little foolish especially as I had remembered that there was a tower of empty paint cans that I'd stacked at the side of the building. Even so, I cowered inside until I saw his Land Rover pull up.

"I'm sorry, Eric," I said. "I think it was a fox or something— or the wind. I suppose I'm a bit jittery with everything that has been happening."

"Can't be too careful, luv," he said grimly but still insisted on patrolling the area with a flashlight.

We went out of the back door with me trailing after him. "The paint cans are down that path, there. I was going to take them to the tip."

Eric shone the beam and sure enough, the paint cans were scattered across the flagstone path.

"At least I wasn't imagining it," I said. "It must have been a fox." I was about to head back inside when Eric gave a shout and waved me over.

Crouching down, he played the beam over a series of fresh muddy footprints that ran alongside the length of the path to the front of the house.

"I don't think these are yours, do you?"

"I haven't been down here for a couple of days . . ." I put my shoe alongside one of the prints. It was a lot larger.

"That's a woman's footprint," said Eric.

I was puzzled. "You think it's fresh?"

Eric nodded. "It's been raining most of the day so anything from yesterday would have been washed away. Let's see where these footprints lead."

I knew my mother didn't particularly care for Eric but to-night I saw another side of him I'd not expected. Eric wasn't so bad, after all.

"I'm so glad you're here," I said and meant it.

The footprints ended at the wrought-iron gate that opened into the main entrance where they joined thin tire marks.

"Those are bicycle tires," said Eric. "You were right. Someone has been snooping. Have you had an alarm put in yet?"

"Next week," I said. "Along with the heating and the blinds."

Eric nodded. "Yeah. I reckon someone was casing the joint. Wasn't there a break-in at Luxton's warehouse last night?"

"I believe so," I said.

"You've got a lot of valuable stuff in there. You should tell Shawn."

"I will."

"I think I should take you back to the Carriage House now."

Eric waited whilst I turned off the paraffin heater and locked up the gatehouse.

As I got out of his Land Rover I thought about Bryan and told Eric about what I'd found in Bryan's camper van.

"No wonder he was snooping about," said Eric. "And no wonder he wanted to talk to Joan."

"Do you know why he came back to see you last night?" I said.

"No idea," said Eric. "But like I told Shawn this morning, he seemed upset."

"Did you know that Bryan was married?"

"Blokes don't discuss stuff like that."

I bid him good night.

Alfred had *still* not returned my car. What's more, when I went up to Mum's office to ask her for news, the sign on her door made it plain that she did not want to be disturbed nor was she hungry. Whether this was because she was actually writing or because she couldn't begin to think about what really was going on with her stepbrother, it was hard to tell.

I left her alone and went into the kitchen to find a note tacked to the fridge saying that Edith expected me at the stables at six a.m. sharp.

I made a quick supper of scrambled eggs and had an early night but I lay awake for a very long time. All I could think about was that first thing tomorrow morning, news of exactly what artwork Alfred had stolen from Luxton's warehouse would be public knowledge.

I just hoped that David was still enjoying his second honeymoon.

Chapter Twenty-three

It was dark and cold when I reached the stables the next morning but the whinnies that greeted me warmed my heart. Despite knowing that Alfred had gone AWOL, I still looked up to his flat in the crazy hope that he had magically returned.

Soon, all thoughts of Alfred and the last few days faded as I fed, watered and mucked out the stables. I found I was thoroughly enjoying myself and even when I tacked up Tinkerbell for Edith, and Jupiter for Lavinia, and they set off for a morning ride, I was happy to stay behind and putter in the yard.

There was one awkward moment when Harry stopped by on his way to school to give Thunder an apple. He asked how Alfred was feeling, but other than that, the satisfaction I got from manual labor lifted my spirits.

Edith had left a list of chores for me in the tack room that mostly involved cleaning tack and repairing New Zealand rugs. I thought back to the time I had dreamed of working with horses but Dad had said it just wasn't practical. He told me there was no money in it. How differently my life would have turned out!

Out of habit, I put the kettle on in the tack room to stop for a morning cup of coffee. Presumably the cracked mug and dried-up jar of Coffee-mate belonged to Alfred.

A knock at the tack room revealed Mrs. Cropper standing in the doorway wearing a dark blue raincoat. She'd swapped her mobcap for a matching headscarf that she had tied tightly under her chin. In her hand was a wicker basket. Instinctively, I looked at the size of her feet. Even though she was wearing galoshes, her feet were far smaller than mine. I had no idea if she owned a bicycle.

"I heard that Alfred was poorly," she said. "I always bring him some coffee and currant buns for elevenses but I thought you might like them instead."

"That's very kind of you." I gestured to the kettle on top of a makeshift cupboard. "I'll turn that off."

Mrs. Cropper set the basket on the sofa and brought out a thermos and Tupperware. The thermos was plaid—orange and black—and reminded me of when Mum used to make Dad a packed lunch for the office. He always got a thermos, too, and the coffee was never very hot.

"Sugar?" said Mrs. Cropper as she unscrewed the plastic cup and poured the milky liquid into it. The coffee looked weak but I didn't mind.

"No, thanks."

She removed the lid from the Tupperware. "Take as many currant buns as you like."

"Thank you," I said. "I'm starving. I only had a banana for breakfast."

Mrs. Cropper made no sign of leaving. She just stood there watching me eat her currant buns and drink her coffee—which was tepid, just as Dad's always was.

"How is Alfred this morning?" she said.

"I don't know," I answered truthfully. "I didn't see him."

"Probably a handful, if he's anything like my Seth when he's feeling poorly."

"I'm sure my mother knows how to manage him." Good answer, I thought to myself as I took a second currant bun. It was no wonder that my clothes were getting tight.

Still, Mrs. Cropper showed no sign of leaving.

"Did you want to sit down?" I said, gesturing to the sofa. "But sit at the far end. There are still a few springs in that bit."

"Thank you, but I won't, dear."

There was a silence. I knew she was bracing herself to say something and I started feeling a bit peculiar. "Is everything alright?"

Mrs. Cropper gave a heavy sigh. "I remember Alfred back in the old days, you know."

"Well, he is unforgettable," I said lightly.

"Alfred had a bit of a temper. He was always baiting the local lads to join him in the ring and then he would beat them to a pulp."

"Oh." I was taken aback. "To a pulp? Surely not, Mrs. C."

"And there was one person Alfred Bushman couldn't stand and that was Bryan Laney."

I had a horrible feeling that I knew where this conversation was going. "He didn't seem to be very popular with any of the men on the estate."

"What's that supposed to mean?" Mrs. Cropper demanded.

"I heard that you were quite a beauty, Mrs. C." Actually I hadn't but I could tell that she would have been a handsome woman. "I would expect any man would feel threatened by Bryan and his unwanted attentions."

Mrs. Cropper looked startled.

"Bryan definitely had his eye on you," I said with as big a

smile as I could muster. "Didn't you get one of the special heart-pendants?"

"Did Iris tell you that?" Mrs. Cropper exclaimed.

"I shouldn't worry. It seems that Bryan was handing out those pendants to everyone he fancied."

"But it was Iris he wanted." A peculiar expression crossed Mrs. Cropper's features. Was it jealousy? "Iris wasn't yet sixteen but he didn't care—and nor did she. Poor Joan."

"*Joan?* Joan Stark? What about Joan?"

"You leave Joan out of all this," said Mrs. Cropper hotly. "She's suffered enough. And Iris didn't care about her, either."

I regarded the elderly woman with curiosity and wondered why was she telling me all this.

"To be honest, Mrs. Cropper," I said. "Whatever you want to say about my mother, you should say to her directly—not to me. If you really must know, she thinks of you as a friend."

Mrs. Cropper turned pink. She seemed embarrassed but just said, "Have you finished your coffee? I've got to get on."

She took the Tupperware and slapped on the lid but not before I'd snatched the third currant bun. I returned the thermos.

"Thank you," I said. "That was delicious."

"If anyone is responsible for any of this, it's Alfred," Mrs. Cropper declared. "And I don't think for one minute that he's got a headache. He's run off. He knows he's been caught. He did Pandora in and Bryan, too. Those Bushmans were a bad lot," she went on. "You should all go away. Go back to where you came from."

Stunned, I watched Mrs. Cropper storm to the door. There was a cry of surprise.

"I'm so sorry," said a familiar voice. "Are you alright?"

I didn't hear Mrs. Cropper's response because I was in shock. David walked in.

Chapter Twenty-four

"Good heavens," he said. "I barely recognized you!"

"What are you doing here?" I said.

Suddenly all my insecurities came flooding back. I was aware of my dirty clothes, my hair clamped under the slumber net and no makeup. My fingers were grimy, nails unkempt and in my hand I was clutching a currant bun.

"A 'How are you?' would be nice." David took a step back and raked in my appearance. I took in his. Smart Florsheim shoes; casual sports coat under a Burberry raincoat. Even though his dark hair was streaked with silver, he was still impossibly handsome but impossibly shallow.

David pointed to the currant bun. "Country living seems to be giving you quite an appetite."

"And a Hawaiian honeymoon has definitely given you a tan," I retorted.

David looked pained. "Let's not go there, Katherine. Please?"

"If you are going anywhere, it's away from here," I said coldly. "Please leave."

"Fine. But you must know why I'm here."

"Nope. No idea." But of course I knew. It was exactly as

I had feared. David had found out about the Hollar drawings. Why else would he turn up?

"I knocked at the Carriage House but no one was there, so I drove up to the Hall and the butler—who reminded me of Anthony Hopkins from *The Remains of the Day*—"

"I'm sure Cropper would be flattered you thought so—"

"He told me I'd find you here." David took in the tack room. "No antique shop after all then?"

I just smiled. Let him think what he liked.

"Is there somewhere private we can talk?"

"I can't think of anything we need to talk about."

"Believe me, you do."

"Right here is fine. Please..." I gestured to the sofa. "Do sit down."

"On *that*?" David pulled a face. "I'm fine standing but first..." He turned away and closed the door. "I don't want us to be interrupted."

I was instantly aware of his charisma and suddenly felt vulnerable.

David pointed to my face. "I see you still wear the pearls."

My hands flew to my ears. They were my standard, everyday earrings and ones I never thought twice about putting on. I had completely forgotten that David had bought them for me. "Mikimoto, yes?" David said. "Remember when I bought them for you in Tokyo?"

I was furious. Angry. I wanted to throw something at him—a metal curry comb would do quite a bit of damage with its sharp edges—but instead, I calmly took both earrings out and gave them back.

David rolled his eyes. "You're being childish, Katherine. They were a gift and an expensive gift at that."

"And I've enjoyed wearing them," I said. "But I don't want them anymore."

David looked at the earrings in his hand. "You're upset. I understand."

"I'm rather busy so what exactly do you want?"

"You really don't want them?"

"No."

He shrugged and slipped the pearls into his pocket. "There was a robbery at Luxton's warehouse on Saturday night," he said. "Four paintings were stolen. Two were topographical drawings by an artist called Wenceslaus Hollar. Both were of Honeychurch Hall."

"Oh? Really," I said. "But surely, you should be talking to the dowager countess, not me." I tried to keep my voice steady but I was a terrible liar and he knew it. "You should talk to her—or Rupert."

David actually laughed. "Nice try, Katherine, but I know you too well. You're playing the ignorance card."

"I'm not playing anything."

David studied my face. "If only you weren't so beautiful."

"As you said to me a few minutes ago, don't go there." But I kept my voice even. "So let's not."

He stared at me in silence. I stared back.

"Look, I'm trying to help you," he said harshly. "Just because things didn't work out between us doesn't mean that I don't care."

"Work *out* between us?" I was astonished. "Work *out*?"

"You just couldn't wait," David said angrily. "You had to have it on your time schedule."

"You are unbelievable!" I cried, finally giving in to my fury. "How does renewing your vows fit into my time schedule?"

David had the grace to look embarrassed. "You can't begin to understand!" In two big strides he was beside me and grabbed my hands. "I'm trying to protect your reputation, you must know that."

I snatched my hands away and stepped back, only to collide with a saddle rack. "I hardly think my reputation matters given Saturday's *Daily Post* exposé! Let me think. What was the headline? 'Honeychurch House of Horrors'?"

"I had nothing to do with that," David protested. "In fact, I begged Trudy to leave you alone and she did. The article was written by that young reporter girl—Ginny something."

"And rewritten by your wife."

David shook his head vehemently. "No. Trudy wouldn't do that. It was one of the conditions I made about us getting back together."

"Wow! So I was a condition," I said. "I'm flattered."

"You can believe what you like," he snapped. "But I'm only trying to help."

I didn't know what to say. Did I believe that Ginny had lied? Possibly. Did I believe that Trudy had promised to keep her word to get David back? Yes. Absolutely.

"Kat," he said gently. "I know those drawings were on the watch list."

"Not sure I follow."

"Do I have to spell it out? The Hollar drawings were on the watch list from the robbery in 1990."

"Really?"

"Apparently, they were brought in and registered by Eric Pugsley," said David. "He signed them in. He lives on the estate. I wonder how he came to get them?"

"I wonder."

"They must have been here all the time."

"I wouldn't know."

David's face was flushed, a sure sign that he was getting angry. "What do you want me to do? They've been stolen for the second time—"

"Along with some other pieces of art," I pointed out. "Maybe they'll never be found."

"Maybe your Uncle Alfred may never be found, either."

"Maybe not," I said. "And then what?"

"Surveillance footage of the warehouse," said David. "CCTV. We'll be watching all points of entry naturally—airports, ports, train stations."

"Good idea."

A tick started to flicker in David's jaw. "Well, we'll need to interview the dowager countess of course—we'll have to tell her the paintings were already listed as stolen—along with the *Titanic* Steiff mourning bear and a whole other list of items, which I cannot quite recall at this precise moment."

"You wouldn't dare!" I exclaimed. "That would kill her. Leave Edith out of this."

"It would add to the series of Honeychurch scandals, I would think." David forced a sigh. "I'm just doing my job and you know I'm very, *very* good at doing my job."

"And I think you should allow us to do ours, sir."

Shawn flung open the door and strolled into the tack room.

Chapter Twenty-five

I wasn't sure whether I was pleased or horrified at Shawn's sudden appearance. I wondered how much he had heard. I didn't even know if Shawn was aware of the insurance scam—it had happened so long ago.

"Detective Inspector Shawn Cropper." Shawn stretched out his hand. I noticed a smudge of jam at the cuff. "And you are . . . ?"

"David Wynne," said David. "Art and Antiques Unit."

"So soon!" Shawn seemed impressed. "I only just heard half an hour ago that there might be items from the dowager countess's collection that had been among those stolen."

"There were," said David firmly.

"Very good of you to come here and help us out. In fact, we're honored!"

"My pleasure. Well—"

"But I can assure you, we are working closely with Newton Abbot," Shawn went on smoothly. "And naturally, if we need the help of a man as great as yourself, we will be in touch."

"Oh, I'm quite sure we will be in touch," said David pointedly.

Shawn reached into his pocket. "My business card. Feel free

to call any time." Then, to my astonishment, Shawn turned to me. "Sorry I got caught up. Is everything alright, darling?"

"Yes." I nodded. "David was just leaving."

David looked from me, then to Shawn. Shock registered on his face before he seemed to compose himself. "Ah. I see. Not quite your type Katherine but I'm happy for you. It didn't take you long."

"I think you should leave, sir," said Shawn curtly. "Unless you want to be arrested for trespassing on private property? I'm sure you saw the warning signs when you came in through the front gates?"

I saw a flash of sadness cross David's features but then it was gone. He turned to go but paused. "I never meant to hurt you, Kat," he said quietly. "I know you'll never believe me, but it was . . . just too difficult. All of it."

And with that, he vanished. I was exhausted and sank onto the sofa. I didn't even notice the lack of springs or the abundance of dog hairs. To my horror, I found my eyes were swimming with tears.

Shawn thrust a grubby handkerchief into my hand. "Sorry about the smell of bananas," he said.

I managed a smile. "Yes. I've noticed that a lot."

"My mother-in-law," he said ruefully. "She helps with the laundry and she buys this disgusting fabric softener with a fruity fragrance. The twins love it."

"Thank you," I said. "I'm alright. Really I am."

"Good." Shawn paused for a moment and then gently squeezed my shoulder. "What was all that about, Kat?"

"Nothing." And it was better to say absolutely *nothing*. With Alfred on the run, David chasing the drawings and the horrible conversation I'd had with his grandmother earlier on, the last person I wanted to confide in was a police officer.

But Shawn's boyish gallantry had touched my heart. "Thank you."

"For what?"

"For coming to my rescue."

"As you may or may not know the dowager countess's Hollar drawings were two of the items stolen." Shawn briskly changed the subject. "I hope her ladyship was insured. I know she was counting on selling them to repair the plasterwork ceiling."

So it seemed that Shawn didn't know about the scam in 1990. I wasn't sure if this was good news or bad.

"Newton Abbot is confident they'll be able to identify the perpetrator despite the fact that he was wearing a balaclava." Shawn studied my face. "Are you sure you don't have anything to tell me?"

"No. Why?"

"Your mother's MINI was found in Heathfield Business Park," said Shawn. "Very close to Luxton's warehouse. I don't believe in coincidences."

I couldn't look Shawn in the eye. I was almost certain that my own car would be seen on CCTV sooner or later. I hated lying to him but didn't know what else to do.

"How is Ginny?" I said. "Have you seen her yet?"

"Not to talk to," he said. "Roxy is staying with her for the moment just in case."

"You mean . . ." I was horrified. "You expect her attacker might come back?"

"We're not taking any chances," said Shawn.

"Roxy and Ginny are good friends, aren't they?"

At this, Shawn's expression hardened. "From childhood—like most of us around here. We'll be taking disciplinary action once this is all over."

Despite what Roxy had done, I felt sorry for her. She was a good policewoman.

"I think someone was spying on me last night." I went on to tell Shawn about the paint cans and the footprints in the mud.

Shawn looked concerned. "And you didn't think to call?"

"I couldn't get hold of you—"

"Did you leave a message?"

"I changed my mind. I thought I was imagining it but I asked Eric to come over. He felt it might have been someone casing the joint. All my stock is there."

"Just be careful, Kat." Shawn thought for a moment. "I would have said with the break-in at Luxton's warehouse there could be a gang going around."

I definitely wanted to steer clear of talking about Luxton's and changed the subject.

"Did you find out any more about Bryan's wife?" I asked.

"Yes. All very interesting," he said. "She was his fifth wife."

"Fifth!"

"They met at one of these treasure hunt meetings just five years ago. She's secretary of the Plymouth Detector Club; manages their Facebook page and all that sort of thing."

"But why on earth didn't Bryan say so?" I exclaimed. "Why all the secrecy?"

"I have no idea," said Shawn.

But I did.

Bryan still wanted to be seen as a lothario!

"And before you ask," Shawn went on. "Yes, Mrs. Laney has a firm alibi for Saturday night. She was giving a presentation on metal detectors at Torpoint Community College. It was posted on Facebook so she's in the clear."

"Did she say anything else?"

"Obviously, she was upset but not as much as I would have thought," said Shawn. "It sounded like he was a bit of a rogue. But she did mention the receipt book."

"The one in the Ziploc bag?"

"Apparently it has been in Bryan's family for centuries. He was worried that Rupert would insist it belonged to the Honeychurch Hall English Civil War collection."

"He had a good point," I said.

"It proved that one of Bryan's ancestors—a wealthy farmer in fact—gave the earl their silver to support the king but he was never paid back. Bryan believed part of the Honeychurch mint should belong to him."

I found that hard to believe and said so. "But that was centuries ago!"

"People don't forget, Kat," he said. "You're dealing with families who were born here and never left. Families listed in the *Domesday Book*. There's something else..."

I could tell by the tone of his voice that I might not like the something else.

"Mrs. Laney was convinced Bryan was seeing another woman—someone here."

I thought back to the cheap champagne, the two glasses in the sink and the Valentine's card. "But who?"

"Someone who still held a candle for him," said Shawn. "Not my grandmother, in case you were wondering."

"Nor my mother," I said. "Then who?"

Shawn frowned and stepped over to the window and took something off the ledge. "Aren't these your pearl earrings?"

David hadn't taken them after all.

"I noticed you weren't wearing them." Shawn dropped the earrings into my hand. I was about to say I didn't want them but then I began to wonder.

"The Valentine's card," I said slowly. "Bryan had given it—"

"Allegedly."

"*Allegedly*. So perhaps his visitor had given it back to *him* in a fit of pique." Just like I had given my earrings back to David. "And maybe . . . just maybe . . . the pendant necklace that you found in the shrubbery by the culvert could have been one that Bryan had given her, too."

"The attack had been particularly violent," said Shawn thoughtfully. "It felt personal."

"Believe me. I can understand how that could happen," I said as I thought of David.

An awkward silence fell between us.

"I actually came to find you this morning because I wanted you to know that her ladyship has found Pandora's thank you letter."

"I'm so relieved Edith came forward," I said. "So my mother is in the clear?"

"Not quite," said Shawn. "We need to match the handwriting in the letter to that in the flyleaf of *Lady Chatterley's Lover*. In fact, we'll be asking for samples of everyone's handwriting—"

"Everyone?"

"Well, those still living," said Shawn. "Like Alfred, for example."

"Alfred? Whatever for?"

"Just to eliminate him from our inquiries."

"That tired old line," I said, attempting a joke but deep down I was worried.

"They teach us those special phrases at the police academy." Shawn's face softened. "Kat, if you change your mind about anything, anything at all—call me."

"I know. I will." But I knew I wouldn't.

Chapter Twenty-six

"We have to find Alfred," I said to my mother at lunch-time. "Don't you have any idea where he's gone?"

We were sitting in the kitchen eating a ham and cheese sandwich, or rather I was. Mum seemed to have lost her appetite. She looked pale and drawn.

"Of course I don't," Mum snapped. "And anyway, I daren't leave the house. What if her ladyship comes back with grapes or something?"

"She just might."

"Oh, Katherine, what if... what if Alfred has gone? You know, *really* gone. Done a runner?"

It was exactly what I had been dreading. I hadn't been sure whether to tell Mum about David's appearance but in the end I thought she would welcome the distraction.

Mum's jaw dropped. "How gallant of Shawn," she enthused. "He can be so pompous but... well, I am surprised."

"It was very sweet of him," I said.

"He actually brought my MINI back this morning," said Mum. "When I saw him standing at the door I almost had a heart attack."

"That's the voice of a guilty conscience," I teased.

"Are you alright about it all now?"

"About what?"

"About *David*."

"Yes. I'm completely over it," I said and I was. "But we will have a problem. David is on the warpath. He knows about the drawings."

"How silly of Eric to sign his name when he dropped them off," Mum said with scorn. "He left a paper trail."

"It was hardly Eric's fault."

"Oh. My. God." Mum put her head in her hands. "We're ruined—but wait—perhaps it's better if Alfred doesn't come back at all."

"I think it would be for the best," I said. "Shawn wants to see samples of everyone's handwriting so he can compare the thank you letter and the signature in *Lady Chatterley's Lover*."

"Fine. I've nothing to hide."

"Shawn said something else." I told Mum about the fifth Mrs. Laney. "Apparently they were keen treasure hunters."

"What a cheek!" she fumed. "Bryan invited me back to his camper van for a tot of rum, you know."

"You didn't mention that bit."

"I said no."

"Was this before you hit him?"

"Yes."

"Wait—he asked you for a tot of rum. Not a glass of champagne?"

"Bryan? Champagne? No. Why?"

"Does Mrs. Cropper drink champagne?"

"I have no idea."

"She came to see me this morning in the tack room," I said. "But I don't want you to get angry. I'm just the messenger."

As I filled her in on Mrs. Cropper's views on Alfred's temper,

Mum got angrier and angrier. "The nerve! And she said she was my friend!"

"I don't think she is any friend of yours," I said. "But I do think she is hiding something. "I brought up Joan Stark and Mrs. Cropper got very defensive. Said to leave Joan out of it and that she'd suffered enough."

"Right. Let's go and pay Joan a visit," said Mum.

"I think Bryan went to see her on Saturday," I said.

"And look where that got him? Dead as a doornail." Mum shook her head with frustration.

"Personally, I think it's a waste of time. And besides, we daren't leave the Carriage House in case Edith comes."

"Rubbish. I'm not waiting around here. I'll write a note on the door. You don't have to come with me, but I'm going."

Chapter Twenty-seven

Mum duly scribbled three notes that said, *Alfred is sleeping and not to be disturbed,* one for the front door, one for the door in the carriageway and one that led directly from Cromwell Meadows to the kitchen. "I think we've covered all our bases."

Twenty minutes later we turned into the entrance to Sunny Hill Lodge and sped up a very grand drive lined with deciduous shrubs.

I don't know what I had been expecting but it definitely wasn't this.

Sunny Hill Lodge was a gracious Georgian house with large bay windows, a portico and exquisitely manicured grounds. A pergola, which would be blooming with wisteria in the spring, stretched the length of one wing.

Mum pulled up outside the portico entrance with its perfectly clipped boxwood topiaries that flanked the front entrance. A line of luxury cars—Lexus, BMW, Range Rover— were parked on the far side of the gravel where there was a spectacular view of Dartmoor.

"Good grief," said Mum. "How on earth can Joan afford all this?"

"Good question," I said.

"You don't think her ladyship is contributing to Joan's living accommodations, do you?"

"Another good question."

We mounted the stone steps and walked into a small vestibule. A glass door showed the hall beyond. It was lavishly decorated. I mentally calculated the value of the antique furniture, paintings and rugs. They must have cost thousands and thousands of pounds.

Mum tried the handle but the door was locked. I pointed to the bell and a panel of buttons. "It's a secure facility."

Mum hit the buzzer.

A young woman who couldn't be more than twenty-five emerged from a side door. She was dressed in a tailored suit and waved a greeting.

"I have to put in the code," she said through the glass door and tapped a sequence with perfectly manicured nails. There was a loud click and the door swung open.

"Welcome to Sunny Hill." She beamed.

Mum and I stepped inside. Classical music played quietly in the background and there was a pleasant smell of lavender.

"What a lovely place," said Mum.

"Yes. It is, isn't it?" She smiled. "I'm Carla. Have you come to visit a resident?"

"Joan Stark," said Mum.

Carla frowned. "Stark? Let me find the manager for you," she said. "Who shall I say is visiting?"

"I'm Iris Stanford—although Joan would remember me as Bushman—"

"If she does remember . . ." I said. "Which she might not."

"And of course," said Mum grandly. "I'm sure you recognize Kat Stanford."

Carla smiled politely. Clearly she did not and that was

hardly surprising. I must have looked a terrible sight. I'd not thought to change my clothes after my morning at the stables. I hadn't even put on a slash of lipstick. All I'd done was remove my slumber net and tied my hair back into a thick ponytail.

"She doesn't always look so awful," said Mum.

Carla gave another polite smile. "Please wait here," she said and disappeared through a door marked OFFICE.

"I wonder where the residents are?" said Mum in a whisper. "They probably keep them out of the way."

We stood in the hall for what seemed like ages. Mum checked her watch at least three times. "What are they *doing?*" she grumbled.

Finally, another elegantly dressed woman emerged from the office. She was in her late fifties with short gray hair and reminded me of my old math teacher at school.

"I'm Margery Rook. Oh! Goodness!" The manager clutched her throat in surprise and turned pink. "Aren't you Kat Stanford from *Fakes and Treasures?*"

"Yes. I am."

"Goodness, a celebrity." She turned on Carla who had followed her out. "Why on earth didn't you tell me?" she scolded. "This is Kat Stanford, Carla."

"Sorry, Mrs. Rook." But Carla still hadn't a clue who I was nor did she seem to care.

"I am so sorry," gushed Mrs. Rook. "And to have kept you waiting out here for all this time! Please, follow me and do call me Margery. Carla—ask cook to make us some tea and bring a selection of cakes—whatever the residents are having today. Naturally."

"Yes, Mrs. Rook."

As we walked along the thick carpet, Mrs. Rook regarded Mum keenly. "Are you considering Sunny Hill Lodge?"

"Me?" Mum seemed horrified. "My mind is as sharp as a tack, thank you very much."

Mrs. Rook shot me a sympathetic look. "Of course it is, dear. Of course it is."

I stifled a smile.

"It's always a good idea to put your name down ahead of time," Mrs. Rook went on. "We have a two-year waiting list."

"I expect it moves quite quickly," Mum said dryly.

"Actually, no," said Mrs. Rook. "Some of our residents are in their nineties. They adore it here." The manager threw open the office door. "Please. After you."

We stepped into a luxuriously furnished office overlooking a formal rose garden. I could imagine that in the summer, the air would be filled with their scent.

"Do sit down." Mrs. Rook perched on the edge of a pretty armchair covered in a pink-and-white-striped Regency fabric. Mum and I took the pink sofa and sank into a sea of feather cushions and pillows.

"How much does it cost to live here?" Mum asked bluntly.

"We cater to the upper levels of society," said Mrs. Rook carefully. "We do offer payment plans, naturally, but very few of our guests feel the need to."

How on earth had Joan or Edith—if she was supporting her—managed to afford to live here for so many years?

"I hope you don't think this forward of me, Kat—I hope I can call you Kat?" Mrs. Rook said in a fawning voice. "But every summer we have a charity fund-raiser. It's a black tie dinner—that kind of thing. I wondered if you might consider being our toastmaster?"

"Kat would love to," Mum said. "Wouldn't you?"

I really did not want to. Ask me anything you like about

an antique and I can tell you but being a witty toastmaster was not one of my fortes. "I'll need to check my schedule."

"Wonderful!" Mrs. Rook smoothed her skirt down over her knees. She cleared her throat. "What relation did you say you were to Joan Stark?"

"Friends," said Mum. "I've known Joan since we were teenagers."

"I see. Just friends."

"We understand that she has advanced Alzheimer's," I put in. "So I'm quite sure that she won't recognize my mother."

Mrs. Rook bit her lip. "I really don't know how to tell you this."

"Is she dead?" Mum demanded.

"I knew this day would come," Mrs. Rook said quietly. "The thing is, there is no Joan Stark living here. There never was."

Chapter Twenty-eight

"But . . . but . . . that's not possible," said Mum.

"I can assure you we have not broken any laws," said Mrs. Rook hastily.

"Laws?" Mum and I exchanged puzzled looks.

"She's been a mystery to us, as well."

"But we were told she's been living here for years," Mum exclaimed.

There was a knock on the door and a woman in her sixties, dressed in a smart black-and-white uniform, appeared bearing a silver tray of bone china teacups and saucers and a plate of delicious-looking homemade cakes.

"Ah, here is Brown. Just put the tray down on the table. Carla will pour."

"Very good, m'lady," said Brown and did so. She made the slightest of curtseys and exited the room as Carla returned.

"The residents like the idea of staff," Mrs. Rook said. "It makes them feel at home."

Mrs. Rook waited until Carla had set out the tea tray and poured three cups.

"I think I could do with something stronger," Mum muttered. For once, I agreed.

"On Saturday a man came looking for Joan, too," said Mrs. Rook. "Carla—what was the name of the gentleman?"

Carla frowned. "I think it was...Bill, Bob...?"

"Bryan Laney?" I said.

"That's right," Carla said. "He seemed very nervous. He had even brought flowers. It was rather sweet actually."

"What did he say when you told him there was no Joan Stark living here?" I asked.

"He asked if she might have been registered under another name..."

"This an exclusive facility," Mrs. Rook chimed in. "We know all our residents. We would have known if Joan Stark had had another name. I told him that."

"He did say it was too posh for Joan," Carla went on. "And then he asked if there were other residential homes. I gave him a list—there are three in the South Hams—and off he went."

"It doesn't seem Joan's kind of place." Mum nodded thoughtfully. "Perhaps we made a mistake, too, and she is somewhere else?"

"I don't know, Mum." I recalled the care parcels that Muriel in the post office used to give Vera to take to her mother and I distinctly remembered how Alfred's predecessor would visit Sunny Hill Lodge every Friday. Mum and I used to joke about it.

"Do you remember a William Bushman?" said Mum.

"William?" Mrs. Rook said sharply. "Of course!"

"So he *did* come here?" I was confused. "Why would William come here if Joan wasn't here? What aren't you telling us?"

"You can leave, Carla," said Mrs. Rook quickly. "Thank you."

"Very good, Mrs. Rook." And Carla...left.

Mum and I sat patiently whilst Mrs. Rook's face underwent a series of expressions ranging from confusion to fear.

"Alright," she said. "And you say you're friends? Not family members?"

"Yes. Friends. What is going on?" Mum demanded. "Is Joan alright?"

"I don't know," said Mrs. Rook. "I've never met her. I don't even know if she's still alive."

Mum and I exchanged looks of astonishment.

"I can assure you that no one has broken any laws," Mrs. Rook said again.

"So you keep saying," said Mum.

"I don't know when William started bringing the care parcels," she said. "It was during Mrs. Nash's—that was my predecessor—time. She passed away four years ago."

"I'm stunned," I said to Mum. "Do you think William was in on it?"

"But why? What could he possibly gain?" said Mum. "It makes no sense."

"William was very popular with the residents," Mrs. Rook went on. "He always came on Friday for bingo. He was the caller, of course. Then one day, he didn't show up and we never heard from him again."

"But why would he do that?" I said again.

"We didn't think to question why," said Mrs. Rook. "We were just happy that he wanted to spend time with the residents. As I say—we've done nothing wrong. Nothing at all."

"But didn't you think to tell William there was no Joan Stark here?"

"I don't know what Mrs. Nash told him," said Mrs. Rook. "All I know is that Mrs. Nash said that the care parcels were to be distributed among the residents."

"I find that hard to believe," said Mum coldly. "Didn't it ever cross your mind to trace the packages? To find out where the real Joan Stark could be?"

"We assumed she must have died." Mrs. Rook reddened. "It was just magazines and chocolates. Sometimes some lovely French soap. I honestly don't know what all the fuss is about."

Mum got up. "We're going."

Mrs. Rook leapt to her feet, clearly flustered. "You're not going to tell Mr. Pelham-Burns, are you?"

"It depends," Mum said.

"Who is Mr. Pelham-Burns?" I asked.

"He's the chairman of the board," said Mrs. Rook, looking decidedly nervous.

"Of course not," I said.

"And we can count on you for our fund-raiser?"

"I need to check my calendar," I said. "But I'll be in touch."

Mum was already out the door.

"You need a code!" Mrs. Rook shouted.

I caught Mum up at the front door banging numbers at random on the security panel.

Carla materialized behind us and calmly said, "Allow me." There was a loud buzz and Mum took off across the car park like some wild animal freed from a cage.

She didn't speak until we were halfway down the drive.

"That wretched Mrs. Cropper," Mum snarled as she put her foot to the pedal. "She knows. She knows all about Joan. She has to."

"But why? I just don't understand why anyone would create such a lie. I mean—did poor Vera not know the truth about her mother?"

"That's what we're going to find out."

"Eric must know something, too," I said. "They all grew up together."

"So Eric was in on it as well," said Mum with disgust. "After all, Joan is his mother-in-law."

"No, I don't think so," I said. "He told me that Bryan asked where she lived and Eric told him Sunny Hill Lodge. He would hardly have told him that if she didn't."

"Unless he was throwing you off the scent."

Mum had a point.

"We're outsiders, Katherine," said Mum grimly. "Why should we be told anything that doesn't concern us?"

"So who do you think broke the news to Joan about her daughter's death?" I said.

"Remember Vera's funeral?" Mum said. "We never gave it a second thought that Joan wasn't there."

"But where is Joan now?" I wondered. "I mean—where does she live? She can't be local otherwise people would know, wouldn't they?"

"I bet she was the one who attacked Bryan," said Mum.

"But how would she know that Bryan was back in the neighborhood?"

"That wretched Mrs. Cropper," Mum said. "I bet she told her."

"What shall we do?" I said.

"I'm going to have a talk with my friend *Peggy*, that's what I'm going to do."

Chapter Twenty-nine

Mrs. Cropper was rolling out pastry on the kitchen table as Mum burst into the room.

"We've just been to Sunny Hill Lodge, *Peggy*," she declared.

All the color drained out of Mrs. Cropper's face. "Oh," she whispered.

"Just what on earth is going on?" Mum cried. "Does her ladyship know about Joan Stark?"

"No, no!" Mrs. Cropper clutched at her throat in genuine terror. "Please don't tell her."

"That depends on your explanation," said Mum coldly.

Mrs. Cropper's expression was one of abject misery. "Seth and I tried to keep it quiet. We really did." She looked over at the kitchen door. "Harry will be back from school any minute."

"I'll close it," I said and did so. "Why don't we all sit down and have a cup of tea?"

"I think I might need something stronger," Mrs. Cropper whispered. "There's some sloe gin in the pantry."

"I'll get it," I said and did that, too.

Mum gestured for Mrs. Cropper to sit down. I poured three glasses of sloe gin.

Mrs. Cropper knocked back her glass in one go. She took a deep breath. "Joan never had Alzheimer's."

"Clearly. That much we know," said Mum.

"Vera was my niece," said Mrs. Cropper. "I just wanted to protect her, that's all."

"That's quite a spectacular story," I pointed out. "I would be devastated if I had been Vera."

"It started out as such a small white lie," Mrs. Cropper went on.

I looked at Mum pointedly. "As lies often do."

"Joan was evil. She was a horrible person and a horrible mother," Mrs. Cropper said passionately. "She caused endless grief to her ladyship."

"Like what?" Mum demanded.

"You wouldn't know what she was really like just visiting the Hall in the summer months," said Mrs. Cropper. "But she flung herself at every man to make Bryan jealous—even her ladyship's brother, Lord Rupert. That was the last straw."

"So why would you tell Joan that Bryan Laney had come back to Little Dipperton?" I asked.

Mrs. Cropper gasped. "I did no such thing."

"You must have done!" Mum declared. "The phone call that morning in your kitchen. It was a hang-up. Someone asking for Bryan Laney and demanding to know my name."

Mrs. Cropper bristled with indignation. "Yes. It's true. She did call me but I did not tell her about Bryan being here. I would never do that."

"Well, how did she find out?" Mum demanded.

"Joan told me she saw it on Facebook."

"Facebook!" Mum and I chorused.

"She said something about liking some treasure hunting

club page," said Mrs. Cropper. "I wouldn't know. I don't like Facebook. Everyone knowing everyone's business."

"How would you know?" said Mum. "There's no Internet here and you don't have a computer."

"So?" Mrs. Cropper sneered. "Nor do you!"

The two women were acting like children.

"Did you know that Bryan was married?" I asked Mrs. Cropper.

Her jaw dropped. "No!"

"It's his fifth wife," Mum declared.

"Fifth!" Mrs. Cropper exclaimed. "Does Joan know?"

"How would we know if Joan knows," said Mum. "So you *are* in touch with her? Was it *you* who started the rumor about her Alzheimer's?"

"Alright. I'll tell you everything." Mrs. Cropper seemed defeated. "To be honest, it's a relief."

We sat down at the table.

"When Bryan joined the Navy—that would have been the same summer as the Pandora business—Joan was gutted." Mrs. Cropper gave a heavy sigh. "You see, after the ball, they'd run off together but a week later, she was back home. She said that Bryan was going off to sea to make a lot of money and that he'd come back for her. Of course, we all knew what a cad he was but Joan refused to believe us. He'd come home on leave; they'd have a bit of a fling and then he'd go off again for another nine months or so—always keeping her dangling. I told her to forget him but she said she'd had her fortune told and that he was the one for her."

"How silly," Mum said with scorn.

"*You* told Joan her fortune, Iris," said Mrs. Cropper. "Madame Z's Psychic Touch! It was you who said he only had eyes for her."

"But no one believes all that nonsense," Mum protested. "Good grief. How old was she, twentysomething?"

Mrs. Cropper regarded my mother with utter dislike.

"But didn't she get married?" I said. "She had Vera, after all."

"Married my brother," said Mrs. Cropper. "Always running off to meet Bryan when his ship came to port. She as good as killed him. Broke his heart, she did. Abandoned her own daughter. Poor Vera. We brought her up as best we could."

"But didn't Vera want to know what happened to her mother?" I said. "I know I would."

"That's gratifying," Mum muttered.

"But, Alzheimer's!" I was truly astonished "What about the care parcels? Was that your idea to keep up this disgusting pretense?"

"It was Muriel's at the post office," said Mrs. Cropper, who had the grace to look embarrassed. "I just gave them to William."

"And he never said anything?"

"It's none of your business!" Mrs. Cropper was defiant. "I just tried to protect Vera and now she's gone. It doesn't matter anymore, does it? No one need know. No harm done."

"But there is harm done," I exclaimed. "Especially if Joan killed Bryan—"

"I bet she found out he was married and snapped," said Mum.

"What about Pandora, though?" I said.

"Joan wouldn't have known about the double-hide," Mrs. Cropper insisted.

"She would if you are right in saying she had a fling with Edith's brother," I said. "Maybe he told her where the double-hide was?"

"If anyone wanted to hurt Pandora it was you, Iris,"

Mrs. Cropper said. "Everyone knew how angry you were about Pandora wearing your Egyptian costume."

"I was. And I don't deny it."

The two women glowered at each other until Mum said, "Joan did it. I'm sure of it—and she tried to frame me by forging my signature in that book."

"What's all this talk about forgery?" Lavinia strolled into the kitchen with Harry, who was sporting a black eye.

"Oh Harry!" I exclaimed. "What happened?"

Harry grinned. "You should see the other chap, Stanford!"

"Harry has been fighting!" Lavinia fumed. "We've been summoned to the headmaster's office first thing tomorrow morning. When Rupert finds out he is going to be *livid*."

Harry put up his fists and did a quick left-right hook. "Alfred was right. He said they'd be cowards. You should have seen how they scarpered when Max went down."

"You hit Max!" I gasped.

"That lad had it coming," said Mrs. Cropper. "Good for you."

"Alfred is an excellent teacher," Mum chimed in.

"Where is Alfred?" Lavinia went on. "Surely he can't *still* have a headache?"

"It's a migraine, m'lady," said Mum, reverting to her old way of greeting Lavinia. For a brief time they'd been on first-name terms but not anymore. "Still clinging onto life by a thread."

"Well call a doctor for heaven's sake. Cropper will do it—Cropper!" Lavinia yelled.

"There's no need for that," said Mum.

Cropper glided silently into the kitchen. "Here, m'lady."

"Cropper, call Dr. Smeaton," said Lavinia. "Tell him it's urgent and we need him to make a house call right away."

"Oh, surely, not," Mum protested. "Alfred will be as right as rain tomorrow. He just had a chill."

"I thought he had a migraine?"

"It turned into a chill," said Mum quickly. "And besides, Katherine's very happy to help with the horses. She loves it, don't you, Katherine?"

"Yes, I'm helping with the horses and I love it."

"When I tell Alfred about what happened with Max, I bet he'll feel better!" Harry chimed in. "A chap has to teach another chap a lesson—Ouch!"

Lavinia had cuffed Harry around the ear.

"You'll do no such thing. In fact, you can go straight to your room without your milk and cake today, young man."

Harry kept grinning. He seemed to be wearing his black eye as a badge of honor. Lavinia grabbed him by the elbow and roughly steered him out of the kitchen. Harry shot a parting grin over his shoulder. I gave him a military salute.

"The doctor can come tomorrow morning, m'lady," we heard Cropper say. "His wife said he is attending a home birth this evening."

I couldn't make out Lavinia's reply other than "maddening."

The four of us stood in the kitchen.

Cropper looked to Mrs. Cropper with a frown.

"They know about Joan," she said flatly.

He nodded. "Ah."

"And don't say I-told-you-so," Mrs. Cropper said.

Cropper gave her a nod but didn't say a word.

"We should tell Shawn," I said.

"But not her ladyship?" said Mrs. Cropper. "Please don't tell her ladyship."

"I think Shawn should make that decision," I said. "Come on, Mum."

We left the kitchen and headed back to the car. "Where to now?"

"Eric," said Mum. "Maybe he knows where Joan lives."

"Let's stay out of it," I said.

"Suit yourself, but I'm going."

Chapter Thirty

We found Eric watching the hydraulic press slowly squeeze what life was left in his end-of-life vehicles until they were as flat as pancakes. He cut a lonely figure and I thought that out of all the people I'd met at the Hall, Eric seemed to be the one who had surprised me the most. Mum had disliked him from the start but the more I got to know him, the more I realized he had a good heart.

"I wonder if that car crusher could do something for Eric's eyebrows," said Mum. "You know—flatten them out."

The moment Eric saw us coming he stopped the machine and waited for us to pick our way through the mounds of tires and various pieces of discarded machinery. I thought of the tire iron that was used to kill Bryan. Eric's scrapyard wasn't far from where Bryan's camper van had been parked.

"We've come to talk about your mother-in-law, Joan," said Mum bluntly.

"What about her?"

"We know she doesn't have Alzheimer's," Mum declared.

"You don't know what you're talking about," said Eric. "She's up at the care home, Sunny Hill Lodge."

"Have you ever been there?" Mum said.

Eric bristled. "Why?"

"Have you?" Mum insisted.

"It's no business of yours." He scowled. "Let things be."

"So you were in on the lie," Mum said.

"You don't know the half of it," Eric said. "Joan would write to Vera, always asking for money. I never showed Vera the letters. Always the hard-luck story and then she'd disappear again—meet some man or other."

I could see Eric's point but even so, surely that would have been something that Vera should have decided for herself.

"Did you keep her letters?" Mum said suddenly.

"I hid them." Eric gestured to a stack of flattened cars at the far end of the row. "They're probably still in there. I had to hide stuff. Vera was always suspicious. Always thinking I was having an affair."

"Why did you keep them?"

Eric looked uncomfortable. "I kept meaning to tell Vera. You know, one day, like. But—then she died." He regarded us with suspicion. "Why do you want to see them?"

"I think Joan was the one who forged Pandora's thank you letter to her ladyship," I said. "We want to compare the writing."

"Then, that's a matter for Shawn to decide, not you."

"Why?" Mum demanded.

"It's none of your business, that's why." Eric thrust out his jaw. "It's private."

"It is my business!"

"Okay, we understand," I said soothingly. "But will you at least show Shawn Joan's letters?"

"No, I will not," said Eric. "It's best to let things be. What good would it do now?"

"Because we think Joan killed Bryan in a crime of passion,"

said Mum. "Bludgeoned him to death with one of *your* tire irons—in case you've forgotten."

Eric just blinked.

"And she may have kidnapped Ginny..."

"Don't be so bloody daft," Eric exclaimed. "Joan's in her seventies! You really think she bundled Ginny into the back of her own car?"

Mum stood her ground. "Joan must have given you her address."

"Iris..." Eric sounded exasperated. "Let it go."

"At least tell us where she lives?" I said.

"She's got a place in Paignton. Affordable housing. That kind of thing. That's all I know."

Eric switched on the car crusher engine. The noise ended all further conversation.

Mum and I tramped back to the Carriage House. "Eric could be right—at least about Ginny's abduction. We must tell Shawn," I said for the umpteenth time. "Oh—speak of the Devil."

Shawn's panda was parked in the courtyard. He and Roxy emerged from the carriageway.

"Ah, there you are," said Shawn. "We'd like a quick word with you, Mrs. Stanford."

"Good, because we'd like a quick word with you, wouldn't we, Kat?"

I nodded. "We've discovered that Joan Stark has never had Alzheimer's nor does she live at Sunny Hill Lodge."

"How do you know that?" Roxy exclaimed.

"I wish you would let the police do their job," said Shawn crossly.

"Why don't we go inside and put the kettle on," I suggested.

"Did *you* know that your grandmother has been covering for Joan?" Mum demanded.

Shawn's expression was hard to read. "No, to tea, Kat. But thank you."

"We'd like to talk to *you*, Mrs. Stanford, down at the station," said Roxy.

Mum's jaw dropped. "Whatever for?"

"Newton Abbot has come through with their surveillance tape," said Roxy with obvious relish. "You were seen getting out of your car at Heathfield Business Park."

"That wasn't me!" Mum said hotly. "I told you, my car was stolen by joyriders!"

"A bit odd for one person to be joyriding on his own," said Roxy. "Usually they run in packs."

"I wouldn't know," said Mum wearily. "And besides, how can you possibly think it was me in that balaclava?"

Roxy shot Shawn a look of triumph. "We didn't mention anything about a balaclava."

"The same person was seen exiting Luxton's warehouse carrying four large objects that looked very much like boxed-up works of art."

My heart started to thump as I wondered if my car had been spotted, too.

Shawn stroked his chin thoughtfully. "Mrs. Stanford may be right, Roxy. Although the person of interest that we spotted seemed a female, perhaps it was a male of similar build."

Roxy nodded. "Is Alfred Bushman here?"

"He's ill," said Mum quickly.

"We were told he was recuperating at the Carriage House," Roxy said suspiciously. "What's wrong with him?"

"A headache—a migraine—a chill! I don't know," said

Mum with rising hysteria. "Does it matter what's wrong with him? He's just not well!"

"And where is *your* car, Ms. Stanford?" Shawn looked around the interior of the carriageway in mock disbelief. "I see it's not here! I do hope it hasn't been stolen."

I felt I was part of a Victorian farce. I caught Mum's frantic appeal for help.

"I left it at Jane's Cottage." I couldn't believe I had actually lied to a police officer.

"We'll need to take your fingerprints, Mrs. Stanford," said Roxy.

"Of course my fingerprints are going to be in the MINI." Mum rolled her eyes. "It's my car! And Alfred's will be on there, too—oh!" I could almost hear what was going through my mother's mind. The last thing she wanted was for the police to run Alfred's fingerprints. They would discover that his rap sheet was practically a mile long.

"On second thoughts, Officers. I'm very happy to accompany you to the station," said Mum meekly. "Katherine, there is some homemade chicken soup on the Aga for Alfred." She flashed a smile at Shawn. "It really helps with his migraines."

"Do I need to remind you that perverting the course of justice is a criminal offense?" said Shawn sternly.

"You do not need to remind me," Mum declared. "But surely, you should be out catching Bryan's killer instead of wasting your time over a robbery."

"We think the two crimes are connected," said Roxy.

"But—that's ridiculous!" Mum exclaimed.

"Yep. And Pandora Haslam-Grimley, too," Roxy said. "And believe me, this time it's not going to get swept under the carpet."

"You're talking to the wrong person," said Mum, nervous. "Joan Stark—she's the culprit."

"We know all about Joan, thank you," said Shawn. "Gran told me everything."

And with that, he looked at my mother and simply said, "Shall we go?"

As Shawn's panda drove away with Mum in the back, I had an unnerving sense of déjà vu.

Mum had been arrested again—but this time, I had a horrible feeling that she was protecting Alfred. Not just from the Luxton's warehouse break-in, but from Pandora's death, too. Perhaps Edith's thank you letter had contained incriminating clues, after all.

But where did that leave Bryan?

If the Valentine's card in the camper van and the necklace left by the culvert were Joan's—was that proof enough that she killed him?

And then there was Ginny. On a whim, I called Totnes Hospital but I was told she was unable to accept any phone calls and there were no visitors until Wednesday.

Ginny's abduction seemed so strange. Was it really an attempt to end her life or just a warning? Did Ginny really have inside information on decades of Honeychurch scandals? What could she possibly know that would drive someone to do such a thing?

Back in the kitchen I fixed myself a large gin and tonic.

Mum's story—*The American Heiress*—was on the top of the counter. I picked it up and took another look. Now that I knew that Mum had attempted the Derbyshire dialect from *Lady Chatterley's Lover*, it was easier to understand—especially if I read the words aloud.

It was very simply written and taken from the perspective

of a young servant girl at the Hall. At first, I assumed that since
Edith was Lady Honeychurch and she had had an affair with
the gamekeeper, the story must be about her. After all, that had
been the basis for *Forbidden*, the second in my mother's hugely
successful Star-Crossed Lovers series. But when I looked more
closely, it was obvious that this was about Pandora. It was written as part-diary, part-fantasy and mixed up with passages
Mum had copied from *Lady Chatterley's Lover.*

Then, I managed to decipher the most interesting bit.
Pandora—who was called Pansy in this story, struck a young
servant girl called Jean with her riding whip. To add insult to
injury, Pansy had brazenly flirted with Jean's beau. In despair,
Jean sought help from a traveling gypsy who predicted that
Pansy would soon disappear. It didn't take a brain surgeon to
realize that Jean had to be Joan.

The phone rang. Eagerly, I snatched it up hoping it was
Mum but it was David. The minute he recognized my voice
he said, "Don't hang up, Kat."

"What do you want?"

"I wanted to let you know that the Hollar paintings are officially on the Art and Antiques Unit watch list. I didn't want
this to happen. I was hoping you could have told me what was
going on . . ."

"Honestly, David," I said. "I have no idea what is going on.
Just do what you have to do."

"You're making a mistake—"

But I had already put the phone down. I made a silent plea
to Alfred, to please get rid of those stupid paintings, but the
phone rang again.

"Please don't call me anymore," I said.

"Oh, Iris!"

"Mrs. Cropper?"

"It is you, isn't it?" she said urgently. "You must come quickly."

"It's Kat, Mrs. Cropper," I said. "Are you alright? Whatever is wrong?"

"It's her ladyship." There was a pause as Mrs. Cropper struggled to compose her distress. "She's fallen."

"Is she hurt?" I said.

"Cropper is calling for an ambulance," said Mrs. Cropper. "His lordship and Lady Lavinia are with her now but she specifically asked for you."

"Mum's not here—"

"Iris, come to the King's Parlor," Mrs. Cropper urged. "Through the Tudor courtyard. You know the way."

And with that, Mrs. Cropper disconnected the line.

I scribbled a quick note to Mum and left it on the kitchen table. I couldn't imagine her being stuck at Newton Abbot all night, but Newton Abbot was not the little satellite police station where everyone goes home at five.

It was only as I dragged on my coat and raced to the Hall that I realized in all Mrs. Cropper's panic, she had called me Iris.

Chapter Thirty-one

I took Mum's MINI and left it parked behind the servants' quarters. Grabbing an umbrella, I hurried around the side of the building.

I didn't think twice about the side door to the Tudor wing being open but when I reached the Great Hall and found it deserted, I felt a prickle of unease.

The door to the King's Parlor stood ajar but I couldn't hear any voices.

Don't be ridiculous, Kat, I told myself. Although the short trip from the Carriage House to the Great Hall couldn't have been more than five minutes, maybe they hadn't waited for an ambulance and just taken Edith straight to the hospital.

"Mrs. Cropper?" I called out. "Are you there?"

There was no reply. I took out my phone and was about to dial the Hall when my heart skipped a beat.

A figure in a yellow sou'wester cape stepped out of the shadows. She was holding a twelve-bore shotgun.

I was startled by how much Joan looked like her daughter Vera. The same pinched face; the same mean look.

Joan was just a few years older than my mother but the years had not been kind to her. She was rail thin and with her long white hair hanging loose to her shoulders and a wild look in her eyes, she looked insane. I knew I had to keep calm.

I threw my hands up in surrender. "Please don't hurt me!" It wasn't difficult to pretend to be terrified. I was.

"You're not Iris." For a moment, Joan looked confused. "Who are you?"

"I'm Kat Stanford," I said, desperately trying to steady my nerves. "I'm on TV." I had no idea why that thought came into my head. "You've probably seen me there."

"On the telly?"

"That's right," I said. "I used to have an antiques show called *Fakes and Treasures*. Have you ever seen it?"

Joan thought for a moment. "You're Rapunzel."

"That's right." I gestured to my unruly hair. "You wouldn't think it, would you?"

Joan continued to stare at me. She didn't lower the shotgun. "Where is Iris?"

"Iris? I don't know an Iris." I gave what I hoped was a friendly smile. "Actually, I was looking for Mrs. Cropper. Is she here?"

No answer.

"She's your friend, isn't she?" I said.

"Peggy's no friend of mine," said Joan coldly. "She's been spreading lies."

"I've not lived in Little Dipperton for very long so I wouldn't know."

"Peggy liked to pretend she was on my side," Joan went on. "She took my own daughter away from me, you know. Poisoned her against me by spreading lies."

"That's terrible."

"I never got a chance to say good-bye to my Vera!" Joan gripped the shotgun even tighter. "She died. My daughter died."

"That's awful, I am so sorry."

"Where's Iris?" Joan asked again.

"I don't know an Iris," I said again.

"She was with the travelers," said Joan. "Flaunting herself in front of my Bryan every summer. Poisoning him against me."

Bryan. Joan had actually said his name.

"What did this Iris do?" I asked but I could tell that Joan was lost in her own world.

"Madame Z's Psychic Touch. What a load of rubbish."

I had to find some common ground.

"I went to a fortune teller once." Actually, I had never been to one. "I was in love with a man and she promised that we would be together forever but he went back to his wife. Was your man married?"

Joan nodded.

"How many times?"

"Five. He told me he didn't know why he married them and that I would always have a special place in his heart."

I'd heard that tired old line myself from David.

"My old boyfriend even told me to keep hold of my earrings because they were a gift," I said suddenly. "But I didn't want them! I wanted nothing to do with him ever again. Do you know what I mean?"

Joan nodded vehemently. "Yes. Yes. I know. I didn't want anything from Bryan. And then he had the nerve to say, *'Five times married. Five times a fool,'* but it was me who was the fool."

"I know that feeling, too, Joan," I said gently. "Are you talking about Bryan Laney?"

"You know I am." Joan's expression was ugly. "I know you've been with him, I know you have! He could never resist a young girl." I hardly thought at nearly forty that qualified me as "young," but Joan wasn't listening. "You're one of Bryan's tarts.

Admit it! You are! You were at Jane's Cottage with him—I saw you. Sneaking around."

"Bryan was going to help me hang some mirrors," I said calmly. "It turned out that he couldn't even lift a hammer."

The fact that Joan truly believed me capable of having a tryst with a man who had to be thirty years my senior just confirmed that she was as mad as a hatter.

"Did he give *you* a necklace?" Joan said harshly. "Like he gave all the others? Did he ask *you* to wait for him, too?"

"No. He never asked me that. I think he came to Honeychurch to look for the Honeychurch mint."

Joan sneered. "Of course he did. I knew he'd come back. The moment the double-hide was discovered. I just knew it."

"You seem very confident." I was slowly edging my way to the door. If no one was coming, I was going to make a run for it—gun or no gun. "How did you find out?"

"Facebook," said Joan. "Plymouth Treasure Hunters page. His *wife* posted it."

"Ah, Facebook," I said.

"But the last laugh is on me," said Joan triumphantly. "Him and his stupid treasure hunting. He only wanted me because I know where it is."

"What?" I exclaimed. "You really do?"

"Of course I know where it is," said Joan. "Bryan liked to say it was his ancestor who hid the stuff but it wasn't. It was mine!"

"But . . . but where is it?"

"Gone," she declared. "And that's what I told him. It's gone."

"Gone where? You mean someone got to it first? In the double-hide?"

Joan laughed. "It's down the warren well. That's where it is."

Harry had told me all about the warren well. "At Jane's Cottage? I've never seen a well."

"Because it's gone," said Joan gleefully. "Vanished. Disappeared."

"Is that what you told Bryan?"

"He didn't believe me. He was angry—said I'd led him on for years. Imagine! Me! Leading him on!"

"What about the double-hide?" I said. "The tools were found there. I saw them."

"I knew there was a double-hide," said Joan. "My granddad told me but it was Rupert who showed me how to open it."

"The earl?" I said. "You mean Lady Edith's brother?"

"That's right."

"I bet that made Bryan jealous!"

"It did," she said proudly. "But then her ladyship got the wrong end of the stick. Got all upset and threw me out."

"And what about Pandora?" I said.

All the color drained from Joan's face. "It was an accident," she said. "I just wanted to scare her. It was Madame Z's idea. 'You can make her disappear,' that's what she said."

I felt sick. "What do you mean?"

Joan's expression hardened. "Pandora toyed with my Bryan. Thought she could have any man she wanted."

"And that's when you went to see Madame Z?"

Joan nodded. "She told me to teach Pandora a lesson. Give her a fright. So I did."

"What happened?"

"It was her ladyship's birthday ball," said Joan. "There was already an upset because Pandora was wearing the Cleopatra outfit that was meant for Edith." Joan grinned, clearly enjoying herself. "Iris made it. She was livid!"

"What did you do?"

"They were playing that game—Smee, you know, squashed sardines," Joan went on.

"That's hide-and-seek in reverse, isn't it?" I said playing for time. "What are the rules?"

"One person hides and then everyone else searches for the hidden person," she explained. "Whenever someone finds the hidden person, they hide with them in the same place and the hidden group gets bigger and bigger."

"And very cozy," I said. "You need a big house for a game like that. The Hall must have been perfect."

"It was." Joan seemed smug. "Pandora ordered me to show her somewhere really special. So I did."

"Did you know that there was a second hide behind the first?" I asked.

"Yes. Pandora liked that. She liked it a lot." Joan flashed a smile. "So I left her there."

"Did you realize that she couldn't get out?"

Joan didn't answer. "And then Bryan and Iris had a fight and he said, *'Let's get away for a dirty weekend,'* and so we did."

Mrs. Cropper had told me that they'd run off together on the night of the ball.

"You left Pandora in the double-hide," I said.

"I thought she'd find a way out," said Joan with a shrug. "We were only away for a few days but when I went back to check that Pandora had got out, she was dead."

"You knew she was dead?" I was appalled. "Why didn't you tell someone?"

"It wasn't my fault." Joan stuck out her jaw. "I mean, people can stay alive for days without food and water..."

"You think someone else killed her?" I didn't believe this

for a minute but I was running out of ways to keep her talking and it was quite obvious that no one was coming to my rescue. I really was going to have to make a run for it.

"Oh, yes. Definitely."

"Well—it looks like the police have arrested the right person."

Joan's jaw dropped. "Who has been arrested?"

"Iris Bushman has been arrested."

Joan broke into a huge grin. "Good."

"Yes. Apparently Iris left a book in the first hide then forged a thank you letter from Pandora to throw people off the scent. Iris wanted people to believe that Pandora had gone to the Orient. But of course, she's denying it. I mean—no one can prove the book was hers."

"Yes, they can!" Joan exclaimed. "The book has her name written inside."

I knew that Joan couldn't have known that unless she wrote Mum's name herself.

"I just don't know where Iris would have gotten that kind of book from." I pretended to be baffled. "What was it called again? Something about the lady of the manor having an affair with the gamekeeper?"

"Lady Chatterley's Lover," said Joan.

"Really?" I feigned surprise. "That makes *Fifty Shades of Grey* look like a children's story these days, doesn't it?"

Joan was beginning to relax. I could see her fingers loosening their grip on the shotgun.

"I wonder if Iris found the book in the hayloft when she was up there with Bryan?" I mused.

Joan stiffened but didn't comment.

"And of course, the police are certain it was Iris who abducted the young reporter." I tried to make my voice sound as casual as I could.

"Yeah. Well, she did," said Joan.

"I think that Ginny knew too much and Iris was scared that it was going to come out in the *Daily Post*."

"Yeah. That Iris, she's ruthless," said Joan. "Always been good at covering her tracks."

"I think she's going to get a big shock when she knows that Ginny Riley survived to tell her stories."

"She survived?" Joan went very still. "But she can't have done."

I could see from Joan's face that she still had no idea who I really was but suddenly, she sprang into action. In two quick strides, Joan tripped the mechanism behind the Dobson painting. The linenfold paneling popped open.

"You really think I'm that stupid?" Joan shouted. "I know who you are. You're Iris's daughter."

My stomach turned right over. "No, I'm not."

"Peggy told me." Joan laughed. "But I enjoyed talking to you." She released the safety catch on the shotgun and gestured for me to get into the hide. Now I knew how Joan had forced Ginny to get into her own car.

I realized that no one would know where I was. I would face the same sentence as Pandora had all those years ago. Joan had been playing me along all the time. How could I have been such an idiot!

"Joan, you're making a mistake by doing this," I said. "I know you didn't mean for Pandora to die—"

"Yeah well, accidents will happen."

"And Bryan—I can understand how upset you must have been—"

"I guess I just snapped." She smiled again.

Mrs. Cropper was right. Joan was evil. No wonder Eric had kept Vera away from her.

"Give me your phone," said Joan. "And your car keys. It's the red MINI, right?"

Shaking, I did as I was told. "Joan—seriously—"

"Off you go." She pushed me to the entrance to the first priest hole. "I can push you if you'd prefer."

"Is this what you did to Pandora?" I said.

"Oh, no. She was very happy to climb in," Joan declared. "Good-bye Rapunzel."

Chapter Thirty-two

With no phone and no light it took me a while for my eyes to adjust to the darkness. I heard a groan.

Someone else was down here.

Hunched in the corner was the outline of a figure.

I heard another groan.

"Katherine?" came a whisper.

"Mrs. *Cropper*?" I couldn't believe it. I felt my way to her side.

"Oh, Katherine," she whimpered.

"Are you alright?"

"My ankle. I think it's broken," she said. "I'm sorry. Joan made me call. She wanted to see Iris."

"It's okay," I said. "I'm glad it's me and not my mother. Don't worry. Someone will know we are here. Did you tell your husband?"

"Seth has his rotary meeting tonight," said Mrs. Cropper.

"What about the rest of the family?" I said. "Edith? Lavinia? Rupert?"

"They don't know we're here, either. What about Iris?" Mrs. Cropper said hopefully. "Did you tell her where you were going?"

"My mother has been arrested," I said. "She's at Newton Abbot police station. She could be held all night."

"What about Alfred? You must have told him?"

Of course I couldn't have done but I didn't want to alarm Mrs. Cropper so I lied and said I'd left him a note.

I was struggling to come to terms with the fact that we were in serious trouble.

"Joan did everything, didn't she?" whispered Mrs. Cropper. "Pandora, Bryan—Ginny."

"Yes."

"And to think I thought it was my Seth. Poor Seth."

I had to find a way out. "Is there anything you remember about the double-hide?" I said. "Something—no matter how small—when you were growing up?"

"Seth is the one who was into all that type of thing," said Mrs. Cropper. She shivered. It was cold down here and I could tell she was in pain.

"Poor Pandora," she went on softly. "What a horrible way to die. Stuck in here. Knowing that people were around you but they couldn't hear your cry for help."

We fell silent again. I put my arm around Mrs. Cropper's shoulders to try and comfort her but was really doing it for myself. I was absolutely terrified.

"Did you crawl over here?" I said to Mrs. Cropper.

"Yes."

How could Pandora have gotten to the back of the hide with a broken neck?

I got to my feet. "I've just thought of something."

Tentatively, I felt my way to the chimney breast and touched the coarse brickwork. My hands found cold iron. I had discovered a rung. Reaching up, I found another.

Perhaps, just *perhaps*, this was the beginning of a crude

ladder that would take me up and out. It then occurred to me that when the tools had been left during the English Civil War, Joan's and Bryan's ancestors had actually hidden down here. Maybe there was another way out? It seemed a long shot but it was all I had and worth a try.

I made my way back to Mrs. Cropper to share my theory. "What do you know about the fireplaces here?"

"Each chimney on each floor has a damper that opens into the flue," she said. "I was just a girl when the chimney sweep used to come and of course, it was before this wing was sealed off—"

"Tell me about the damper."

"It's an iron door. It controls the draft," said Mrs. Cropper. "You open it by pulling on a chain that lifts the latch. Every flue has one or two but in this house, because of the hearth tax, there are more flues than chimneys—that's what the builders used to do—use the flues to link new chimneys to old."

"Do you think I can open the damper from outside the flue?" I said. "And then crawl inside?"

"Yes. Most of the dampers have a smoke shelf," Mrs. Cropper said. "I only know there are handholds inside the flue. If you could get inside, then you can climb down and get out through one of the fireplaces."

It was just as well I wasn't afraid of heights.

"Okay. I'll see what I can do," I said. "I'm going to have to leave you here."

"Just don't forget me," she said, attempting a weak joke.

Slowly, I began the climb, fighting down my claustrophobia every step of the way. I was in a narrow shaft between the outside wall of the house and the chimney stack.

It was completely and utterly dark. I was doing everything by touch, one rung at a time—reaching up with my hands and then placing one foot—and then the other before heaving myself up; making sure each rung held. With every step I stopped to brush my fingertips across the brickwork, hoping to feel the edges of a damper.

I felt nothing.

But there *had* to be something. Why else would the iron rungs be fixed to the outside of the flue?

I'd counted nineteen steps until, to my horror, one rung swung away from the wall. With a cry, I hung on desperately as my feet scrabbled to find the rung below.

And then I knew what had happened to Pandora.

She, too, must have tried to climb out this way but had probably been hampered by her Egyptian costume.

Pandora had fallen and broken her neck and that was why her body was found so far away from the entrance to the double-hide in such a grotesque position.

What a truly awful way to die. Joan had claimed she'd not had anything to do with Pandora's death other than showing her how to get in. And maybe, in this she was telling the truth.

I daren't move. Praying that the entire rung wouldn't come away from the wall; conscious of the thick dust and cobwebs from decades of disuse going up my nose and getting into my hair. Clutching the end that was bolted to the brickwork, I made one last attempt at finding the damper.

And then my fingers felt the cool, gratifying touch of metal.

I dug my fingers under the lip.

The door wouldn't budge. The latch was probably jammed or rusted together.

I hung there, desperate.

Thinking.

Mrs. Cropper had mentioned a chain.

I reached over as far as I dared, sweeping my hand left and right until, to my utter relief, my fingers found the chain. I had to tug it several times until I heard a click, stuck my fingers under the lip again and opened the door. A murky light spilled into the shaft.

"I've found it, Mrs. C.," I called down. "I'm going for help."

The opening was only just large enough for me to haul myself into it. Mrs. Cropper was right, there was a smoke shelf. I sat there for a moment to catch my breath.

Looking up I saw a faint dab of sky and noticed more rungs continued up to the very top of the chimney.

I couldn't believe how enormous this flue was and what an extraordinary maze of blackened tunnels led off from this one chimney. "Coffins of black," that's what William Blake's poem called them in his "Songs of Innocence—The Chimney Sweeper." The thought of those poor orphan boys sweeping chimneys all day was too awful to think about.

I guessed I'd climbed to the second floor. Carefully, I crawled into one of the smaller flues. I didn't even know if any of the fireplaces had been boarded up. But I had to try to find a way out.

I didn't want to think that one tiny slip could send me plunging down to the cold stone hearth beneath—but where—into the King's Parlor or the Great Hall?

This time it was easier. I only had to climb a few feet up before I came to the damper. To my relief, I opened it without any problem at all and squeezed inside. Down below, I saw the fire basket. The room seemed bathed in a soft, yellow light. Carefully, I braced my back against one side and my hands and feet against the other and slowly shimmied my way down, scrambling the last few feet and landing on my bottom in the fire basket that was, thankfully, empty.

"Golly, Stanford," I heard a familiar voice say. "I thought you were Father Christmas for a moment!"

Never had I been so happy to see Harry. He was sitting up in bed reading *Biggles and the Leopards of Zinn.*

"Reporting for duty, sir," I said, giving him a quick salute.

"I see you are wearing camouflage," he said. "Was the mission to the bunker a success?"

"Yes, you could say it was."

"Good. We'll debrief in the morning," Harry said and settled back to his book as if my descending from his chimney was an everyday occurrence.

Fifteen minutes later and after many false starts down endless corridors, I was hurrying through the galleried reception and collided with Rupert.

He sprang back, horrified. "Good heavens! What on earth is going on? You're covered in black soot!"

Lavinia and Edith emerged from a side door from where I could hear the blare of a television set. There were more cries of dismay. I swiftly filled them in on everything that had happened.

"I'll call Shawn and an ambulance," said Lavinia.

"I'll rescue Mrs. Cropper." Rupert broke into a trot across the marble floor.

"We shall go after Joan," said Edith coldly.

"She could be anywhere by now," I said. "She had a head start and took my mother's MINI."

"You go and get your car, pick up Alfred at the stables—I just saw him checking the horses, thank God—and then come back for me."

"Alfred is back?" I cried. "At the stables?"

"Yes, girl! What do you think I meant?" said Edith impatiently. "We need a bit of brawn and we certainly won't get that from my son."

Chapter Thirty-three

Alfred acted completely normal when he picked us up. If anything, he looked remarkably cheerful, which led me to believe that he had successfully hidden the drawings.

"Where's Iris off to?" he demanded as I climbed into the back of the Golf and Edith took the front seat. "I passed her speeding through Little Dipperton."

"That wasn't Iris," I said and told Alfred about my encounter with Joan Stark.

"Bloody hell!" he exclaimed. "Leave it to Alfred. Where do you think she's going?"

"Just drive, Alfred!" Edith shouted and slammed the dashboard. "We're wasting valuable time."

As we tore out past the gatehouses and turned into Cavalier Lane, the headlights caught a flash of metal. "I think that was Joan's tricycle," I said as I clung to the rear door handle and held on for dear life. Joan must have abandoned it.

We took three hairpin bends without slowing down. The Golf fishtailed on the wet road but Alfred didn't flinch. His hands gripped the steering wheel; his foot was hard on the accelerator.

"Shouldn't we change gears?" I said as Alfred repeatedly

shifted from first to second despite the ear-splitting protests coming from the poor engine.

Edith started to laugh. "Good heavens, Alfred," she hooted. "Anyone would think you were driving a getaway car!"

I caught Alfred's eye in the rearview mirror. He winked.

"But where are we going?" I wailed.

"Rupert got Joan's address out of Mrs. Cropper," said Edith. "Some hideous housing estate in Paignton."

"Where's Iris?" Alfred said. "She wasn't at the Carriage House."

"She's been arrested," said Edith cheerfully. "Can't you drive any faster?"

"Arrested!" Alfred exclaimed. "Why?"

"It's too long a story to go into now," I said as we approached a roundabout and Alfred just shot right over the middle hump.

As we entered the Paignton suburbs, we encountered a bit of traffic but that didn't slow Alfred down until suddenly he slammed on his brakes.

"Bloody hell!" he said. "There's Iris's MINI!"

The car had been abandoned at a traffic light and was holding up half a dozen motorists who were sounding their horns.

Alfred's eyes met mine again in the rearview mirror. They danced with laughter. "I reckon she ran out of petrol."

"There she is! That's Joan!" I shrieked as I spotted a yellow caped figure hurrying along the pavement. "I forgot to tell you—she's got a shotgun!"

Alfred wasn't fazed. He pulled over and stopped the car, leapt out and set off at a jog.

"I'll help him—"

"No! Stay!" Edith commanded as if I were Mr. Chips. "Alfred knows what he's doing. I must say he's very fit for his age."

Edith and I watched open-mouthed as Joan jaywalked

across the road. Cars screeched to a halt, horns blared but she didn't seem to notice.

She made her way toward another roundabout and clambered over the barrier.

Alfred was closing in.

Joan pulled out the shotgun from under her cape.

"Oh! I can't watch!" I cried as Alfred vaulted over the barrier.

The shotgun got caught in Joan's cape. She screamed. Alfred yelled and promptly brought Joan down in a rugby tackle. The pair tumbled to the ground in a flurry of limbs and flashing yellow PVC.

"I always remember that as one of Alfred's signature moves in the boxing ring," Edith mused.

"I think that's a rugby tackle."

"Who cares?" Edith's grin was so wide I realized she had all her teeth and made a mental note to tell Mum. She had always wondered.

Alfred straddled Joan and turned to us, waving the shotgun aloft.

"Bravo! Bravo!" Edith yelled and we both began to clap. "This is the most fun I've had in ages."

Lavinia must have been successful in contacting the police because minutes later there was a cacophony of sirens and a convoy of police panda cars converged at the roundabout surrounding it completely.

"Thank God." I turned to Edith. "It's over."

"Yes. It's over," she said grimly. "Justice for poor Pandora—and for Bryan—although I never really cared for him. He drove the poor girl to it—but that's no excuse." She paused for a moment. "There is something I have been meaning to tell you."

"I hate it when people say that," I said.

"It was Pandora who gave me *Lady Chatterley's Lover*," said Edith. "She bought it when she was traveling in Italy. I got rid of it, of course," Edith went on. "I couldn't have that in the house but not through any sense of being a prude. I find D. H. Lawrence's work far better than *Fifty Shades of Grey*."

"I agree," I said.

"I was a fool," Edith continued. "I'd confided in Pandora about my love affair with Walter. She kept dropping silly hints to my brother—saying wasn't I just like Lady Constance of Wragby Hall and remarking on the physical resemblance Walter had to Mellors. Rupert was already suspicious..." For a moment, sadness washed over her graceful features. "But of course, the rest you know."

"What happened with the Cleopatra costume?" I said. "My mother was so upset."

"Poor Iris. Yes, Pandora deliberately stole the costume your mother had worked so hard on. Pandora had to be the center of attention, you see." Edith gave a heavy sigh. "It was all so long ago. Age is a funny thing, Katherine. Most of us can move on after having our hearts broken. Cousin Edward—the man I did marry—was a good man. I never forgot Walter but I saw that time in my life for what it was. Young love and infatuation and it was wonderful." She paused again. "Joan never could let go."

Edith's words struck a chord. I was not like Joan. I could move on—and now that Alfred had gotten rid of the drawings, I wouldn't need to have anything more to do with David. I was free at last.

An hour later we dropped Edith back at the Hall. Rupert told us that Mrs. Cropper was on her way to Totnes Hospital and that he had dragged Cropper out of his rotary meeting.

Fortunately, her ankle had just been badly sprained but they were keeping her under observation overnight.

The courtyard was a blaze of light when we pulled into the carriageway. Mum came scurrying out to meet us.

"Where on earth have you been? Alfred! Oh! Oh! Is it really you?" And she promptly burst into tears.

I was feeling pretty emotional myself as I watched them embrace.

"You daft bat," said Alfred affectionately. "Told you it would be alright, didn't I? Just got one more thing to take care of tonight and we're dandy."

"Good God, Katherine!" Mum gawked. "You're completely covered in black paint."

"It's soot, actually," I said. "A long story but I've been up a chimney."

"Oh. Well, whilst you've been doing *that*," said Mum dismissively, "I've been fighting for my freedom. Then, suddenly, there is a phone call and a policewoman who I've never seen before says she'll give me a ride home."

"We were right about Joan, Mum."

"I knew it! Let's go inside and you can tell me everything over a gin and tonic."

Chapter Thirty-four

"Katherine—are you awake?" Mum knocked on my bedroom door. "Shawn's downstairs and he wants to see you."

It was Tuesday morning. I hadn't realized just how traumatic the events of the last few days had been nor how deeply I had needed to sleep.

"Now?"

Mum opened the door a crack and smiled. "He said it was very important. Perhaps he's going to ask you out on a date?"

"Very funny," I mumbled. "Give me five minutes."

"I think you'll need more than that if you want to make yourself presentable. At least you got rid of all that soot."

I climbed straight into my jeans and a sweater and just pulled my hair back into a ponytail.

When I entered the kitchen, Shawn was chatting to Mum holding a mug of coffee in his hand.

"Good news." He beamed. "Ginny confirmed that Joan was her abductor."

"That *is* good news," I said.

"Apparently, Joan paid Ginny an early morning visit to tell her that she'd read her article and that she had more information to sell."

"That wasn't what I expected," I said. "I would have thought she was afraid of her own secrets getting out."

"Joan needed the money," said Shawn. "As it is she's been claiming all kinds of benefits that she's not entitled to. Gran told me that after her brother—that would be my great-uncle—died..."

"I must write that down for my family tree," said Mum.

"Well—put it this way, Joan was penniless. She never could hold down a job so the council gave her a house."

"Sponging off the government," said Mum. "That's why this country's going to the dogs."

"Joan promised Ginny even bigger stories—"

"Joan was always manipulative," Mum declared. "Look at the way she tried to frame me!"

"Everything was going well until Ginny mentioned Alzheimer's," said Shawn. "To quote Ginny's words—*Joan went psychotic.*"

"But Ginny's decades younger than Joan," Mum said. "How on earth did Joan overpower her—enough to bundle her in the back of her car and dump her off on Dartmoor?"

"Joan had a shotgun," I said. "According to Bryan, she was a crack shot."

"A crackpot if you ask me," Mum muttered.

"And those deep scratch marks we saw in the boot of Ginny's car," said Shawn. "They were from her tricycle."

"What's going to happen to the series for the *Daily Post*?" I asked. "Is Ginny still going to write her exclusives?"

"I have no idea," said Shawn. "She was pretty shaken up. But that's not the only reason I am here."

Mum winked at me across the room and mouthed the words, "A date!" I ignored her.

"The most extraordinary thing happened last night," said

Shawn. "Someone broke into Luxton's warehouse and returned all the artwork."

"*What?*" I was horrified.

"They really need to get a new alarm system installed," Mum declared.

"So it looks as if the dowager countess will be able to sell the Hollar drawings at the auction, after all."

"That's wonderful," said Mum. "Isn't that wonderful, Katherine?"

"Amazing," I said bleakly.

"Well—I'd better get on," said Shawn. "I have a number of reports to write up what with Bryan, Pandora, Ginny and two break-ins—I always laugh when someone tells me that nothing ever happens in Little Dipperton."

I saw Shawn to the front door. "And you're certain that the Hollar drawings were among the items returned?"

"Yes. It was confirmed."

"Will you continue to look into it?"

"Since they've been put back and—to be honest—I've got my hands full with all these other cases and Newton Abbot aren't bothered—probably not."

"So they aren't going to look at the CCTV footage?" I just had to ask.

Shawn regarded me with suspicion. "Apparently not." He hesitated for a moment. "Kat—I feel I have done you a disservice and I apologize."

"Whatever for?"

"I thought you were protecting your mother or Alfred over all this business and I was wrong. I'd like to make it up to you. Perhaps we can have a drink one evening."

"Lovely!" I said with forced heartiness. At any other time, I would have been happy at the invitation but not now—and especially not after the auction that would probably be attended by a bevy of officers from the Art & Antiques Unit. I could see them swarming in with David at the helm.

I returned to the kitchen to find Alfred had slipped in through the back door.

He was tucking into a huge breakfast of scrambled eggs, toast and jam and looked as if he hadn't slept all night—which I suspected, he hadn't.

"I don't know how you can eat at a time like this," I said with dismay. "The police have just been here."

"He knows," said Mum.

Alfred just laughed. "Oh ye of little faith."

Mum hovered over him as if he were a god. "More tea, Alfred?"

"What's going on?" I said suspiciously. "You do realize what just happened, don't you?"

"You'll see," said Mum, shooting a knowing look at Alfred.

I dragged out a chair and sat down. "I'm too tired to argue."

"There is something I've been meaning to ask you," said Alfred suddenly. "I was looking at those drawings and I noticed something. They're topographical drawings, right? They were done to record as accurately as possible the properties and grounds..."

"I didn't know you were so knowledgeable, Alfred," I said.

"Alfred knows a lot about the art world," Mum chimed in.

"I've been doing a bit of research and you said that Warren Lodge burned down in the English Civil War, right?"

"Yes."

"Then Jane's Cottage was built on the foundation?"

"I suppose so."

"Ah—but you see, it wasn't built on the exact foundation,"

said Alfred. "I reckon it was moved about twenty-five yards farther south."

"How can you tell?" I asked.

"Ah! That's a secret," said Alfred.

"What else did you notice?"

"The warren well isn't there anymore. But it is in the drawing."

Joan had said her ancestor had put the silver in the warren well and it had disappeared. Harry had said that the warrener always had a well because they needed water for the rabbits for skinning carcasses and cleaning the skins. Was it distinctly possible that the well was still there—but under the floor of Jane's Cottage?

"Of course!" I rushed over to plant a kiss on a very startled Alfred's forehead. He turned pink with pleasure.

"Thank you, thank you!" I raced out of the kitchen shouting, "I have to go."

Of course Bryan had been snooping around Jane's Cottage. He probably had his suspicions all along but he could hardly start digging up the floor.

I didn't want to get anyone's hopes up—let alone my own but in the end I thought it best to share my theory with Rupert and I was glad I did.

Enlisting Eric's help and armed with spades, pickaxes and a wheelbarrow, the three of us spent hours at Jane's Cottage pulling up the old floors but we found absolutely nothing. It was so disheartening.

Around four-thirty, just when it was beginning to get dark, I stepped outside to take a break. I was so disappointed and felt more than a little foolish. I'd been so sure about finding the warren well under the floor of Jane's Cottage—and so had Rupert.

Joan was right. The well had vanished.

I heard a rustle in the undergrowth—probably a rabbit—and turned to see the old brick privy in the trees.

On a whim, I just had an idea. Retrieving a flashlight from the cottage I headed back to the privy and looked for a way inside. Ivy and vines had crept into the crevices and in the summer months, it would have been almost impossible to see the building at all.

The wooden door was half off its hinges, most of the roof tiles had gone and it really was little more than a shell. The frame was rotten and the door just flopped forward. I heaved it aside and stepped into the darkness.

Along the back wall was the privy itself.

It was made of wooden slats but instead of one hole to sit over, there were two. After all these years, I couldn't imagine there would be anything gross down there but even so, I braced myself to take a peek below.

Both holes were filled to the brim with leaves and detritus and dried up—yuck. I hunted around for a long stick and started poking and prodding at the surface. The hole on the left was disgusting and once I'd picked off the surface, it released the most terrible stench. With tiles missing from the roof and all this rain the contents didn't bear thinking about.

But the other hole was different. It contained nothing but rubble and stones.

Call it a hunch, but I just kept picking away with my stick until I saw red brick. I scraped along and found more. And then more—until I knew I'd uncovered the cylindrical rim of the warren well.

I charged back to Jane's Cottage just as Rupert and Eric were loading the tools back into Eric's Land Rover.

"I'm sorry," said Rupert. "We've made a mess of your floors.

I'll personally replace them for you—what?" He took one look at my face and broke into a wide grin. "You've found it, haven't you?"

The space in the privy was small for the three of us but Eric and Rupert managed to dismantle the wooden loo to give us more room. I held the flashlight and the two of them dug with spades in a fever of excitement.

After just twenty minutes, Rupert gave a cry of surprise. "Look! It's here. By God, I don't believe it!"

Eric and I crowded in to look. There, about six feet down, tucked into a recess that had been cut out of the well wall was a large, but very dirty, earthenware pot.

"Kat—will you do the honors?" beamed Rupert.

With the two men holding onto each leg, I leaned down and prized the pot loose.

It was filled to the brim with silver coins.

Chapter Thirty-five

News of the discovery of the famous Honeychurch mint filled the front pages of both the *Dipperton Deal* and the *Daily Post* that Saturday morning.

Bryan's widow generously allowed the newspapers access to the receipt book that was in Bryan's possession showing that it wasn't just the wealthy who had supported the Royalist cause—but "people of all persuasions" who had contributed what little they had and expected repayment.

The tools discovered in the double-hide were given lavish descriptions as to their purpose and confirmed that the Honeychurch clan had played an important and dangerous role in supporting the king all those centuries ago.

But, as an antique dealer, what was utterly thrilling was that among the silver pennies, shillings, half-crowns and crowns minted at the Hall, were six extremely rare solid silver Declaration Pounds dated 1643.

Set up initially as the new mint for the doomed King Charles I's victory over Cromwell, each coin bore the words, LET GOD ARISE AND LET HIS ENEMIES BE SCATTERED, symbolizing the king's belief in the absolute monarch to rule by divine right. Charles was beheaded for high treason against the people just six years after the coin was created.

Last year just one Declaration Pound had fetched a staggering fifty-six thousand pounds at Duke's of Dorchester auction house. Edith parted with three and put the rest in the Museum Room.

The plasterwork in the King's Parlor could now be restored, after all.

As to the discovery of Pandora Haslam-Grimley's body, it was deemed an unfortunate accident—the result of a game of Smee that went wrong. Bryan's death, however, was told in lurid detail in the *Daily Post* but since he had not literally grown up on the Honeychurch Hall estate and Joan had left the area as a young woman, his death warranted just a short paragraph in the *Dipperton Deal*.

Joan may not have suffered from Alzheimer's but she was diagnosed with paranoid schizophrenia and was currently awaiting arraignment.

Surprisingly, there was nothing written by Ginny Riley.

As for David, he turned up with his team of experts just before the Hollar drawings came up for sale and dramatically called a halt to the proceedings only to discover that the drawings on offer were crude fakes.

To say that David was left with the proverbial egg all over his face was putting it mildly.

"I told you to trust Alfred," whispered Mum. "Although he's not very happy. He could have done flawless copies but he thought David needed taking down a peg or two."

That evening, we all celebrated a victory in the library with champagne, including Shawn and the twins. Roxy was noticeably absent.

"She'll be disciplined, of course," said Shawn. "A police officer must be impartial at all times. I think she's learned her lesson."

Harry bounded in, bursting with excitement. "Guess what?" he exclaimed. "Max, Jed, Emerson, Ronan and Callum have asked me to go with them to Paignton Zoo tomorrow. Can I, Father?"

It would seem that Harry's show-and-tell with the Honeychurch mint and stories of buried treasure had made him the most popular boy in the class.

"Of course," said Rupert. "And perhaps they'd like to come back here for some of Mrs. Cropper's homemade cake afterward."

"Wicked!" Harry beamed.

I saw Lavinia blanch, but she didn't say a word.

The next morning I got a call from Ginny. "I just wanted to let you know that the *Daily Post* won't be running the Honeychurch series, after all."

It had been the one thing I still dreaded. "I know everyone will be happy, but what changed?"

"Trudy Wynne asked me not to report David's snafu and the cost of all the manpower that went into the operation," said Ginny. "In exchange, she agreed to the series being dropped." Ginny took a deep breath. "Actually, she offered me a job at the *Daily Post* and I accepted."

"Congratulations," I said but deep down I knew it would really change her.

"Don't worry," she said. "I did a lot of thinking out on Dartmoor when I honestly thought I wasn't going to make it. I did Roxy a great wrong by abusing her confidentiality and you've always been a good friend to me. I'm sorry."

Later, as Mum, Alfred and I sat at the kitchen table reliving the last few days, I said, "So where *are* the original Hollar drawings?"

"Where do you think?" Alfred chuckled. "Back in the King's Parlor where they belong."

"Her ladyship is so happy," said Mum.

"And we are, too. Mum, will you join me in a toast?"

We raised our glasses and cried, "To Alfred for saving the day."

He grinned and said, "I told you to trust me."

Murder at Honeychurch Hall

Hannah Dennison

Available to buy in ebook and paperback

If the stones of the house could talk . . .

When Kat Stanford abandons a successful television career to help her mother, Iris, move into a rustic carriage house in Devon she quickly discovers that, behind the well-trimmed hedgerows, Honeychurch Hall is populated by more eccentrics than Kat ever met in all her time in London.

The Dowager Countess, Lord and Lady Honeychurch, their precocious seven-year-old heir, his missing nanny, a brooding stable manager, a housekeeper with an extensive designer shoe collection . . . Everyone seems to harbour a secret – and Kat's mother may be hiding the darkest of them all . . .

Deadly Desires at Honeychurch Hall

Hannah Dennison

Available to buy in ebook and paperback

When the body of a transport minister is discovered in the grounds of the Honeychurch Hall estate, suspicion as to his unusual demise naturally falls on the residents. After all, who could possibly want a high-speed train line and rolling stock depot built in their front yard?

News of the murder soon reaches local resident Kat Stanford's nemesis Trudy Wynne. A ruthless tabloid journalist and the ex-wife of Kat's discarded lover, Trudy is out for revenge. She is also interested in exposing – and humiliating – Kat's mother Iris, who is secretly the international bestselling romance writer Krystalle Storm.

As the body count begins to build, Kat becomes inextricably embroiled in the ensuing scandal. Is the minister's death the result of a local vendetta, or could it be connected to her mother's unusual past?